KWAME NKRUMAH—CONTRIBUTIONS TO THE AFRICAN REVOLUTION

AF063999

KWAME NKRUMAH

CONTRIBUTIONS TO THE AFRICAN REVOLUTION

Doreatha Mbalia

PANAF

Kwame Nkrumah: Contributions to the African Revolution

First published 2011 by Panaf Books

© 2011 Panaf

16 St. Cuthbert's Street
Bedford MK40 3JG.UK

All rights reserved.
No part of this volume may be reproduced,
stored in a retrieval system, or transmitted
in any form or by any means, electronic,
mechanical, photocopying or otherwise,
without the prior permission of Panaf Books.

Pb   9780901787064

Printed by Lightning Source

Contents

List of Photographs vi

Introduction 1

Part One: Nkrumah's Theoretical Contribution
                 to the African Revolution

    Chapter 1   Books and Pamphlets 11

    Chapter 2   The Conakry Letters 39

Part Two: Nkrumah's Practical Contribution
                 to the African Revolution 81

    Chapter 3   The Cabinet Minutes 83

    Chapter 4   Nkrumah's Parliament Speeches 97

    Chapter 5   Nkrumah's Conference Speeches 121

    Chapter 6   The *Daily Graphic* 143

    Chapter 7   Conclusion 155

Photographs 163

Bibliography 173

Index 179

About the Author 185

List of Photographs

1/2	Nkrumah speaks at the African Freedom Fighters' Conference, June 1962	163
3	Nkrumah opens the All-African People's Conference in Accra, December, 1958	164
4	Nkrumah speaks at the All-African People's Conference, December 8, 1958	164
5	Nkrumah with Emperor Haile Selassie c. 1960	165
6	Nkrumah and W.E.B. DuBois c. 1960	165
7	Nkrumah and Modibo Keita of Mali at the signing of the Ghana-Guinea-Mali pact, April 1961	165
8	Nkrumah with Gamal Nasser, Sékou Touré and Modibo Keita at the Casablanca Conference, January 1961	165
9	Nkrumah and Sékou Touré in Conakry, Guinea	166
10	Nkrumah with Fidel Castro	166
11	Nkrumah opens the Conference of Pan-African Journalists, November 1963	167
12	Osagyefo Dr. Kwame Nkrumah	167
13	Nkrumah with Mohammed Ali	168
14	Nkrumah with Chou En-Lai, 1964	170
15	Nkrumah with Gamal Nasser at the OAU meeting of African Heads of State, Cairo, July 1964	170
16	Nkrumah with Chairman Mao Tse Tung	171
17	Nkrumah with Nehru	171
18	Kwame Nkrumah Prime Minister of Ghana	172
19	The casket of Nkrumah at his funeral, Guinea, May 1972	172

Introduction

Kwame Nkrumah made an indelible mark on Africa in particular and the world in general: there is no single individual who contributed more to Africa and its people than Nkrumah. In theory and in practice, his great contribution was to the African Revolution, the struggle to bring about a liberated, united, and socialist Africa (Pan-Africanism) primarily and to worldwide socialism secondarily. It was his view that the former should precede the latter, that the achievement of African unity would, in turn, contribute significantly to worldwide socialism. In regard to a socialist African union, Nkrumah writes: "I have often been accused of pursuing 'a policy of the impossible'. But I cannot believe in the impossibility of achieving African union any more than I could ever have thought of the impossibility of attaining African freedom" (*Africa Must Unite* [AMU], p. 170). In the same work he addresses the skeptics who thought that Africa would never unite, who pointed to language and other differences as a way of accusing Nkrumah of devising "a policy of the impossible". Nkrumah's response was always the same: "The forces that unite us are intrinsic and greater than the superimposed influences that keep us apart" (AMU, p. 221). In regard to worldwide socialism, he writes: "A united socialist Africa will be a bulwark for world socialism. It will add strength to the progressive and socialist forces, for peace and socialism" (Milne, *The Conakry Years*, p. 121).

Nkrumah's theory and practice were dynamic, evolving significantly between 1965 and 1972, the final seven years of his life, most of which he spent in exile from his country, Ghana. This evolution accelerated the African Revolution in advancing both its theory and its practice. For example, prior to Nkrumah the theory of the African Revolution did not regard scientific socialism as the only viable economic system for the development of Africa and for the advancement of *all* Africans, wherever they happen to be born. Most significantly, there was neither a philosophy nor an ideology designed and articulated for African people. In that regard, it might be said that Nkrumah did for Africans what Marx and Lenin did for Europe and what Mao Tse-Tung did for China at their respective moments of social revolution in the early and mid twentieth century. And, of course, the development of an ideology for African people was essential if the African Revolution had any chance of success. As Nkrumah saw it, a monolithic ideological unity would give direction to the energies of African people and guide Africans toward collective action in pursuit of Pan-Africanism. Additionally, Nkrumah contributed to Pan-Africanism an extensive, detailed exposure and examination of the enemy, capitalism, especially in its guise of neo-colonialism; the idea of the unity of Africa as the *only* solution for the survival (not just the freedom and development) of Africa and its people; and in his final years, reasoned argument for the idea of armed struggle as a tactic for achieving Pan-Africanism.

The practice of Pan-Africanism, actual attempts to unite Africa and make it a homeland for all African people in the service of all African people, was also advanced under the leadership of Kwame Nkrumah. In traditional Africa, Pan-Africanism essentially meant "unity of development" within different regions. These regional states resulted from the need for African people to create larger political kingdoms in order to provide a greater quality of life for the people. Even with the introduction of Islam into Africa, Africans continued to strive for larger states. So while the introduction of Islam into Africa gave impetus to the emergence of class contradictions, as evidenced in the roles of kings and chiefs, this merely gave new direction to the pursuit of unity. Even the brutal disruption of African development caused by slavery and colonialism did not divert the pursuit of unity. It merely gave rise to resistance movements, movements of liberation that ultimately required unity. These kept alive the Diasporan Africans' longing to return to Africa as reflected in the early "Back to Africa" movements of Paul Cuffee, and later the DuBoisian conferences and the practical building attempts of Marcus Garvey and the Universal Negro Improvement Association (UNIA), whose rallying cry was "Africa for the Africans, Those at Home and Abroad". Although those attempts were unsuccessful in returning large numbers of Africans to their homeland, the UNIA did, for example, mobilize and unify African people around the world into one organization; it illuminated the creed that all African people, no matter where they are born or raised, are Africans and belong to the African nation.

It was Kwame Nkrumah who truly gave Pan-Africanism its home—the most significant practical advancement of the African Revolution. For a home is a base from which measurable acts in regard to a united, socialist Africa can be executed and documented. The first practical step initiated by Nkrumah was a series of conferences designed to accelerate the liberation movements going on throughout Africa and to plant the seed of unity in the minds of the leaders of Africa. Another significant practical step was the conception of, but most importantly the launching of, the Organization of African Unity (OAU), Nkrumah's structural apparatus for building a united Africa. Then too there were the training facilities for youths and young freedom fighters from throughout Africa. These accomplishments, and many more, on behalf of all Africans, advanced Pan-Africanism in a practical way.

For the purpose of this study, Nkrumah's theoretical and practical contributions to the African Revolution are approached through a segmentation into five fundamental elements: identity, enemy, objective, strategy and tactics.

On the question of identity, Nkrumah writes: "All peoples of African descent, whether they live in North or South America, the Caribbean or in any other part of the world are Africans and belong to the African Nation" (*Class Struggle in Africa*, p. 87fn). This question of identity was critical, not only because all Africans were needed for the African Revolution, but more importantly because those born outside of the continent had to be brought to the realization that they were in fact Africans who just happened to be born in the Diaspora. As Kwame Ture (formerly, Stokely Carmichael) stated, the only significant difference between those born at home and those born in the African Diaspora is that one group was taken from the land, the other had their land taken from them. Nkrumah states in *The Spectre of Black Power*:

> It must be understood that liberation movements in Africa, the struggles of Black Power in America or in any other part of the world, can only find consummation in the political unification of Africa, the home of the black man and people of African descent throughout the world. (*The Struggle Continues*, p. 14; *Handbook of Revolutionary Warfare*, p. 427)

Nkrumah called out to all continental and Diasporan Africans to make both a quantitative and qualitative contribution to the African Revolution. In "Message to the Black People of Britain", Nkrumah writes: "What is Black Power? By Black Power we mean the power of the four-fifths of the world population which has been systematically damned into a state of underdevelopment by colonialism and neo-colonialism" (*The Struggle Continues*, p. 13; and *Handbook of Revolutionary Warfare*, p. 429). With Africans from throughout the world united in the struggle, Nkrumah was convinced that Africa, and consequently its people, would be free: "real black freedom will only come when Africa is politically united. It is only then that the black man will be free to breathe the air of freedom, which is his to breathe, in any part of the world" ("Message" in *The Struggle Continues*, p. 14; and *Handbook of Revolutionary Warfare*, p. 430).

The enemy that Nkrumah says has damned four-fifths of the world's population is capitalism, in all its forms. According to him, capitalism "is but the gentleman's method of slavery" (*Consciencism*, p. 72). Capitalism overseas is imperialism and it manifests itself in three different forms: colonialism, settler-colonialism, or neo-colonialism:

> Imperialism, which is the highest state of capitalism, will continue to flourish in different forms as long as conditions permit it. Though its end is certain, it can only come about under pressure of nationalist wakening and an alliance of progressive forces which hasten its end and destroy its conditions of existence. It will end when there are no nations and peoples exploiting others; when there are no vested interests exploiting the earth, its fruits and resources for the benefit of a few against the well-being of the many. (*Consciencism*, p. 57–58)

In *Handbook of Revolutionary Warfare* (hereafter "HRW"), Nkrumah writes: "The people will have no equitable share in national reconstruction and its benefits unless the victory over imperialism in its colonialist and neo-colonialist stages is complete" (HRW, p. 29–30). Of the colonial stage, he writes: "I have always regarded colonialism as the policy by which a foreign power binds territories to herself by political ties with the primary object of promoting her own economic advantage" (*Ghana: The Autobiography of Kwame Nkrumah* [hereafter "Autobiography"], p. vii). In explaining the new form of colonialism, he states: "the essence of neo-colonialism is that the State which is subject to it is, in theory, independent and has all the outward trappings of international sovereignty. In reality its economic system and thus its political policy is directed from outside" (*Neo-Colonialism: The Last Stage of Imperialism* [hereafter "N-C"], p. ix). This particular manifestation of capitalism:

> ... is the worst form of imperialism. For those who practise it, it means power without responsibility, and for those who suffer from it, it means exploitation without redress. (p. xi)

In *Handbook of Revolutionary Warfare*, Nkrumah further describes the condition of states under neo-colonialism:

> A state can be said to be a neo-colonialist or client state if it is independent *de jure* and dependent *de facto*. It is a state where political power lies in the conservative forces of the former colony and where economic power remains under the control of international finance capital. In other words, the country continues to be economically exploited by interests which are alien to the majority of the ex-colonised population but are intrinsic to the world capitalist sector. Such a state is in the grip of neo-colonialism. It has become a client state. (HRW, p. 8)

And for a client state to exist, neo-colonial puppets are required—individuals who might seem to be in the service of the state, but who in fact serve the purposes of capitalist interest. Such 'puppets' says Nkrumah are the "true class enemy" of African people (*Class Struggle in Africa*, p. 15), and Nkrumah's attention turned again and again to addressing and illuminating the iniquities of the client-state condition (as will be shown in Part I).

A people's objective is always based on two elements: the identity of the people and the enemy of the people. As African people, Africans can only struggle for their rightful land base—Africa. Because of capitalism, particularly in its forms of colonialism and neo-colonialism, the African people's objective must be Pan-Africanism: the liberation and unification of Africa under a socialist economic system. Nkrumah saw that independent, isolated states would never be allowed to develop according to their own needs. In a speech at the closing session of the Casablanca Conference, a meeting of the most progressive states in Africa in January 1961, Nkrumah states:

> I can see no security for African States unless African leaders, like ourselves, have realized beyond all doubt that salvation for Africa lies in unity ... for in unity lies strength, and as I see it, African States must unite or sell themselves out to imperialist and colonialist exploiters for a mess of pottage, or disintegrate individually. (*Revolutionary Path*, p. 138)

His clear understanding of the need for continental unity and continental socialism made it possible for Nkrumah to expand the Marcus Garvey/UNIA definition of Pan-Africanism. For Africa to serve its people, it must be socialist. Thus, in *Handbook of Revolutionary Warfare* (1969), Nkrumah writes: "At the core of the concept of African unity lies socialism and the socialist definition of the new African society" (HRW, p. 28). But as early as 1959, Nkrumah makes clear that this will be the path of economic development for Ghana: "We aim at creating in Ghana a socialist society in which each will give, according to his ability, and receive according to his needs" ("Speech at Accra Arena", 12 June 1959 in HRW, p. 28). According to Nkrumah, socialism implies:

1. Common ownership of the means of production, distribution and exchange. Production is for use, and not for profit.
2. Planned methods of production by the state, based on modern industry and agriculture.
3. Political power in the hands of the people, with the entire body of workers possessing the necessary governmental machinery through which to express their needs and aspirations. It is a concept in keeping with the humanist and egalitarian spirit which characterised traditional African society, though it must be applied in a modern context. All are workers; and no person exploits another.
4. Application of scientific methods in all spheres of thought and production.

For those struggling to achieve the Pan-African goals of continental unity and continental socialism, organization is the key. Not any kind of organization will do, however. Organizations throughout the world must become interlocked, ideologically and strategically, in executing the African Revolution. Nationalist groups, struggling for reforms within their particular geo-political territories, will not solve Africa's problems, and Nkrumah urged that "These isolated battles must be fought as part of the great revolutionary, liberation struggle, and within the framework of our politico-military organisation" (HRW, p. 88). Nkrumah saw that only through a global, organized effort can African people hope to solve their problems on a permanent basis. No single organization or individual could accomplish this objective. Nor could it be accomplished by mere political organization.

That Nkrumah moved from the tactic of non-violent, positive action to recognition of the need for armed struggle is not a surprise. As Nkrumah explained, "There is no fundamental difference between armed struggle as such and organised revolutionary action of a civil type. The various methods of our struggle and the changing from one method to another should be determined mainly by the circumstances and the set of conditions prevailing in a given territory" (HRW, pp. 49–50). Tactics are determined by the enemy's action. Only principles are permanent and unchanging. If there is no recourse other than armed struggle, if the choice is between remaining colonized and neo-colonized, exploited and oppressed or achieving liberation, then the enemy leaves the people no choice but to take up arms: "Revolutionary warfare is the logical, inevitable answer to the political, economic and social situation in Africa today. We do not have the luxury of an alternative. We are faced with a necessity" (HRW, p. 42). While Nkrumah was in power and during his stay in Guinea, some states still trying to free themselves from colonialism—those in "Portuguese Africa", for example—were being bludgeoned. Other states, having won their independence, had to protect themselves from neo-colonialist inspired coups d'état and assassination attempts against their leaders. To defend themselves effectively, armed struggle was required. Nkrumah came to believe that Africans must train themselves accordingly:

> [No] one is born or is not born a natural revolutionary fighter. The problem is not whether revolutionaries are naturally suited to Africa, or Africa to revolutionary warfare. Predestination of this sort never exists. The fact is that revolutionary warfare is the only way in which the total liberation and unity of the African continent can be achieved. (HRW, pp. 20–21)

"The people's armed struggle", he said, is "the highest form of political action" (HRW, p. 52). Nkrumah believed that the people's identity is derived from the ancestral land base, not merely from their birthplace. The land base that Africans justly claim, of course, is continental Africa. What luck! For Africa is a rich continent still, though her wealth has been exploited for hundreds of years. Since the fifteenth century Africa's great wealth has been owned, controlled and exported to other parts of the world by merchants, mercenaries, colonialists, and neo-colonialists. Nkrumah's saw that Africa must be unified and socialist so that its wealth will benefit all of its people, those at home and those abroad. A continental socialist government will demand and command fair trade prices for its resources. Its wealth will come back to the people in the forms of free education, free health care, guaranteed housing, guaranteed food, a living wage. Moreover, that power to negotiate fair prices on a world market transfers to the social reality of African people: the power to demand fair treatment of its people wherever they happen to live in the world. Nkrumah understood that only a united, socialist Africa could provide a permanent solution to the exploitation of Africa's wealth, the exploitation of its people's labor, and the oppression of its people. He never stopped writing and speaking about it. The overthrow of Nkrumah's Ghanaian government on February 24, 1966, only strengthened his resolve to fight for Pan-Africanism.

The purpose of this book is to examine Kwame Nkrumah's theory and practice of the African Revolution: first to measure their impact on Africa, its people and the rest of the world from 1957 to 1972; and second to consider whether they remain viable for today's Pan-Africanists. In Part I of this book Nkrumah's theory is examined through his writings: his major books and pamphlets, as well as his correspondence during the years of his exile in Conakry, Guinea. In Part II, Nkrumah's practice is examined in terms of his deeds, the practical steps he took in regard to the African Revolution. Here this includes Nkrumah's addresses to conferences as well as newspaper articles, minutes of government-level meetings and 'write-ups' of ceremonies and banquets at which Nkrumah shares his theory with an audience. The conclusion reflects briefly on the state of the African World today, and urges that Nkrumah's enduring Pan-Africanist philosophy continues to offer the solution to the many ills confronting Africa and its people.

~ ~ ~ ~ ~

Part One

Nkrumah's Theoretical Contribution to the African Revolution

1

Books and Pamphlets

Kwame Nkrumah's theory of the African Revolution is articulated in his major, published works: *Towards Colonial Freedom* (1945), *Africa Must Unite* (1963), *Consciencism* (1964), *Neo-Colonialism: The Last Stage of Imperialism* (1965), *Handbook of Revolutionary Warfare* (1968), and *Class Struggle in Africa* (1970). Elements of the theory include the questions of identity, enemy, objective, strategy, and tactics, and all are discussed in these major works. In some of the earlier works, however, these elements appear in embryo form or are left undeveloped; others, such as tactics, will undergo a fundamental change in later works.

While not usually considered major, two additional works are compelling enough to include in this study: "The Spectre of Black Power" and "Message to the Black People of Britain" [both published in 1968 and reprinted in *The Struggle Continues* (1973) and in *Revolutionary Path* (1973)]. In clarifying the definition of the African Revolution, they too help to advance Nkrumah's theory.

TOWARDS COLONIAL FREEDOM (1945)

Towards Colonial Freedom (hereafter "TCF") is Kwame Nkrumah's earliest, seminal published work on the form of capitalism flourishing in Africa during the first half of the twentieth century. First published in 1945, it was written as his dissertation while he was a student at the University of Pennsylvania, and reflects the anti-capitalist thinking of Nkrumah when he was just a young man. In fact, many of the fundamental elements of Nkrumaism can be found in this early work: the nature of the enemy, including its machinations; political unity as a prerequisite to economic independence; continental unity, the only permanent way to solve the problems of African people; armed struggle as a tactic capable of defeating the enemy; and socialism as the only viable economic system for a free, united Africa.

In the Preface, Nkrumah writes that the work has a threefold purpose: it "affirms, and postulates as inevitable, the national solidarity of colonial peoples and their determination to end the political and economic power of colonial governments" (TCF, p. xiii); it analyzes "colonial policies, the colonial mode of production and distribution and of imports and exports" (p. xiii); and it serves "as a rough blue-print of the processes by which colonial peoples can establish the realization of their complete and unconditional independence" (p. xiii). He ends the preface with a warning to all colonial peoples that capitalism "knows no law beyond its own [economic] interests" (p. xiv).

In the Introduction, Nkrumah writes that "the basis of colonial territorial dependence is economic, but the basis of the solution of the problem is political" (TCF, p. xv). This belief is one espoused until his death. In *Handbook of Revolutionary Warfare*, he writes: "Without political unity, African states will never commit themselves to full economic integration, which is the only productive form of integration able to develop our great resources fully for the well-being of the African people as a whole" (p. 40). Because the solution to the economic exploitation of Africa and its people is political, "political independence is an indispensable step towards securing economic "emancipation" (p. xv). Another axiom held steadfastly was that this political independence is possible only if there is continental unity: "this point of view irrevocably calls for an alliance of all colonial territories and dependencies. All provincial and tribal differences should be broken down completely" (p. xv). He also warns Africans not to be fooled by the machinations of colonialism, because:

> ... beneath the 'humanitarian' and 'appeasement' shibboleths of colonial governments, a proper scrutiny leads one to discover nothing but deception, hypocrisy, oppression and exploitation" [as reflected in] such expressions as 'colonial charter', 'trusteeship', 'partnership', 'guardianship', 'international colonial commission', 'dominion status', 'condominium', 'freedom from fear of permanent subjection', 'constitutional reform' and other shabby sham gestures of setting up a fake machinery for 'gradual evolution towards self-government'. (TCF p. xvi).

Such expressions are nothing more than a "means to cover the eyes of colonial peoples with the veil of imperialist chicanery" (TCF, p. xvi). Interesting too is Nkrumah's early recognition of the capitalists' attempt to promote a unified Africa with an eye toward "the ease" of exploitation: "the 'Pan-Africanism' of Jan Smuts ... is a subterfuge attempt to give assistance to the annexationist powers to exploit Africa on a wider scale" (p. xvii, note).

Under the section, "Colonialism and Imperialism", Nkrumah exposes the disguises that veil capitalism in Africa by explaining the true nature of colonialism and by differentiating between the two forms of colonies existing in Africa at the time: settlement colonies and exploitation colonies. Of the former he writes, "a settlement colony is one in which the geographical and racial environment is not very different from that of the 'mother country'" (TCF, p. 3, note). An exploitation colony "consists typically of groups of business men, monopolist combines, cartels, trusts, administrators, soldiers and missionaries—all of which are thrust and dumped into conditions and environment quite different from their home country" (p. 3, note). No matter the type, however, the *raison d'être* was economic exploitation. Nkrumah quotes Albert Sarraut, Colonial Secretary of State for France in 1923, who clearly articulated the purpose of colonial imperialism: "The origin of colonization is nothing else than enterprise of individual interests, a one-sided and egotistical imposition of the strong upon the weak" (p. 4). After a lengthy discussion of the history of colonialism, Nkrumah outlines the objectives of colonialism:

> (i) to make the colonies non-manufacturing dependencies; (ii) to prevent the colonial subjects from acquiring the knowledge of modern means and techniques for developing their own industries; (iii) to make colonial 'subjects' simple producers of raw materials through cheap labour; (iv) to prohibit the colonies from trading with other nations except through the 'mother country'. (TCF, p. 10)

The consequences of colonialism were devastating to the economic and social fabric of African life. It killed the arts and crafts; it thrust capital loans upon colonies in order to finance the infrastructure for the ease of exploitation; and it imposed western cultural religious and social norms into the life and culture of the people. But the introduction of this form of capitalism into Africa did not mean that Africa became a capitalist territory. Capitalism, introduced into the colonies, did "not take the 'normal' course it took in western countries. Free competition did not exist, monopoly control of all resources of the colonies demonstrates the perversion of finance capitalism" when introduced into Africa (TCF, p. 14). This is why Africa could never become a capitalist territory, even if it so wished. It could only become a satellite of, i.e. a colony of, the West; for the "finance capitalist and investor [will always] find the easiest and richest profits not from establishing industry in the colonies, which would compete with home industries ... but by exhausting the natural and mineral resources of the colonies" (p. 14). Of course, this type of set-up benefits only the capitalists and creates total dependence in the colony. That is why "it is a common economic experience that wherever there is economic dependence there is no freedom" (p. 17).

In the section entitled "The Land Question", Nkrumah examines the various ways in which land was stolen from the African and exploited. Overall, the "African is robbed of most of his lands, through legal extortion and forced concession" (TCF, p. 21). Several devices are used to confiscate the land: "legal" enactments; ordinances; ninety-year leases; and military defense acts (TCF, pp. 21–23).

Under "Colonial Policies: Theory and Practice", Nkrumah examines the types of colonies created in Africa, such as protectorates and trusteeships. All are disguises for naked exploitation. Moreover, any so-called "humanitarian" act on the part of the 'mother country' was executed to facilitate exploitation:

> The colonial powers build hospitals because if the health of the colonial subjects is not taken care of it will not only jeopardize their own health but will diminish the productive power of the colonial labourer. They build schools in order to satisfy the demand for clerical activities and occupations for foreign commercial and mercantile concerns. The roads they build lead only to the mining and plantation centres. In short, any humanitarian act of any colonial power towards the 'ward' is merely to enhance its primary objective: economic exploitation. If it were not so, why haven't the West African colonies, for instance, been given the necessary training that provides for complete political and economic independence? (p. 27)

Even in this earliest work Nkrumah recognises that strength lies in political unity beyond local state boundaries. Under the heading, "Apology for Apologetics", he states:

> The political and economic predicament of Liberia demonstrates the fact that unless there is a complete national unity of all the West African colonies it will be practically impossible for any one West African colony to throw off her foreign yoke. Russia and the United States of America are a conglomeration of different peoples and cultures, yet each has achieved political unity. Cultural and linguistic diversities are by no means inconsistent with political unity. (p. 33)

He also reveals a strategy for reaching the objective of continental unity: "The West African colonies, for example, must first unite and become a national entity, absolutely free from the encumbrances of foreign rule" (p. 33).

As there is negative and positive in everything, in "What Must Be Done", Nkrumah lists the positive results of imperialism in Africa:

> (a) the emergence of a colonial intelligentsia; (b) the awakening of national consciousness among colonial peoples; (c) the emergence of a working class movement; and (d) the growth of a national liberation movement. (p. 39)

Most importantly, in this section, Nkrumah outlines action steps that must be taken in order to break free from the yoke of colonialism. The most significant of these is the inevitability of war: "under imperialism war cannot be averted and a coalition between the proletarian movement in the capitalist countries and the colonial liberation movement, against the world front of imperialism becomes inevitable" (TCF, p. 41). Interestingly, this early position in regard to tactics is exactly the same as Nkrumah's last position: armed struggle.

At the end of *Towards Colonial Freedom*, Nkrumah arrives at the best economic system that will ensure the development of all African people—socialism: "Thus the goal of the national liberation movement is the realization of complete and unconditional independence, and the building of a society of peoples in which the free development of each is the condition for the free development of all" (p. 43). The concluding statement is this clarion call: "PEOPLES OF THE COLONIES, UNITE: The working men of all countries are behind you" (p. 43).

Here in Nkrumah's earliest major publication are the seeds of the African Revolution that will reach fruition in his last, *Class Struggle in Africa*. First, that the enemy of all colonial and working-class peoples is capitalism, in all of its forms. Second, that political independence is a prerequisite for economic independence. Third, that Africa can never become a 'united states' of *capitalist* Africa. Fourth, that wherever there is economic dependence there can never be freedom. Fifth, that capitalists will use any machination in order to realize their profit objectives. Sixth, that it "will be practically impossible for any one West African [or African] colony to throw off her foreign yoke" (p. 33). Seventh, that therefore continental unity is called for. Eighth, that armed struggle cannot be averted. Ninth, that socialism is the only economic alternative for Africa. And, tenth, that a worldwide strategy is required in order to defeat capitalist-imperialist powers. Both foresight and genius are revealed by Nkrumah at this early point in his political life.

AFRICA MUST UNITE (1963)

That Nkrumah and his struggle on behalf of Pan-Africanism had come to the attention of capitalists and their agents prior to the writing of *Africa Must Unite* is not surprising. According to one writer, "The FBI began files on Nkrumah in January 1945, perhaps as a result of Nkrumah's sponsorship of the Council on African Affairs conference in April 1944" (Sherwood, pp. 106–7). However, after the publication of *Africa Must Unite*, it is reasonable to assume that intelligence agencies in the USA, Great Britain, Israel and South Africa intensified their surveillance efforts. In fact, the writing of the work and the founding conference of the Organization of African Unity nearly coincide.

Africa Must Unite [hereafter "AMU"] thoroughly and persuasively argues for a united, socialist states of Africa. Significantly, Nkrumah dedicates the book to his friend and mentor, George Padmore, a Pan-Africanist who helped Nkrumah to understand that the future of Africa and its people depend on unification. The thesis of the work appears in the introduction, where Nkrumah writes: "Our freedom stands open to danger just as long as the independent states of Africa remain apart" (AMU, p. xvii). The evidence of this danger was all around.

That freedom for African countries is synonymous with unification (and socialism) is a point that Nkrumah will emphasize until his death. It is a unification that can be built on existing commonalities, for Nkrumah was "convinced that the forces making for unity far outweigh those which divide us" (AMU, p. 132). Later, he writes that Africa with its islands is just one Africa:

> We reject the idea of any kind of partition. From Tangier or Cairo in the North to Capetown in the South, from Cape Guardafui in the East to Cape Verde Islands in the West, Africa is one and indivisible. (AMU, p. 217)

Neither is language is a barrier to unification, since all are Africans: "The fact that I speak English does not make me an Englishman" (AMU, p. 217), for "[t]he forces that unite us are intrinsic and greater than the super-imposed influences that keep us apart", p. 217). The most far-reaching outcome of a united Africa is "the dignity of Africa" (p. 221) and the strengthening of "its impact on world affairs" (p. 193). In other words, a new image of Africa will emerge and with it a new African personality.

What should be the objectives of a united, socialist African continent? Nkrumah clearly articulates these goals in *Africa Must Unite*: "An over-all economic planning on a continental basis" (p. 218) including a common currency; "a unified military and defence strategy" (p. 219); and "a unified foreign policy and diplomacy" (p. 220) in order "to give political direction to our joint efforts for the protection and economic development of our continent" (p. 220). Economically, colonial African states had been forced to labor on behalf of their colonial masters, with Africa's vast resources vacuumed out and emptied into Europe. Ghana's cocoa, for example, was never processed at home, "not a single chocolate factory" was built in Ghana (pp. 26–27). Moreover, while Ghana produced palm oil, the manufacture from it of soap and edible fats took place in Great Britain. Why should individual states "trade" with Europe on Europe's terms when they can trade with one another to the mutual benefit of each state and the continent as a whole? Continentally, "an African Common Market, devoted uniquely to African interests, would more efficaciously promote the true requirements of the African states" (p. 162). Moreover, "custom barriers can be eliminated; differences in domestic structures accommodated" and a single continental currency must emerge (p. 157). Remarking on the absolute necessity of unification, Nkrumah writes:

> Because of the enormously greater energy, both human and material, that would be released through continentally integrated planning, productivity increase would be incomparably higher than the sum of the individual growths which we may anticipate within the individual countries under separatism. (AMU, p. 171)

Not only would Africa benefit from unification, but also the very survival of Africa and its people is dependent on unification. This was Nkrumah's belief. And he took every opportunity to advocate on behalf of this belief—through books, newspaper articles, speeches, conferences, and individual meetings with heads of state inside and outside of Africa. Evidence of Nkrumah's push for unification among African heads of state is plentiful. In December 1960, after His Imperial Majesty Haile Selassie I, Emperor of Ethiopia, visits Ghana, the two heads of state issue a joint communiqué which stated "that a Union of the African States is a necessity which should be pursued energetically in the interests of African solidarity and security" (p. 147). In October 1961, a similar one was issued by the president of Somalia and Nkrumah. Patrice Lumumba visited Ghana in August 1960, and Nkrumah writes that during his visit Lumumba "agreed then to work in the closest possible association with other independent African states for the establishment of a Union of African States" (p. 148). This would become a pattern—Nkrumah's influencing African heads of state (and those born outside of the continent as well) to acknowledge African unity as the only possible solution to the problems experienced by African people worldwide. Nkrumah worked diligently to get as many heads of state as possible first to agree to a united states of Africa and, second, to issue joint public statements to that effect.

Nkrumah saw that unity was necessary for the survival and development of Africa, but he was also convinced that unity was the solution for all peoples of the world: for example, that South America and the Caribbean must unite. In *Africa Must Unite*, he tells of Simon Bolivar's regrettably unsuccessful attempt to unite the South American colonies (p. 188). As well, Nkrumah writes of "federation of the British West Indian territories" (p. 189). According to Nkrumah, such a unity is not only the natural evolution of a people, but also "is the only answer to the present poverty and stagnant agricultural societies of the Caribbean world" (p. 189).

Talking and writing about unity is one thing; taking practical steps to bring about unity is another, and Nkrumah did both. Genuine, practical steps were taken to realize his goal of Pan-Africanism. Guinea, Mali, and Ghana formed "the nucleus of the United States of Africa" (AMU, p. 142). These three countries even went so far as to start "an African Common Market" (p. 143), and Nkrumah proposed that they "erect for the time being a constitutional form" (p. 220) that especially allows them "to formulate a common policy in all matters affecting the security, defence, and development of Africa" (p. 221). Moreover, "in July 1961 customs barriers between Ghana and Upper Volta were removed" (p. 157). It was Nkrumah's belief that "the linking together of neighboring brother states [was] the best means of promoting the welfare of the people throughout the whole continent" (p. 86); and he hoped "that other states in Africa will follow suit, and that we need not wait until the entire continent has seen the light of brotherhood. A start can be made with as little as two, three or four states willing to submit themselves to a sovereign union" (p. 86). In fact, he challenged newly independent states to "form a kind of African civil service pool, standing at the service of emerging African states and ready to serve the new Union of African States" (p. 96).

Nkrumah saw socialism as the mode of production that would enable "full employment, good housing and equal opportunity for education and cultural advancement for all the people up to the highest level possible" (AMU, p. 119), not, as with capitalism, just an opportunity for only a small percentage of the population to advance. As today's western, capitalist support of an African Union verifies, it was Nkrumah's commitment to socialism, not African liberation and unification, which most riled imperialists. This socialist path had to be prevented at all costs because it, if successfully achieved, would mean an end to neocolonialism and any other form of continental exploitation. In his attempt to establish a socialist united states of Africa, Nkrumah knew that Africa would need the help of established socialist countries such as the Soviet Union, China, Poland, Czechoslovakia, and Yugoslavia, so he went about forging "new links" with them (p. 108). More imminently threatening than this problem, but perhaps not as costly, was Nkrumah's push for world peace at one of the most active times for western capitalist countries. Nkrumah avows that Ghana will cooperate with "any living organism that can be counted on effectively to promote international peace" (p. 194). In September 1961, he attended the Belgrade Conference of Non-Aligned Countries in Yugoslavia, along with representatives from twenty-four other countries (p. 198). It was a meeting of all those interested in peace. There Nkrumah states that Ghana's foreign policy is three-pronged: "African independence, African unity, and the maintenance of world peace through a policy of positive neutrality and non-alignment" (p. 200). Nkrumah's threefold interests are clearly connected: crushing "imperialism and the recent offshoot neo-colonialism [is] in the interest of world peace … [and a] united Africa would be able to make a greater contribution towards the peace and progress of mankind" (p. 202); and he condemns imperialism for being "a fundamental cause of war" (p. 202).

Nkrumah does not speak of imperialism and neo-colonialism in the abstract; he specifically identifies those countries that are pursuing the policies of a new form of imperialism. As described by Nkrumah, the All-African People's Conference held in Cairo in 1961 (largely the brainchild of Nkrumah) "warned independent African states to beware of neo-colonialism, which was associated with the United Kingdom, the United States of America, France, Western Germany, Israel, Belgium, the Netherlands, and South Africa. It also warned states to be on their guard against imperialist agents "in the guise of religious or philanthropic organizations" (AMU, p. 139). These western powers will try "to divide Africa into fictitious zones north and south of the Sahara which emphasizes racial, religious and cultural differences" in order to facilitate exploitation" (p. 188). Nkrumah could have added "language differences" to the list. Of those countries most dangerous to unity, because of their proximity to other African countries, is South Africa. According to Nkrumah, its "building up [of] a military machine comparable with those of the foremost nations of Western Europe ... presents a most ominous danger" (p. xvii). Therefore, most important to the survival of each individual African country in the face of such danger was the commitment of African states to form a socialist union. In Nkrumah's thinking, if the Soviets could do it in "little over thirty years" then so could Africans.

Perhaps no other incident more clearly demonstrated the danger of 'balkanization' than the Congo debacle, the tragic outcome of which was the assassination of Patrice Lumumba. According to Nkrumah, it was "a valuable object lesson ... on the imperative need for unity" (AMU, p. 139). Africa must unite or perish!

CONSCIENCISM: PHILOSOPHY AND IDEOLOGY FOR DECOLONIZATION (1964/1970)

To wage a successful revolution, a people must have a philosophy—a world view, an outlook on the world, and an ideology—a guide to an objective based on that world view—taking into account that people's history and culture. In *Consciencism*, Nkrumah offers both.

Philosophies are based on either idealism or materialism. All materialist philosophies have at their core a tool called dialectical and historical materialism. Fundamental to materialism is the idea that matter is primary and gives rise to consciousness, that matter has the power of self-motion, that everything is governed by scientific law, that everything is thus knowable. Fundamental to dialectics is that everything and everyone is interconnected, that everything and everyone changes, that there is a quantitative buildup in things and people that leads to a qualitative change, that there are contradictions (negative and positive) in everything. Materialism and dialectics come together to form dialectical materialism. Historical materialism is nothing but dialectical materialism applied to the development of society. It is the materialist's conception of history, with the economic system playing the primary, determining role since it is that which ensures the survival of society's citizens. Therefore, an economic system primarily is responsible for the kinds of ideas prevalent in a society. An inherently unfair economic system, such as capitalism, will spawn unfair ideas. An inherently fair economic system, such as socialism, will spawn fair ideas.

Maoism, Marxist-Leninism, and Nkrumaism are materialist ideologies which have at their core materialist philosophies. Thus they employ the tool of dialectical and historical materialism. In *Consciencism* [hereafter "C"], Nkrumah discusses at length the elements of dialectical and historical materialism. These elements are also discussed in many other works and, in some cases, are mistakenly made synonymous with Marxism-Leninism. Because they are readily accessible, we need not take time discussing these principles here. What is primary in this review of Nkrumah's philosophical work is the way(s) in which the philosophy and ideology for African people must differ from the materialist philosophies embodied in the ideologies of Maoism or Marxist-Leninism.

Nkrumah names the philosophy for African people "philosophical consciencism". According to him, it is "the map in intellectual terms of the disposition of forces which will enable African society to digest the Western and the Islamic and the Euro-Christian elements in Africa, and develop them in such a way that they fit into the African personality" (C, p. 79). Another way to state this philosophy for African people is to pose the following question: In order to build an Africa that is for the people, how can Africans apply dialectics to their unique experiences as Africans, being, first, conscious of the fact that they have been influenced by Islam and Euro-Christianity; being, second, conscious of the fact that remnants of traditionalisms still exist in their societies; and being, third, conscious of the fact that because of these experiences, they suffer a personality, i.e. identity, crisis?

The essence of this question appears in statement form on the same page: "Philosophical consciencism is that philosophical standpoint which, taking its start from the present content of the African conscience, indicates the way in which progress is forged out of the conflict in that conscience" (C, p. 79). The statement reflects Nkrumah's belief that there is a crisis in the African world, and it hints at a blueprint that will resolve the crisis. Nkrumah never presents such a blueprint; but that African people suffer from a "Crisis of the African

Personality" resulting from the years of exploitation and oppression, he makes very clear. That liberation from their exploitation and oppression is vital, he again clearly articulates; and that applying dialectics to a people's own unique experience is an essential part of the liberation process again is made clear. However, a step-by-step, fully articulated plan for this liberation is not presented in *Consciencism*.

Unclear too is the distinction that Nkrumah makes between philosophical consciencism and other materialist philosophies. While he does state that it is essential to apply dialectics to a people's own unique experiences, he himself does not make this application. He writes in the last paragraph of *Consciencism* that "philosophical consciencism is a general philosophy which admits of application to any country. But it is especially applicable to colonies and newly independent and developing countries" (C, pp. 117–118). Clearly, however, philosophical consciencism is meant to be a philosophy for areas such as Africa that have experienced colonialism. Unlike the Soviet Union, for example, Africa cannot consider an evolution from a traditional reality to feudalism to capitalism to socialism. In fact, different parts of Africa had their societies interrupted at different stages of their development. At the time of contact with Europe, some areas were traditional; others, tributary. Then too the experience of colonialism negates the continent's capitalist chances since the western world's power would always relegate Africa and other colonial areas to the position of satellite areas, feeder regions, or neo-colonial territories.

More importantly, why would Africans want to adopt a capitalist reality? The whole idea of the African Revolution is to make conditions fair and just for all of the people, not just a few. So, Nkrumah writes:

> ... a people can only be redeemed by lifting themselves up, as it were, by the strings of their boots. ... It is only a socialist scheme of development that can meet the passionate objectivity of philosophical consciencism. (C, p. 113)

Nkrumah makes a point of saying that socialism must be applied to Africa in "regard to the experience and consciousness" of Africans, to Africa's "actual material conditions", to Africans' "experience and our consciousness" (C, p. 114). But socialism is like dialectical and historical materialism: tools, one philosophical and the other economical, which must be applied to particular conditions. Though the tools are universal, like a hammer and a nail, what you build, when you build, and where you build depend on the particular geopolitical environment as well as on the needs of the people living in that particular environment. As Nkrumah himself will later say, there is no such thing as African socialism.

The next concept that Nkrumah tackles in *Consciencism* is ideology. African people need a theoretical guide, a map, that will show them the way out of the exploitative and oppressive reality of colonialism, neo-colonialism, domestic colonialism, racism and sexism—all the ills that have befallen them. An ideology is a theoretical guide: "a body of connected thought which will determine the general nature of our action" and which will unify "the society which we have inherited, this unification to take account, at all times, of the elevated ideals underlying the traditional African society" (C, p. 78). In his description of ideology, Nkrumah writes:

> The ideology of a society is total. It embraces the whole life of a people, and manifests itself in their class-structure, history, literature, art, religion. It also acquires a philosophical statement. (C, p. 59)

In *Consciencism*, Nkrumah does not name this ideology. Later, those who subscribe to Nkrumah's political theories will call this ideology *Nkrumahism* or *Nkrumaism*, for two reasons: first, because of the unique history of Africa and its people and, second, in recognition of the political, economic, social, and moral theoretical and practical contributions that were best articulated and practised by Kwame Nkrumah.

What specifically will an African ideology do for African people? It will show them how to take the positive from their three experiences—Islamic, Euro-Christian, and traditional—and unite them to create a new African reality; a new Africa, free from exploitation; and a new African personality:

> African society has one segment which comprises our traditional way of life; it has a second segment which is filled by the presence of the Islamic tradition in Africa; it has a final segment which represents the infiltration of the Christian tradition and culture of Western Europe into Africa, using colonialism and neocolonialism as its primary vehicles. These different segments are animated by competing ideologies. But since society implies a certain dynamic unity, there needs to emerge an ideology which, genuinely catering for the needs of all, will take the place of the competing ideologies, and so reflect the dynamic unity of society and be the guide of society's continual progress. (C, p. 68)

Nkrumaism will also cohere the struggles of African people into a monolithic union. Without such an ideological unity to guide Africans in building a united, socialist motherland as well as to guide them in sustaining and nurturing themselves until they are truly liberated, Africans will be left struggling to survive day by day—divided, dependent, and without an agreed-upon plan as to how they can overcome their problems permanently. Ideological unity, then, is the most effective weapon to unite the energies of African people in order to guide them toward collective action in pursuit of Pan-Africanism.

Nkrumah, in the final portion of *Consciencism*, uses set theorems to demonstrate that this forging is possible. But the process of forging the three experiences is not laid out. How can the three disparate experiences be forged together? Is Nkrumaism an overarching, superceding ideology that recognizes these three disparate realities? What are the essential features of Nkrumaism that makes it pertain to Africans only: same identity, same enemy, same objective, same strategy, same tactics? What is the first step that Africans must take in forging these realities? What is the second step, the third, and so on? Present day and future Nkrumaists must continue to clarify and develop Nkrumaism to make it a clear and useful liberating ideology.

There are further questions for both present and future Nkrumaists to ponder. While ideological unity seems the most effective tool to direct the motion of Africans toward Pan-Africanism, is the achievement of such unity realistic or even necessary for reaching the initial phase(s) of Pan-Africanism? Is the difficult task of forging the diverse experiences of African people required in order to liberate, unite and launch a socialist Africa? Is it sufficient for Africans to tolerate diversity and recognize the legitimacy of myriad experiences?

Can Africans agree on the following: the co-existence of a plurality of religious beliefs in Africa, the only necessary element being one's commitment to Pan-Africanism; the liberation and unification of Africa under a socialist economic system; the embracing of the principles of humanism, collectivism, and egalitarianism; the struggle to push the positive; the commitment to education on all levels and in all sectors of the population; and, finally, the adherence to the laws of the socialist state?

Affirmative answers to these questions may facilitate and expedite the building of Pan-Africanism. For Africans must eliminate all obstacles in order to have a clear, unencumbered path to Pan-Africanism.

In *Consciencism* Nkrumah moves beyond merely criticizing imperialism in all of its disguises. Rather, he advocates a liberated, united, socialist continent and attempts to demonstrate how it will emerge, ideologically. Despite its shortcomings, Nkrumaism, as presented in *Consciencism*, is an ideology that Nkrumah creates and presents to African people as a map to guide all African people toward Pan-Africanism. And, as in all of his works, he clearly and straightforwardly criticizes capitalism and imperialism and neo-colonialism. In fact, he shows that one gives birth to the other: "Imperialism, which is the highest stage of capitalism, will continue to flourish in different forms as long as conditions permit it" (C, p. 57). The only way to end imperialism is to make sure that "there are no vested interests exploiting the earth, its fruits and resources for the benefit of a few against the well-being of the many" (p. 58). Neo-colonialism is not substantively different from capitalism and imperialism: they all are economic structures under which the few exploit the many. Capitalism is the term used to describe an economic system which operates in a defined territory and which exploits the labor of its own citizens on behalf of a few. It "is a development by refinement from feudalism" and "is but the gentleman's method of slavery" (p. 72). Imperialism is capitalism extended abroad, so that now not only are citizens of the capitalist country being exploited, but also citizens of someone else's country are being exploited. Neo-colonialism is a particular form of imperialism whereby the leadership of exploited countries is corrupted and serves as puppets for capitalist countries.

> In neo-colonialism ... the people are divided from their leaders and, instead of providing true leadership and guidance which is informed at every point by the ideal of the general welfare, leaders come to neglect the very people who put them in power and incautiously become instruments of suppression on behalf of the neo-colonialists. (C, p. 102)

In distinguishing between colonialism and neo-colonialism, Nkrumah writes: "Neo-colonialism is negative action playing possum" (C, p. 100). Nkrumah was not blind to the intent of imperialists to re-colonize African countries as they, one by one, gained independence. He stated that "any oblique attempt of a foreign power to thwart, balk, corrupt or otherwise pervert the true independence of a sovereign people is neo-colonialist" because the foreign power is seeking "to subordinate [the interests of a sovereign people] to those of a foreign power" (p. 102). In fact, Nkrumah was one of the first statesmen, if not the first, to recognize that "neo-colonialism, much like post-slavery in the United States, is a greater danger to independent countries than is colonialism" because "colonialism is crude, essentially overt, and apt to be overcome by a purposeful concert of national effort", p. 102). On the other hand, neo-colonialism is a surreptitious attempt by imperialists to come back (if they had left) into a former colony in order to control it—back-door colonialism, so to speak.

Three other statements in *Consciencism*, articulated in a more developed form in Nkrumah's later works, must nevertheless have proven noteworthy to neo-colonialists. First, that "The passage from the ancestral line of slavery via feudalism and capitalism to socialism can only lie through revolution" (C, p. 73). Second, that "Capitalism at home is domestic colonialism" (p. 74), a term that Malcolm X popularized in the USA. Third, that "The emancipation of the African continent is the emancipation of man" (p. 78). In essence, what these three statements signal is that the former colonialists must ready themselves for battle, at home and abroad; that all exploited and oppressed people are linked in their revolutionary fight to free themselves; and that any oppressed people's liberation contributes to the liberation of humanity.

Undoubtedly, the capitalists/imperialists took note of Nkrumah—especially since there were those listening throughout the African continent, throughout the African Diaspora, throughout the non-western world, and, indeed, those exploited and oppressed throughout the developed, western world.

NEO-COLONIALISM: THE LAST STAGE OF IMPERIALISM (1965)

With the publication in 1965 of *Neo-Colonialism* [hereafter "N-C"], Nkrumah was one of the earliest to expose the machinations of the capitalist world. When capitalists understood that they could no longer operate in the same manner in regard to their colonies, they devised another plan of exploitation: "all former colonies which have now become independent, including particularly South Africa, are subject in some degree to neo-colonialist pressures which however much they wish to resist they cannot entirely escape, struggle as they may" (N-C, pp. 20). What is neo-colonialism? Instead of having their agents visible and of European descent, the imperialists schemed to present a new "front"—a so-called puppet front. Handpicked Africans serve as the clients of the imperialists; they become the leaders of former colonies and simply allow the imperialists to continue to exploit the newly independent countries, sacrificing their own people's needs for their selfish, individualistic desire for wealth and power. "The essence of neo-colonialism", writes Nkrumah, "is that the State which is subject to it is, in theory, independent and has all the outward trappings of international sovereignty. In reality its economic system and thus its political policy is directed from outside" (p. ix). In other words, neo-colonialism is a new form of colonization. It is, in fact, "the worst form of imperialism" because neo-colonialism "means power without responsibility and for those who suffer from it, it means exploitation without redress" (p. xi).

Under colonialism, the enemy at least was visible and, from time to time, forced "to explain and justify" its position (N-C, p. xi). Under colonialism, one country controlled a colony or colonies. Under neo-colonialism, however, "control may be exercised by a consortium of financial interests which are not specifically identifiable with any particular state" (p. x). Nkrumah cites the Congo as an example of a country controlled by "great international financial concerns" (p. x). Another pitfall of neo-colonialism is multilateral aid that filters through international organizations such as the International Monetary Fund (IMF) and the World Bank. Nkrumah exposes this type of aid as a "trap", with "U.S. capital as [the organizations'] major backing" (p. 242); and:

> ... these agencies have the habit of forcing would-be borrowers to submit to various offensive conditions, such as supplying information about their economies, submitting their policy and plans to review by the World Bank and accepting agency supervision of their use of loans. (N-C, pp. 242–243)

What all this means in essence is the control of the newly independent state's economy. Once the country receives aid, it relinquishes its right to self-determination. Redress from wrongs committed as a result of neo-colonialism becomes even more difficult to obtain. Nkrumah writes that neo-colonialists now have "the right to meddle in internal finances, including currency and foreign exchange, to lower trade barriers in favour of the donor country's goods and capital; to protect the interests of private investments", and so on and so on (N-C, p. 243).

But neo-colonialism could never be successful if it remained solely an economic matter. How can an organization (or a corporation), a consortium of financial institutions, or a small group of people and its African puppets keep millions of people under its boot? Nkrumah asks this question himself. The answer is by controlling and influencing the religious, ideological and cultural spheres of a country (N-C, p. 239): "To ensure success … , the imperialists have made widespread and wily use of ideological and cultural weapons" (pp. 245–246). What are examples of such weapons? They are the same weapons used within their own territories. The media, for example, is a potent weapon. Nkrumah writes: "One has only to listen to the cheers of an African audience as Hollywood's heroes slaughter red Indians or Asiatics to understand the effectiveness of this weapon" (p. 246). Then too there is "the enormous monopoly press, together with the outflow of slick, clever, expensive magazines" (p. 246). There is also the international capitalist journalism which puts out "a flood of anti-liberation propaganda" or anti-communist propaganda (p. 247). Moreover, the Peace Corps, the CIA, the US Information Agency (USIA) and "Hollywood"—all of these agencies of the US are, according to Nkrumah, arms and weapons in the service of neo-colonialists (p. 247). Nkrumah also writes that "Perhaps one of the most insidious methods of the neo-colonialists is religious evangelism" (p. 247) and cites the anti-nationalist influence of "largely" American religious sects: "Typical of these are Jehovah's Witnesses … busily teaching … citizens not to salute the new national flags" (p. 247).

Of course, as a last resort, there are the military bases and military advisers that are found throughout Africa. Sometimes, when accepting aid— or as "the departing colonialists" privilege, what accompanies it (or what is granted) —is the "setting up [of] military bases or stationing troops in former colonies and the supplying of 'advisers' of one sort or another" (N-C, p. 246). Neo-colonialists will try in every way and at all costs and at all times to thwart the people's efforts to resist exploitation and thereby to "save" the African world.

What is the remedy? The African Revolution. A liberated, united socialist Africa and, eventually, worldwide socialism: "A continent like Africa, however much it increases its agricultural output, will not benefit unless it is sufficiently politically and economically united to force the developed world to pay it a fair price for its cash crops" (N-C, p. 9). In fact, because neo-colonialist "financial and economic empires are pan-African, they can only be challenged on a pan-African basis. Only a united Africa, through an All-African Union Government can defeat them" (N-C, p. 36). As far as Africa is concerned, capitalist unity is neo-colonial unity. A united capitalist Africa will just facilitate the neo-colonialists' exploitation of the continent. Socialism is the only economic system that will lift Africa from the depths of its poverty for all of its people and make it a powerhouse to be reckoned with. But first Africa must become an industrial socialist power. Second, not only must "the socialized modes of production and tremendous human and capital investments involved call for cohesive and integrated planning" (p. 11), but also "Africa will need to bring to its aid all its talent and ingenuity in order to meet the challenge that independence and demands of its peoples for better living have raised. The challenge cannot be met on any piece-meal scale, but only by the total mobilization of the continent's resources within the framework of comprehensive socialist planning and deployment" (p. 11). It will mean a total continental reorganization of the production process "so that each country can specialize in producing the goods and crops for which it is best suited" (p. 27). Of course, *Africa Must Unite* is the Nkrumah work which best describes this method of continental production and exchange. *Neo-Colonialism*'s interest is in exposing the enemy of Africa and all other developing areas of the world. And it does it well.

In the introduction to *Neo-Colonialism*, Nkrumah writes: "This book is therefore an attempt to examine neo-colonialism not only in its African context and its relation to African unity, but in a world perspective" because "neo-colonialism is by no means exclusively an African question" (N-C, p. xvii). It is in the context of his world influence as well as in the context of his influence on the African world that Nkrumah is most threatening to the capitalists: "When Africa becomes economically free and politically united, the monopolists will come face to face with their own working class in their own countries, and a new struggle will arise within which the liquidation and collapse of imperialism will be complete" (N-C, p. 256). For the capitalists, another disturbing

Nkrumah revelation is that the US is "the world's leading imperialist power" which "lays successor claim to the so-called vacua which the retiring colonial powers are said to leave behind" (N-C, p. 56). Nkrumah goes further, pointing out the US's roles in Vietnam and the Congo as ones of "rabid neo-colonialism" (N-C, p. 56).

In the wake of this new colonialist power that has emerged in Africa, there are eight important objectives that must be undertaken, according to Nkrumah:

1. Nkrumah, and all other Pan-Africanists, must exert "mass pressure" on every African leader to make "it impossible for him openly to oppose African unity" (p. 24);
2. Africa must unite;
3. Afro-Asian solidarity must be strengthened (p. 253);
4. Relationships must be forged with "our Latin American brothers" (p. 253);
5. "The support of the growing socialist sector of the world" must continue its support of the developing world (p. 253);
6. "Support for liberation and anti-colonialism inside the imperialist world itself" must grow (p. 253);
7. Nkrumah, and others like him, must continue their exposure of the people's enemy;
8. All sectors of the world's masses must be educated about the nature of neo-colonialism because it is not a leader but the masses who are the makers of history.

In regard to this last point, Nkrumah writes, "for when all is said and done, it is the so-called little man, the bent-backed, exploited, malnourished, blood-covered fighter for independence who decides. And he invariably decides for freedom" (N-C, p. 254). The fight against neo-colonialism is ultimately a world-wide class struggle between the "haves" and the "have nots" (N-C, p. 255).

HANDBOOK OF REVOLUTIONARY WARFARE (1968)

With each succeeding work, Nkrumah more deeply penetrates into the inner workings of capitalism. *Handbook of Revolutionary Warfare* (hereafter HRW) must have been more troubling to the capitalists/imperialists than Nkrumah's previous works for three reasons. First, it demonstrates that the 1966 coup d'état that deposed Nkrumah's government in Ghana and exiled Nkrumah to the neighbouring state of Guinea was not sufficient to silence him. Second, it evidences Nkrumah's maturing class consciousness in regard to the nature of capitalism and imperialism. Third, it serves as a manual or map for Africans to use to destroy neo-colonialism and to set up a continental, socialist united states of Africa with all of the machinery necessary to ensure the union's success.

After the overthrow in 1966, Nkrumah becomes co-president of Guinea and produces his most class-conscious theoretical work to date. Although more politically conscious people listen to Nkrumah after the coup, the coup has let puppet leaders of Africa and the world "off the hook"—they no longer have to pay "lip service" to the African Revolution. The politically conscious know that Nkrumah's likely CIA-inspired overthrow proves that what Nkrumah said in *Neo-Colonialism* is correct. Neo-colonialists will do whatever is in their power to hold on to the former colonies. In *The Handbook of Revolutionary Warfare*, Nkrumah wastes no time in repeating his messages of unity and exposing the nature of the enemy. However, he relegates only Chapter One of Book One to the enemy. Rather, he realizes that time is so precious in the struggle for Pan-Africanism that he must come to the point:

> Time is running out. We must act now. The freedom fighters already operating in many parts of Africa must no longer be allowed to bear the full brunt of a continental struggle against a continental enemy. (HRW, p. 42)

Nkrumah understands that "independence" struggles are not simply national independence struggles. If successful, they are part of a two-part war that ends in a union of socialist states. Also, he recognizes that the enemy is not confined to one western nation. Several nations, including Israel, are actively involved with, or provide material support for, colonial powers. And he knows that the enemy does not just operate in one African country; it operates continentally. The key question to address, then, is what must Africa do right now in light of "the world strategy of imperialism"? Heretofore, he had placed great hope in the leadership of Africa. No longer. The answer seems clear after his overthrow: Africa must form a guerilla revolutionary army to fight for Africa. Indeed, this purpose is clear from the dedication of *The Handbook of Revolutionary Warfare*: "the guerilla is the masses in arms".

In "Book One, Know the enemy", new, insightful points are included, reflecting Nkrumah's post-coup, sharpened class consciousness. For example, he writes that the myth of capitalism in regard to everyone enjoying affluence was revealed in "the establishment of a 'welfare state' as the only safeguard against the threat of fascism or communism" (HRW, p. 4). In essence, "the welfare state is the internal condition, neo-colonialism is the external condition, for the continued hegemony of international finance capital" (p. 12–13). Another example is his point regarding the United Nations: "The imperialists even make use of the United Nations Organisation in order to camouflage their neo-colonialist objectives" (p. 7). As a last resort, neo-colonialists "set up a bogus 'progressive' party", as they did in Guinea-Bissau and Angola, in order to set the stage "for negotiations, autonomy and the formation of a puppet government" (p. 10). Along with assassinations, the coup d'état is the neo-colonialists' last resort (p. 11). In a speech made at the Opening of the Second Conference of African Journalists on November 11, 1963, Nkrumah prefigured his own coup d'état in defining neo-colonialism and in telling his audience how it works. The machinations of the neo-colonialists are key in this speech:

> They see to it that the political power remains in the hands of indigenous reactionaries.
> They manoeuvre to control the Army, the Police and even the Intelligence Services.
> They see to it that the economic institutions of the country are in the hands of their agents, and that economic production is completely controlled by private foreign capital leaving only the less profitable infrastructure in the hands of the indigenous population.
> They divide the Trade Union and other popular movements.
> When they have gained full control, in this way, of a client or puppet state, with a client or puppet administration, then they are in a position to do what they like to the territory, its government and its people.
> If they cannot get their own way, then they engineer political and military coups, to overthrow the regimes and install new reactionary regimes which will carry out their orders.
> Both the basic nature of neo-colonialism and the accumulated experience of liberation movements in Africa, Asia and Latin America indicate clearly that the only way for the broad masses to eradicate neo-colonialism is through a revolutionary movement springing from a direct confrontation with the imperialists, and drawing its strength from the exploited and disinherited masses. (HRW, p. 16)

Prior to the February 1966 overthrow, Nkrumah had been working to get "heads of state" to agree to unify. But once ousted, he understood clearly that a grassroots movement involving armed struggle would be the only way to prevent Africa's re-colonization (HRW, p. 18). He writes: "revolutionary warfare is the key to African freedom and is the only way in which total liberation and unity of the African continent can be achieved" (p. 20–21); and that armed struggle is not a choice, neither is it moral or immoral. Rather, "it is a scientific historically-determined necessity" (p. 19). No one wants war. However, freedom is the objective, and if war is the only way to achieve this objective, then so be it. Nkrumah is not going to stop. He will not be silenced. Instead, he is revving-up the African Revolution, calling for "the formation of the All-African People's Revolutionary Army" (p. 23).

Book One, Chapter Two concentrates on Pan-Africanism. Most of the text in this chapter is a reiteration of his earlier declarations of a liberated, unified, socialist Africa: "in unity lies strength. African states must unite or sell themselves out to imperialist and colonialist exploiters for a mess of pottage, or disintegrate individually" (HRW, p. 35). Also repeated is the point that it makes no sense to unite if socialism is not the economic system that prevails: "Only under socialism can we reliably accumulate the capital we need for our development, ensure that the gains of investment are applied to the general welfare, and achieve our goal of a free and united continent" (p. 29). In other words, if Africa unites under capitalism, Africa will be a continental slave to neocolonialism, the agents of which will use any means to prevail. One of its earliest tactics is to entice leaders to "sell out" their people and become puppets of neo-colonialism. Sometimes, neo-colonialists can corrupt not only an individual, but also an entire organization. This is the case with the Organization of African Unity (p. 36–38).

Book Two is most important. It lays out the plan for the African Revolution, with the understanding that "Africa is one; and this battle must be fought and won continentally" (HRW, p. 43). Strategically, Africans must see the continent not as a geopolitical area of more than fifty microstates, but as a vast territory divided according to their present condition in the struggle against neo-colonialism. Therefore, "our continental territory [must be] considered as consisting of three categories of territories which correspond to the varying levels of popular organisation and to the precise measure of victory attained by the people's forces over the enemy" (p. 43). The three categories are as follows: liberated areas, zones under enemy control, and contested zones (i.e., hot points). This is Nkrumah's zonal theory. Each of the zones is described. Of particular interest are the enemy-held and contested zones because these need to move to the status of liberated territories. The significant difference between the enemy-held and contested zone is "only one missing link: a handful of genuine revolutionaries prepared to organize and act" (p. 49). In order to help change zones to liberated ones, an All-African People's Revolutionary Party (AAPRP) is needed "to co-ordinate policies and to direct action" (p. 56). Moreover, an All-African People's Revolutionary Army (AAPRA) is needed "to unify our liberation forces and to carry the armed struggle through to final victory" (p. 56). Lastly, there must exist an All-African Committee for Political Coordination (AACPC) "to act as a liaison between all parties which recognise the urgent necessity of conducting an organised and unified struggle against colonialism and neo-colonialism" (p. 57).

In this protracted struggle for Pan-Africanism and against neo-colonialism, there is a role for everyone, "for the people are the makers of history" (HRW, p. 75): peasants, workers, students, women, the national bourgeoisie, revolutionary outsiders. All must be politically educated and play a role in defeating the enemy. Peasants must be organized because they "form the overwhelming majority of our population" (HRW, p. 76); workers too since they are "the essential labour force for the continued existence of neo-colonialism" (p. 81). Of particular significance is the role of African women, who "have already shown themselves to be of paramount importance in the revolutionary struggle" (p. 89). In fact, according to Nkrumah, "the degree of a country's revolutionary awareness, may be measured by the political maturity of its women" (p. 91). Another sector of vital importance is the youth, for young people are the spark for revolution. So, "in liberated areas, students must constantly guard and revitalise the revolution. On our youth depends the future of Africa and the continent's total liberation and unity" (p. 88).

The last part of *The Handbook of Revolutionary Warfare* concentrates on "some of the fundamental elementary principles and techniques of guerilla warfare" (HRW, p. 103). Most of the space in this final section is dedicated to the organization of a guerilla army: "The fully-trained guerilla is armed both ideologically and physically for the revolutionary struggle. The tactics of guerilla warfare rest in the main with him. With the support of the masses, and with unified direction of the revolutionary party, he is invincible" (p. 122).

Nkrumah ends *The Handbook of Revolutionary Warfare* with a call to action, a call that could not but send shivers through the neo-colonialists: "People of Africa, arise! Defeat imperialism, neo-colonialism and settler domination. Stand together and unite in the revolutionary struggle. Forward to victory. We shall conquer" (HRW, p. 122).

THE SPECTRE OF BLACK POWER and *MESSAGE TO THE BLACK PEOPLE OF BRITAIN* (1968)

In 1968, Nkrumah writes two additional works: "The Spectre of Black Power" (pamphlet) and "Message to the Black People of Britain" (essay), both reprinted in *The Struggle Continues* [hereafter "Struggle"]; sections also included in *Revolutionary Path* ["RP"]). Both are considered major works in this study because they extend the political line of Nkrumaism.

In "The Spectre of Black Power", Nkrumah reaches a breakthrough in his theory of the African Revolution. It is this work, more than any other, which clarifies the concept of "Black Power", collapsing all "Black Power" struggles around the world into one struggle—the African Revolution. Here Nkrumah clearly and meticulously links Africans born in the Diaspora with the Pan-

African Movement. Black Power, according to him, is insubstantial, vaporous, unless it is part and parcel of the struggle to achieve a socialist united Africa and worldwide socialism:

> What is Black Power? I see it in the United States as part of the vanguard of the world revolution against capitalism, imperialism and neo-colonialism which have enslaved, exploited and oppressed peoples everywhere, and against which the masses of the world are now revolting. Black Power is part of the world rebellion of the oppressed against oppressor, of the exploited against the exploiter. It operates throughout the African continent, in North and South America, the Caribbean, wherever Africans and people of African descent live. It is linked with the Pan-African struggle for unity on the African continent, and with all those who strive to establish a socialist society. (RP, p. 426; Struggle, pp. 39–40)

Therefore, Black Power is merely ephemeral if not linked to the African Revolution, according to Nkrumah. Chronicling the history of this link, Nkrumah substantiates the connection between those abroad and those at home. In fact, he asserts that "Pan-Africanism has its beginnings in the liberation struggle of African-Americans, expressing the aspirations of Africans and peoples of African descent" (RP, p. 421; Struggle, p. 34). Those Africans first enslaved on the continent and then marched to the coast to await embarkation struggled, every step of the way, to return to their homes. While packed like "herrings in a barrel" during the Atlantic Crossing, Africans still struggled, sometimes jumping overboard and other times commandeering the ship in order to return home. Then, once in the West, there were the early attempts to return by those like Paul Cuffee, Alexander Crummell and Martin Delany. Nkrumah documents the dominant role played by Africans in the Americas in organizing the many African conferences held for the sake of Mother Africa: "From the first Pan-African Conference, held in London in 1900, until the fifth and last [Pan-African] Conference held in Manchester in 1945, African-Americans provided the main driving power of the movement" (RP, p. 421; Struggle, p. 34). With the foundation laid by Diasporan Africans, Nkrumah could build Pan-Africanism in a practical way once he returned to Ghana in the late 1940s. Beginning in April 1958 with the First Conference of Independent African States in Accra, Nkrumah takes Pan-Africanism to "its true home": Africa.

The importance of "The Spectre of Black Power" lies in Nkrumah's insistence that there is only one way to achieve Black Power—the African Revolution: "Just as there is only one true socialism, scientific socialism, the principles of which are universal and abiding, there is only one way to achieve the African revolutionary goals of liberation, political unification and socialism"

(RP, p. 423; Struggle, p. 35). Moreover, as he had written in *Handbook*, the only way to achieve unity and socialism on the African continent is through armed struggle; it is the only tactic that will rid Africa of the neo-colonialist "stranglehold over the economic life of our continent" (RP, p. 423; Struggle, p. 34). Africans have no other choice but to fight, and there is no room for fear. It is for these reasons—the dialectical relationship between the Black Power Movements in the Diaspora and the African Revolution as well as the necessity of fearlessness—that Nkrumah dedicates this pamphlet to revolutionaries who showed themselves brave in the face of the enemy: Ernesto Che Guevara, Ben Barka, and Malcolm X. In addition, he frames the pamphlet with words intended to rally all Africans for the fight. After the dedication, he inserts a poem (RP, p. 421; Struggle, p. 33):

> *"We could mourn them but they don't want our tears;*
> *We scorn death knowing that we cannot be defeated".*

Toward the end of the pamphlet, Nkrumah again readies Africans for the struggle ahead—like a general about to lead his men and women into war:

> For us in Africa, for the people of African descent everywhere, there can be no turning back, no compromise, no fear of failure or death. Africa must and shall fulfill her destiny. Even though revolution must reach its goal of unity and socialism. We have taken the correct road, even though hazardous. We face death as we face life with head up, eyes lifted, proud and unafraid. The seed dies that life may come forth. So, we may meet death knowing that we cannot be defeated. (RP, p. 428; Struggle, p. 42)

"Message to the Black People of Britain" also adds to Nkrumah's theoretical contribution to the African Revolution. While much of it repeats his belief, articulated in "The Spectre", of the importance of Diasporan Africans to the Pan-African Movement, there are two new and important elements emphasized in this work. First, and most important, is that any African is a citizen of Africa, any and every part of Africa and the rest of the Pan-African world. There is no such thing as an "alien" African:

> I want you all to understand that I am not in exile in Conakry. Every country and town in Africa is my home, and so I am at home in Conakry, Guinea, as I would be at home in any part of the black world. (RP, p. 431; Struggle, p. 14)

Secondly, Nkrumah exposes the traitorous relationship that some African leaders have with the neo-colonialists, a relationship that he will explore in more depth in *Class Struggle in Africa* (1970) and in his Conakry Letters:

The tragedy is that some African heads of state are themselves actually aiding and abetting imperialists and neo-colonialists. In February 1967 Malawi became the first independent African state to conclude a trade agreement, and later to establish diplomatic relations with South Africa. (RP, p. 431; Struggle, p. 17)

South Africa—the very country that was killing and raping Malawi's sisters and brothers in Africa, particularly those living in Angola, Namibia and Zimbabwe!

CLASS STRUGGLE IN AFRICA (1970)

The last major work that Nkrumah publishes before his death is *Class Struggle in Africa* (1970). Ironically, it is published in the same year in which Guinea and the Democratic Party of Guinea (PDG) witness "the most dangerous [attempted overthrow]—on 22 November 1970" (Milne, 1978, p. 189). Dedicated to the "workers and peasants of Africa", *Class Struggle in Africa* [hereafter "CSA"] exposes the neo-colonialist African puppets, would-be puppets, and political puppetry in general.

Once again Nkrumah aims to educate his readers about the true nature of capitalism, in all its guises, to expose its vicious, anti-people objective so as to prepare Africans for its ultimate destruction: "Imperialism is moribund capitalism; neocolonialism is moribund colonialism. Both sharpen the contradictions in their nature, which eventually lead to their destruction" (CSA, p. 71). From embryo forms of capitalism (such as slavery, tributary systems, feudalism) to more modern forms such as neo-colonialism, class divisions are fomented by capitalists in order to facilitate the exploitation of environments and peoples, natural and human resources, throughout the world. In Africa, these class divisions that existed were "blurred" during colonialism but during national independence struggles they "reappeared, often with increased intensity, particularly in those states where the newly independent government embarked on socialist policies" (p. 10).

A class is a group of "individuals bound together by certain interests which as a class they try to preserve and protect" (CSA, p. 17). The class which has the most wealth has the most power and dominates the society; it is the class that rules: "The ruling class possesses the major instruments of economic production and distribution, and the means of establishing its political dominance, while the subject class serves the interests of the ruling class, and is politically, economically and socially dominated by it" (p. 17). In a capitalist (colonial or neo-colonial) society, the wealthy, powerful class that dominates is a small group of people, less than 1% of a population. This small class constructs a state to its liking for the sole purpose of exploitation, and dominates it: "In capitalist states, the government represents the exploiting class" (p. 17).

During the struggle for independence in African countries, the defeated or about-to-be defeated colonialists had to think of a way to survive. The only way to do so was to come up with a person who was willing to serve as a puppet to lead a country, a puppet that the old colonialist could manipulate. No matter how many Nkrumahs were overthrown or how many Lumumbas murdered, a puppet still had to be found and installed so that exploitation could continue. The puppet leaders of the world who sell their people out to the highest bidder form the foundation of neo-colonialism. These indigenous bourgeoisie are the "true class enemies" of the people and serve as a weight around the necks of the emerging people's revolutions around the world (p. 15). They make it possible for "international monopoly finance" to continue "to plunder Africa and to frustrate the purposes of the African Revolution" (p. 63). So the first thing Africans must do is to expose the puppet (p. 63) as nothing but a "reactionary bourgeoisie" (p. 84), a slave of the capitalist world, who serves as "a bridge for continued imperialist and neocolonialist domination and exploitation" (p. 85). Class struggle in Africa, and indeed throughout the world, must be waged.

Tribalism and racism are machinations of neo-colonialism, so we must not become distracted by them. Nkrumah writes that racism "is inseparable from capitalist economic development" (CSA, p. 27), the removal of capitalism ensures the removal of race oppression. Tribes too emerged as a historic development and "may ... remain" (p. 60). But "tribalism—tribal politics ... should be fought and destroyed" (p. 60) because it is an instrument of neo-colonialism: "Many of the so-called tribal conflicts in modern Africa are in reality class forces brought into conflict by the transition from colonialism to neocolonialism. Tribalism is the result of, not the cause of, underdevelopment" (p. 59).

So, what must be done to unmask the neo-colonialists, to expose the indigenous bourgeoisie, and to free the African masses? Nkrumah's answer once again is the African Revolution—the struggle that must be waged in order to liberate and to unite Africa, and to create a socialist economic system in order to serve its people, those at home and those abroad. It is a Revolution that requires us to regard all people of African descent as Africans. There should be no divisions among us that hold back the African Revolution. For example, the 'balkanization' that resulted from the Berlin Conference of 1884–1885 must be exposed as "artificial territorial boundaries created by imperialism" (CSA, p. 67). Moreover, descriptors such as Nigerian, American, Canadian, Brazilian, Jamaican should not impede the Revolution, for the goal—because it is the only hope for survival, as reggae artist Judy Mowatt sings—is a continent, not an island. There is, therefore, "no justification for the victimization and the expulsion of migrant African labour from one territory to another. In Africa there should be no African 'alien.' All are Africans" (p. 66). The African Revolution, according to Nkrumah, embraces and envelops all people of African descent because "all peoples of African descent, whether they live in North or South America, the Caribbean, or in any other part of the world are Africans and belong to the African nation" (p. 87 footnote).

In the late 1960s, prior to writing *Class Struggle in Africa*, Nkrumah was well aware of the "Black Revolution" being waged in the USA. He was the first to understand that there was only one Black Revolution and that was the African Revolution involving the liberation and unification of a socialist Africa ("The Spectre of Black Power"). It was Nkrumah who taught this lesson to Kwame Ture (Stokely Carmichael) and Malcolm X, among others:

> ... until Africa is united under a socialist government, the Black man throughout the world lacks a national home. It is around the African peoples' struggles for liberation and unification that African or Black culture will take shape and substance. (CSA, p. 87–88)

So what if Africans don't speak the same language or, if by historic circumstances, they don't share the same borders: "The notion that in order to have a nation it is necessary for there to be a common language, a common territory and a common culture, has failed to stand the test of time or the scrutiny of scientific definition of objective reality" (CSA, p. 88). What is most critical is the "community of economic life" (CSA, p. 88).

Africans, those at home and those abroad as Marcus Garvey stated, must have as their primary goal, Pan-Africanism. Nkrumah writes: "The total liberation and unification of Africa under an All-African socialist government" (CSA, p. 80) will not only help "people of African descent everywhere", it will "at the same time advance the triumph of the international socialist revolution, and the onward progress towards world communism, under which every society is ordered on the principle of—from each according to his ability, to each according to his needs" (p. 88).

Although Africa and its scattered people are Nkrumah's primary concern, they are not his sole focus. Nkrumah's conception of the African Revolution encompasses more than Africa. The exploitation of the masses of the people worldwide by a handful of greedy people is also a part of this Revolution. So, he makes it plain that when he talks of socialism, he is not referring to "African socialism" which he perceives as a meaningless and irrelevant term since there is no such thing as "a form of socialism peculiar to Africa" (CSA, p. 26). Socialism is an economic system based on the premise that the masses of the people own the major means of production in a society and control the distribution of the goods which emerge from that production process. Therefore, Nkrumah, as a humanist concerned about the welfare of humanity, advocates worldwide socialism. It is critical for the "peoples of the less industrialized areas of the world", those of Africa, Asia and Latin America (p. 82). It is just as critical for those residing in the developed nations of the world who are themselves being exploited by capitalism. Therefore, there must be a "world revolutionary process" to link "the three main streams: the socialist world system, the liberation movements of the peoples of Africa, Asia and Latin America, and the working-class movement in the industrialized, capitalist countries" (p. 82).

In regard to the African Revolution, Nkrumah's major works represent the assimilation, advancement, and refinement of Pan-Africanism in general and, in particular, Garveyism, the theory put forth by Amy Ashwood Garvey, Amy Jacques Garvey, Marcus Garvey and millions of others in the Universal Negro Improvement Association (UNIA). For example, questions such as the nature of the economic system best suited for Africa and the nature of the struggle that must be waged to reclaim Africa were either left unaddressed in Garveyism or were not clearly understood at the turn of the twentieth century. Nkrumah's advancement and refinement of the elements of the African Revolution were desperately needed in the wake of the colonialist and neo-colonialist ploys in Africa. And, as always, in any historic epoch, the objective and subjective conditions, as well as the consciousness of the people, groom someone to step up to address their needs. Kwame Nkrumah fulfilled this historic necessity by supplying the theoretical model for the reclamation of Africa. This would be extended even further during his final years in Conakry, Guinea. The body of his correspondence during those years illuminates the particular details of the African Revolution and reflects Nkrumah's most progressive thinking, that which precedes his death on April 27, 1972.

~ ~ ~ ~ ~

2

The Conakry Letters

In regard to the nature of imperialism, the 1966 Ghana coup d'état sharpens the understanding of Africans and colonial subjects everywhere in general and Nkrumah in particular. That is, the act, the coup, proves correct the theory that Nkrumah espoused in *Neo-Colonialism* and other works: that the imperialists will use everything in their power to continue to exploit and that no single state in Africa will ever be secure until Africa unites. However, far from solving the problem of Nkrumah's influence on the world, the coup only increases the problem. He intensifies his efforts to expose the enemy and to achieve the objective of Pan-Africanism. Moreover, his worldwide reputation and popularity soars.

After the coup, Nkrumah is made co-president of Guinea (CY, p. 6). He writes his most profound works in Guinea. He understands that only revolution—armed struggle—is the answer to neo-colonialism. Additionally, he is in touch with those who are actively engaged in armed struggle, particularly the revolutionary leader Amilcar Cabral, assassinated in Conakry less than one year after the death of Nkrumah.

Nkrumah's increased consciousness and the consequent evolution of his theory on the African Revolution are well represented by his correspondence while in Conakry, Guinea. Even his language and style are characterized now by a "no nonsense" approach to neo-colonialism and worldwide capitalism. Overall, then, Nkrumah's post-coup letters provide a useful tool by which to measure his heightened concern for Africa and African people, as well as to measure his clearer understanding of the viciousness of the enemy.

June Milne, Nkrumah's literary executrix, compiled the collection of Nkrumah's correspondence during the post-coup years in Conakry, and which has been held at Howard University, Washington, DC. This, the June Milne Collection, provided the source of Milne's own book on Nkrumah's latter correspondence—much of it conducted between herself and Nkrumah—published as *Kwame Nkrumah: The Conakry Years* (1990) [hereafter "CY"]. That volume offers profound insight into Nkrumah's thinking during the years 1966–1972. However, the increased consciousness of Nkrumah during these years is further illuminated by looking also at the (hitherto) unpublished letters in the Milne Collection. The following discussion thus highlights significant passages from both published and unpublished letters, as well as unpublished sections of published letters. The presentation (and discussion) of these invaluable letters is arranged chronologically, divided into five time periods: 1966, 1967, 1968, 1969, and 1970–72. Within each period, the discussion is separated into several categories: first, the sections or letters which demonstrate his understanding of the enemy, neo-colonialism; second, those which reflect his belief that only armed struggle can destroy neo-colonialism; third, those which document his growing worldwide reputation; and, fourth, as a consequence of the three preceding ones, those which illustrate his danger to neo-colonialism.

1966

While on his way to Viet Nam to meet with Ho Chi Minh, Kwame Nkrumah is overthrown on February 24, 1966. In Peking, he learns of the coup d'état. Ahmed Sékou Touré, president of Guinea, sends him a letter the next day in which Touré proposes "to call on all progressive African countries to hold a special conference and take all adequate measures" (June Milne Collection [hereafter, JMC], Box 154–9, #4). Nkrumah responds to him on the same day, addressing the letter to "My dear Brother and President". This critical letter reflects both Toure's and Nkrumah's clear understanding that the coup was initiated by neo-colonialists:

> It is true, as you say, that this incident in Ghana is a plot by the imperialists, neo-colonialists and their agents in Africa. As these imperialist forces grow more militant and insidious, using traitors to the African cause against the freedom and independence of our people, we must strengthen our resolution and fight for the dignity of our people to the last man, and for the unity of Africa. It is heartening to know that in this struggle we can count on the support and understanding of Africa's well-tried leaders like yourself. I know that our cause will triumph and that we can look forward to the day when Africa shall be really united and free from foreign interference and intrigues and saboteurs and puppets. (JMC, Box 154–9, #4)

Determined to forge ahead with the African Revolution—preferably by being restored to his democratically elected position as president of Ghana, Nkrumah returns to Africa, deciding to go to Guinea because of its proximity to Ghana and because of his close friendship with Sékou Touré. Not long after his arrival (March 3, 1966), Touré arranges a mass rally and proclaims Nkrumah "head of state of Guinea" (CY, p. 6). At the rally, Touré makes clear Nkrumah's stature in the world: "The Ghanaian traitors have been mistaken in thinking that Nkrumah is simply a Ghanaian. He is a universal man" (CY, p. 6). In making him co-president of Guinea, Touré too is signaling to the world the inevitability of the African Revolution and, as such, Nkrumah's position at the helm of the Revolution. Removing Nkrumah as leader from one microstate, this act connotes, does not stop the progress of the Revolution.

The coup clears up things for Nkrumah, sharpening his understanding of the struggle. On April 1, 1966, he writes to Milne: "These are trying days but I regard them as a sort of cleansing process. The issues involved in the struggle are now very clear ... . And the way ahead is now clearly marked" (CY, p. 31). Milne writes that "far from being silenced", as the imperialists expected, "he was showing every sign of continuing to be a thorn in the flesh of the same forces, domestic and international, who had combined to overthrow his government". She notes that, for the imperialists, "Nkrumah and Sékou Touré were a formidable combination" (CY, p. 19). In a letter to Nkrumah dated May 4, 1966, American literary agent Julie Medlock writes: "I hope it has occurred to you as it has to me that your future work on the world scene may turn out to be more important than just being President of Ghana ... indeed, fresh opportunity may be on your doorstep" (JMC, Box 154–6, #37).

Indeed, in Conakry Nkrumah is now free of the time-consuming duties he was mired in as head of state in Ghana. Relieved of the pomp and ceremony and the internal struggle against elitism that necessarily comes with being president, as well as acquiring a newfound, more personal, sense of how dangerous the neo-colonialists are, Nkrumah is free to give his full attention to the African Revolution. And, from the time he arrives in Guinea, he takes every advantage of doing so. Thus, the coup does indeed present Nkrumah with "fresh opportunity", but even more importantly a heightened awareness of the best way to conduct the African Revolution.

In a draft dispatch to Touré and Modibo Keita of Mali, Nkrumah writes: "The events of military rebellion and coup d'état, tragic though they are, have at least revealed a number of facts that were previously concealed and made the issues involved in the African revolutionary struggle more sharply visible" (CY, p. 39). On September 27, 1966, Nkrumah writes to British columnist Pat Sloan, a stalwart Nkrumaist and one of his most faithful comrades in struggle: "Thanks to the so-called Ghana coup, I now see the struggle in its truer perspective" (p. 71).

Not only did Nkrumah see more clearly, but also he felt energized by the coup: "I am 56", he wrote to Milne on August 3, 1966, "but I feel in every way that I am 24, and I mean from head to foot. Everything about my physical body feels new, healthy and strong" (CY, p. 58). Four months earlier, on April 16, 1966, he wrote: "I write so fast, that's why the penmanship is so bad. It is not so bad if I write slowly, taking my time. But the damn brain works so fast the fingers can't catch up with it" (p. 36). Despite the clear mind and rejuvenated body, all was not rosy. The hustle and bustle of being President of Ghana was now replaced with the quiet and comparatively solitary life of a theoretician. On September 27, 1966, Nkrumah writes to Milne: "The path I have taken is a lonely path, full of thorns and thistles, but it must be traversed" (p. 73).

Nkrumah's sharpened class analysis, and this newfound energy, allows him to advance the African Revolution. His ability to do so is due to his no longer having to appease the half-hearted African statesmen, to his no longer having to soft-pedal socialism as the only economic system guaranteed to satisfy the needs of all Africans, and of course to his own clearer view of every aspect of the African Revolution. On March 26, 1966, he writes that "at the moment the imperialists and the neocolonialists are happy. But I shall surprise them" (CY, p. 28). On March 28, 1966, he relates to June Milne what he was planning to say in Vietnam when Ho Chi Minh invited him to Hanoi:

> [T]he only solution to the Vietnam war is for the United States to clear out its presence in Vietnam, north and south. It is now known all over the world that the USA is the aggressor. I have studied this Vietnam question and have a better understanding of its true state and implications. ... I am interested in the Vietnamese war because I am opposed to imperialism and neo-colonialism: and I believe that world socialism can end war and usher in permanent peace for the world. I believe in internationalism, but internationalism must presuppose Asia for Asia, Africa for Africans, and Europe for Europeans.

Later in that letter, he writes, "they want to destroy me and Ghana for we are in the forefront of the African struggle for emancipation" (CY, p. 29). On April 19, 1966, he writes to Milne that "until socialism, and I mean scientific socialism, triumphs over capitalism and imperialism I shall not stop attacking these social evils" (CY, p. 37). Capitalism is the enemy; socialism is the solution.

Second, after the coup, he is convinced that only armed struggle can destroy neo-colonialism. In everything that he writes, to everyone that he meets, he advocates armed struggle as a necessary, historic stage in the struggle against neo-colonialism. Milne writes that soon after Nkrumah and his entourage arrived in Conakry, everyone, "including Nkrumah, had undergone military training with members of the Guinea militia" (p. 15). He is preparing himself for the armed struggle that he is convinced is forthcoming. On April 30, 1966, Nkrumah writes that he has "been thinking and planning of raising a volunteer army when I get to Ghana, not for Ghana but for Africa.

I am now convinced that African unity and socialism can effectively be achieved only by armed struggle" (p. 41). On May 10, 1966, he writes to Milne, "Now I realize that at certain stages in a political struggle one must back persuasion and propaganda by force" (p. 42). In the same letter, he writes that he has "just finished reading Mao Tse-Tung's works on guerilla warfare. Stimulating" (p. 42). On May 18, he writes to Milne that "the nature and character of neo-colonialism are such that there is no other way to fight and overcome them than by guerilla warfare and struggle" (p. 44). On July 8, 1966, again to Milne, he criticizes Jomo Kenyatta and Tom Mboya of Kenya for having "submitted Kenya to neo-colonialist subjugation. You know my conviction and solution: only an armed guerila struggle can end neo-colonialism and imperialism wherever they may be" (p. 53).

By September 1966, Nkrumah has worked out the strategy and tactics of the armed struggle and begins to draft the manual for this phase, later published as *The Handbook of Revolutionary Warfare*. (Nkrumah had written notes for this work before the coup, but they were stolen. See CY, p. 79.) In a letter of September 27, 1966, he writes to Milne that a Pan-African unifying party must be created to guide the All-African People's Revolutionary Army (AAPRA). The AAPRA will act "as its military arm" and both "the AAPRA and the AAPSP [the All-African People's Socialist Party] should supersede the OAU and make it redundant" (CY, pp. 72–73). On October 31, 1966, Nkrumah writes to Milne:

> [The *Handbook*] will show the world how determined I am with African unity. I did that work for the African freedom fighters fighting for the freedom of their countries from colonialism. Indeed it was to be used as a textbook for the freedom fighters who were being trained, and was the basis for lectures to them at various stages of their study. (CY, p. 79)

Earlier, Nkrumah had written that his presence as statesman, President of Ghana, and foremost proponent of Pan-Africanism from 1957–1966 made African leaders at least pay "lip service" to Pan-Africanism. However, now he became more significant to African freedom fighters throughout the world. And it is on the shoulders of these young warriors that the African Revolution rests. They are the spark for Revolution. In *Kwame Nkrumah: The Conakry Years*, Milne writes that "far from sinking into obscurity, Nkrumah's political stature grew, and continues to inspire Africans and people of African descent worldwide" (CY, p. ix–x). The many telegrams and letters from around the world that Nkrumah received after February 24, 1966 are documented in *Dark Days in Ghana* (1968), and some of these and others appear in Milne's published collection. Still others are unpublished. All, however, document his worldwide influence, especially on African youths.

Responding in April of 1966 to a letter from Christine Johnson, an African American, Nkrumah reflects his clear understanding of both the role of young African revolutionaries, no matter where they live in the world, and the benefit which an African Revolution will bring to them:

> When Africa is free and united with one government for the whole of the continent the black man—wherever he may be, either in Africa, West Indies or USA—will discover his personality, his dignity and his honour. Only then will he behave as a complete person, a real human being. (p. 34)

Young Africans from throughout the world listened, understood, and began to espouse Nkrumaism. Milne records that Nkrumah's Convention People's Party (CPP) slogan, "Forward ever! Backward never!", was "widely adopted by liberation movements in Africa" (p. 80, note). And it is a slogan that, still today, is widely adopted by African revolutionaries throughout the world.

Organizations such as the Pan Africanist Youth Movement (PAYM) of Sierra Leone write to reassure Nkrumah that his ideas have not fallen on deaf ears. On March 4, 1966, PAYM writes to both Touré and Nkrumah: "We wish to assure your Excellencies that you are not alone in this great task of achieving Total Independence and Sovereignty for the African Nation that must be. Indeed, never was the whole of Africa so in unison with the Osagyefo when he declared that: 'Until that one government comes to take over the whole of Africa together, there shall be no peace on the African continent'" (p. 22).

S. J. Zwane of Swaziland, living in Tanzania and preparing for the armed struggle to come, belongs to the Ngwane [Swaziland] National Liberatory Congress (NNLC). In June of 1966, he writes to Nkrumah that "the NNLC is the political representative of the forces of African nationalism, which are backed by the forces of Pan-Africanism and international anti-imperialism" (JMC, Box 154–9, #41). People in Jamaica were also listening. Dudley Thompson, a Jamaican senator, writes to Nkrumah on June 22, 1966 about the "neocolonial Government" of Jamaica whose police "storm certain slum areas where the poor but faithful have been resisting the oppressions". He continues by saying that "fingers are being pointed directly at me". Most significantly, however, he states: "I believe the immediate farce will be over in a week or two but unless a new socialist approach to satisfy the hopes of many can be put into effect we shall be lulled by our own Calypso mentality" (JMC, Box 154–8, #66). On July 1, 1966, Nkrumah responds to Thompson by recommending his book on "Neo-Colonialism" (JMC, Box 154–8, #66). Even Kim Il Sung of North Korea is in correspondence with Nkrumah. They exchange letters in March of 1966 (JMC, Box 154–8, #57). Letters to and from Pat Sloan, already mentioned as an Nkrumaist and a teacher at Kwame Nkrumah Ideological Institute (Winneba) when the coup takes place, are very important in revealing the extent of Nkrumah's influence in sharpening the consciousness of all of those in contact with him—even those who were already avowed Nkrumaists. For it is those like Sloan who could help most to advance Nkrumaist theory. On October 3, 1966, Sloan writes that "I am more than ever convinced of the line of NKRUMAISM" (JMC, Box 154–8, #37).

All in all, Nkrumah showed no sign of ceasing his attack on capitalism, neo-colonialism, and imperialism in general. Revolutionaries were even more inspired and in awe of him after the overthrow because he demonstrated an increased level of attack on the enemy. Others had been assassinated or poisoned for far less. In fact, from the beginning of his Conakry years, there were signs of danger. June Milne writes that "several times during the early days of the Conakry period, the envelopes of letters exchanged between him and myself bore unmistakable signs of having been opened and clumsily resealed" (CY, pp. 10–11). Nkrumah resorted to a code system and sealing wax to try to ensure the security of letters (p. 11). On October 4, 1966, Nkrumah writes to Milne that he has "devised a new address by which you can address your letters to me" (p. 75). On November 8, 1966, Sékou Touré wrote to Nkrumah of the US's hand in the kidnapping of the Guinea delegation to the OAU Conference. As a consequence, "the American Ambassador was put under house arrest, and so were other Americans in Conakry. ... All Peace Corps are leaving Conakry. Pan-American Airways no longer stops here" (p. 86). In the same October 4, 1966 letter to Milne, Nkrumah ends with the following wry statement: "The CIA is ever at work". Julie Medlock, one of Nkrumah's most faithful friends, writes a profound and prophetic letter to him on October 22, 1966: "You are already firmly in history as the great apostle of African unity, among other things; must you also risk being a martyr? ... It is your life; you must do what you must do—hopefully, at the right time. May all the Gods of Destiny protect you!" (JMC, Box 154–6, #37).

1967

"The best teacher is the enemy" (CY, pp. 191–192): this sentence Nkrumah asks June Milne to add to *The Handbook of Revolutionary Warfare*, "Book One: Know the Enemy" (27 October, 1967). On January 17, 1967, Nkrumah writes to Milne: "Why does the imperialist world hate me so? (As if I don't know!!) To hell with them. I will continue to expose them" (CY, pp. 114–115). The year 1967 opens with Nkrumah's understanding of neo-colonialism still growing: in a letter to Milne he writes: "We know the nature of imperialism and neo-colonialism inside out" (p. 132). Not only does his understanding of the vicious economic system of capitalism increase, but also he sees clearly the relationship between it and him. The enemy has taught him, and will continue to teach him, well as the year 1967 will demonstrate. Moreover, the struggle against neo-colonialism has become more personal, and this in itself makes for a much clearer understanding of the nature of neo-colonialism and its consequences. In this same letter, he writes: "They forget that the more they attack me, the stronger I get to fight". Far from deterring him, the neo-colonialists' personal interest in him energizes and strengthens Nkrumah. On February 13, 1967, he writes to Milne: "You see why I fight so hard for African unity and socialism. A united socialist Africa will be a bulwark for world socialism. I will add strength to the progressive and socialist forces, for peace and socialism" (p. 121). On April 1, 1967, he writes to Milne that the "qualities in leadership which must be strengthened are bravery, ruthlessness and bitterness. In order for a revolutionary to succeed he must be brave, bitter and ruthless, and also capable of hating his enemies ... . We cannot conquer and overcome neo-colonialism unless we hate those who practise it" (p. 131). Later that month, again to Milne, he writes that in *Neo-colonialism* he "did not rankle or rail enough against the social evils which imperialism and colonialism bring in their train upon the oppressed and the exploited" (p. 140).

Knowing the enemy better helps Nkrumah to know the solution better. He is clearer on the need for socialism. In Ghana, soon after Nkrumah is overthrown, the neo-colonialists devalue the currency and remove Nkrumah's image from it. Nkrumah writes to Milne on August 1, 1967 that he "can see no solution except a 180 [degree] turn to socialism. One can only face such a situation by full-scale socialism" (CY, p. 162). All the hot spots of 1967, for Nkrumah, are struggles that serve as a prelude to worldwide socialism:

> It is all a grand rehearsal for the great 'show' about to come! Vietnam, Middle East, guerilla warfare in Latin America, the restlessness in Africa, Black Power struggle in America, all these events show that the era of man's complete emancipation is about to dawn. (August 1, 1967; CY, p. 168)

The struggles in Africa in particular are "a preparation, or shall I say a grand rehearsal, for the great African Revolution" which will lead to the worldwide revolution for "Europe is decadent. Africa is the hope of the future" (to Milne, August 24, 1967; CY, p. 175). On December 11, 1967, he writes to Milne:

> And when, oh when, all Africa becomes socialist, and with China, Russia and the Eastern democracies, then there will be an avalanche of socialist steam rollers that will snowball out capitalism and imperialism and neo-colonialism to where there will be no return for them. (CY, p. 201)

Africa's enemy is the same enemy—capitalism—which exploits and oppresses the people of the world. When the exploitation is of its own citizens, it is capitalism (or domestic colonialism). When the exploitation is of another country and its people via a corrupt, puppet leader, it is neo-colonialism. Therefore, Nkrumah's clear vision allows him to see the connection between the Black Power Movement in the diaspora and the struggles in Africa: their enemy is the same. On August 10, Nkrumah writes to Milne:

> It is the rotten economic system there [USA] that has brought about Black Power. Black Power is nothing but a violent protest of the have-nots against the haves. It is the poor against the rich ... . The plight of the poor whites and the blacks is the same. They should fight together and make Black Power a real power in the States, irrespective of the colours of the skin. (CY, p. 170)

As Nkrumah's 1970 statement in *Class Struggle in Africa* demonstrates, his understanding of the race issue matures. Only a united, socialist Africa will facilitate the unity of races in the West. Until that time, racism will always present barriers to race unification. No matter his myopia on this question of race in 1967, Nkrumah's recognition of the fact that "the youth of the Western world are completely alienated" (to Milne, August 24, 1967; CY., p. 175), and therefore must spark a socialist revolution, must have rankled the capitalists.

In 1967, Nkrumah is so clear on neo-colonialism as the enemy of all people, and of the USA as the primary culprit among neo-colonialists, that he wishes to distance himself, his people, and Africa from the United States. In a letter to Milne, Nkrumah writes: "In the *Handbook* I used 'United States of Africa', and in abbreviated form it will be USA. NO! Change that to simply 'Africa'. When the time comes we shall know how to re-name the African government, whether People's Republic of Africa or Union of African Socialist Republics" (October 30, 1967; CY, p. 193).

As his stance on neo-colonialism as the enemy had not wavered, but in fact had strengthened, so had his understanding of the solution—the historic necessity of the African Revolution (CY, p. 172). He reads whatever he can on it. On January 17, 1967, he writes to Milne that he has just finished reading *Military Strategy: Soviet Doctrine and Concept* and that "it is terrific. I am going to read it again". Thinking about, strategizing for, and writing about the armed struggle is what Nkrumah is most focused on in 1967. On March 24, 1967, he writes to Milne that the All-African People's Revolutionary Army "is the only hope for Africa now". In fact, the nine coups that occurred that year in Africa are just the preparatory stage for the "formation of AAPRA". For Nkrumah, these coups bode well; he is invigorated by them: "Aren't these exciting times,

June? Everywhere we turn, history is being made, and Africa marches on to her destiny: Union Government, for all Africa, peace and friendship towards all men irrespective of race or colour. Mankind is *one*" (CY, p. 128). Too, the enemy's ideas of "constitutionalism" and "legality" have no place in a neo-colonial environment since these concepts are designed for and defined to benefit the neo-colonialist world. Armed struggle is the only successful avenue in such a climate. So, one must adopt the Tolstoy/Mao maxim: "'The masses worship power, and power grows out of the barrel of a gun'" (p. 129). The same goes for "party politics" and "general elections",: both "are out of the question" (April 14, 1967;, p. 136). What are needed are well-planned insurrections (March 31, 1967;, p. 130) and counter coups (April 14, 1967;, pp. 136–137).

Two powerful statements to come from Nkrumah during 1967 are both in regard to armed struggle. The first is that, whether African leaders agree or not, there are no old colonial, artificial, state boundaries in Africa. The African Revolution does not recognize them,

> ... and so there can be no question of revolutionary forces (e.g. AAPRA) violating a country's sovereignty by entering it for the purpose of the political unification of the continent. The whole of Africa is one, and every part of it belongs to Africa as a whole. (to Milne, April 9, 1967, CY, p. 136).

While still in power, however, Nkrumah had avowed to the Ghanaian Parliament that the freedom fighters studying in Winneba were not intending to overthrow their governments, an act which presupposes continental unification. His tactical theory on the African Revolution clearly had advanced.

A second powerful statement is made shortly after the April 9th one. On April 24, 1967, he writes to Milne:

> Even though the *Handbook* is mainly devoted to the African scene, it must be made clear in it that the defeat of imperialism and neo-colonialism will be final and complete only when guerilla and revolutionary activities against them become global and worldwide. Guerilla and revolutionary activities must be directed against their centres and bastions everywhere. In other words, they must be confronted wherever they are, anywhere in the world, with many Vietnams, Angolas, Portuguese Guineas, Mozambiques etc. This is the only way to victory as I see it now. (CY, pp. 141–142)

Here Nkrumah is advocating World Revolution. And he is very cognizant of the impact of his ideas. Their effect on the neo-colonialists seems foremost in his mind on October 27, 1967 when he writes to June Milne about an idea that came to him regarding the armed struggle: "It has something to do with the armed revolutionary warfare we shall be engaged in when we return. (I wrote something which I have cancelled for security's sake.) Something to do as to how we can politically unite the forces of AAPRA, and all the guerilla and freedom fighters in Africa". He continues, "I have been making notes. I might put it into a statement and call it *The Call at Dawn—The Manifesto of ...* When I see you I shall tell you what should replace these dots" (CY, p. 192).

Of course, such ideas continue to make him a danger to the longevity of neo-colonialism. Since attempts are made to assassinate Nkrumah in Conakry, since letters bear the evidence of being tampered with, since some who profess to be friends and comrades reveal themselves as puppets of the enemy, since those who are close to Nkrumah are convinced of his imminent death by the hands of agents of neo-colonialists, since his faithful cook dies mysteriously, since he is in touch with guerilla fighters like Amilcar Cabral and Black Power advocates like Stokely Carmichael, since he and others continue to work to get him back to Ghana, the neo-colonialists, it must be assumed, did indeed view him as an extremely dangerous foe.

On May 5, 1967, Pat Sloan writes to Nkrumah: "In our 'code' I regularly send [Addo-Osafo] news of you as 'Uncle' and I presume the 'family' with no further 'breakdown' means no further *unsuccessful* coup" (JMC, Unpublished, Box 154–8, #38). On December 28, 1967, Sloan writes of his skepticism concerning a person whom Nkrumah trusts: "This is a pity as the strongest Ghanaian personality left here now is, I suppose, Kwesi Armah who, for obvious reasons I cannot trust (though it *appears* you can)" (JMC, Box 154–8, #38). It is a fact that security leaks were numerous. One in particular led to the arrest of one of Nkrumah's staunchest supporters, Boye Moses. In February of 1967, Moses was "captured in Dahomey ... and flown to Ghana and paraded through the streets of Accra in an iron cage" (CY, p. 105). Another supporter of Nkrumah, the American literary agent and author Julie Medlock, writes on January 5, 1967 about her concern for Nkrumah, and jests about her public support for Nkrumah: "A case in point is my letter to the *Herald Tribune/Washington Post*, attached. After this, I am probably now on the assassination list too, so move over, KNK!" (JMC, Box 154–6, #37). Medlock's published letter to these newspapers is dated January 4, 1967 and includes the line: "Hence it will in time be shown that Nkrumah's political fate has not been determined by any of the things of which he is now accused, but by the desire of inimical foreign forces to get rid of a system they could neither penetrate nor manipulate" (JMC, Box 154–6, #37).

June Milne writes that the corrupt National Liberation Council (NLC) leadership of Ghana did not underestimate Nkrumah's power and influence to return to Ghana; in fact, "their nervousness was shown in the reward of £10,000 which they advertised for [his] capture 'dead or alive'" (CY, p. 105).

According to Milne, there is "evidence in the Conakry files of facilities being provided by Guinean diplomats, who allowed the use of their embassies for the transmission of messages and packages" (p. 105).

Milne also relates how, on April 17, 1965, a counter-coup attempt in Ghana was almost successful. Over 120 men entered Accra, "captured the radio station and Flagstaff House, and forced their way into Christianborg Castle, the administrative headquarters of the NLC" (CY, p. 107). They were captured, however. Two of the men, "Lts Arthur and Yeboah were sentenced to death by firing squad, and Second Lt Poku to thirty years imprisonment" (CY, p. 107). In September of 1967, Nkrumah's hopes were dashed once again when Ekow Eshun was captured and imprisoned in Accra. He had been "engaged in some clandestine operation on [Nkrumah's] behalf" (CY, p. 110).

The NLC's nervousness, together with the attempts to reinstate Nkrumah as Ghana's only democratically-elected head of state, would have intensified the enemy's efforts to render him impotent by any means necessary. Milne details one such (thwarted) effort, when on March 16, 1967 "an attempt was made to kidnap Nkrumah. During the night, a Guinean naval patrol intercepted a fishing trawler within Guinean territorial waters close to Villa Syli. On board were two white men and twelve Ghanaians" who were found to have "detailed information on the layout of Villa Syli, even knowing in which room Nkrumah slept". Milne records that "After the kidnapping scare, security at the villa was stepped up, backed by Guinean naval patrols" (CY, pp. 105–106).

Milne also relates that, in November 1967, one of Nkrumah's most trusted security officers was detained as a suspected traitor, having supplied "information to the NLC through a foreign embassy in Conakry", with suspicion of his activities having been "aroused by his liberal spending of money, always in the form of dollar notes" (CY, p. 110).

The signs of danger surrounded Nkrumah. He knew it. On February 16, 1967, he writes to June Milne that, despite being hounded and maligned, "as long as I have an ounce of breath in me I will continue to expose them [the neo-colonialists] with all the strength at my disposal" (CY, p. 122). Some of that strength resided in the persons of Amilcar Cabral and Stokely Carmichael, two young men who had a deep love and respect for Nkrumah's work on behalf of Africa and its people and, because they did, made Nkrumah's life even more perilous—especially Cabral who, in Guinea Bissau, was engaged in armed struggle against the Portuguese. On June 17, 1967, Cabral visits Nkrumah in Conakry—as is his practice—and together with June Milne they watch a "film of 'Portuguese Guinea' war of liberation". Milne describes the scene: the "projectors and screen erected on seafront office by Guinean Minister of Information. Film in colour, presented by Cabral, the leader of the PAIGC. He, President [Nkrumah] and I sat in front row. Film in French, translated verbally as it went along, by Cabral" (CY, p. 156–157). Of Carmichael, Nkrumah writes: "I have got another admirer and a pupil. He does not want to return to the United States. He wants to remain here and return with me to Ghana to work with me and for me" (to Milne, October 6, 1967; CY, p. 186). In an earlier letter, he writes regarding Carmichael: "The CIA is trailing him wherever he goes. Even here they (American embassy) tried to get his passport from him" (to Milne, September 30, 1967; CY, p. 184).

Other Africans, living at home or abroad, engaged in the African Revolution were in touch with Nkrumah. Being "in touch" with him had a twofold significance. First, it reflected Nkrumah's worldwide reputation and influence, especially with African youths. There were many young warriors actively involved in the African Revolution who were positively influenced by Nkrumah. Secondly, and consequently, this "being in touch" contributed to making Nkrumah a real and viable threat to the neo-colonialists and capitalists in general since young people are the spark for Revolution. Writing from Tanzania on June 1, 1967, S. J. Zwane of Swaziland, Chief external representative of the Swane National Liberatory Congress (NNLC) ends his letter to Nkrumah with the following: "Long live African struggle against imperialism, colonialism and neo-colonialism in all their forms. Forward ever backward never". He signs the letter, "Your Excellency, I am, Yours for a free and united Africa" (Box 154–9, #41). A second letter from Bernard Arthur of the Convention People's Party of Ghana Overseas, Moscow, states: "Our struggle now therefore is to develop the Convention People's Party into a real Marxist Revolutionary Party under the guidance of 'Philosophical Consciencism.' We cannot thus go forward without you, your personal guidance and approval in all our doings" (Box 154–1, #63). The Black Panther Party of Oakland, California also writes to Nkrumah, who responds by sending the group an "article on Black Power" and informing the organization that "you can give it any publicity you like if you want to" (Box 154–2, #32). Milne writes that in the summer of 1967, "racial riots in the United States caused Nkrumah to think about writing a pamphlet on Black Power" (CY, p. 110). Such a consideration reflects Nkrumah's own awareness of his influence on African youths. The enormous respect that they had for him is reflected in a letter dated September 5, 1967 that American author Richard Wright's daughter, Julia Wright, sends asking Nkrumah to write something on Black Power in the USA:

> Osagyefo, this is why I am writing to you. Because you are the only African leader who in his writings has shown an understanding of the plight of the American negro. Because you are the only African leader who has made African-American solidarity a reality by welcoming to

> your Ghana Afro-American freedom fighters of the calibre of DuBois, Hunton and my father. It is because of all this and because of the fact that the majority of Africans have not ceased to look up to you as an ideological as well as political source of inspiration, that I am asking you as my leader and my co-fighter to write a statement, or a few reflections, on the recent upsurge of armed struggle for Black Power in the USA. (CY, p. 177)

Julia Wright, in fact, is correct in her appraisal of Nkrumah's influence on the youth of African descent around the world. On July 20, 1967, Nkrumah writes that "[Ambrose] Yankey [Nkrumah's personal assistant] has just told me that he and the 'boys' heard on the radio that the Black Power movement in America is saying that whether I am in Ghana or not I am their leader" (to Milne: CY, p. 165). In a letter to Milne of September 30, 1967, Nkrumah relates: "I have written the enclosed which I have entitled *The Spectre of Black Power*" (CY, p. 185). It appears under that name as a published pamphlet in 1968 (and is also reprinted in *The Struggle Continues*, pp. 36–43). On the nature of Black Power, Nkrumah writes that he is trying to "educate" Stokely Carmichael in the United States to understand that "Black Power [is] not a racist issue. It is political and economic, and only socialism can make Black Power fulfil its destiny" (to Milne, October 6, 1967: CY, p. 187). The "Black Power people" award Nkrumah with a bronze shield on which is written the following: "To a man whose literary ability as well as that of influencing people has been a source of inspiration to all Black People and has carried you to a position in life worthy of perpetual adoration" (CY, p. 187, note).

Too, Nkrumah is still in touch with African heads of state, although he no longer views them as the leading, or even significant, force in the struggle against neo-colonialism and for Pan-Africanism. On February 16, 1967, he writes to Milne:

> Nationalisation is not to be played with. It cannot be done by halves. It is *either, or*. And here, anyhow, I see that my ideas are taking root. I sent a message to [Julius] Nyerere from here … , that we must embark on nationalisation as a new weapon to fight neo-colonialism. The same message also got through to [Kenneth] Kaunda. A message has gone through to [Joseph Désiré] Mobutu. (CY, p. 122)

And, of course, Sékou Touré consults Nkrumah. When the Guinean Foreign Minister is detained in Abijan, Cote d'Ivoire, Nkrumah writes to June Milne that Touré and a man from the UN "came to see me last night. I tell them to tell U Thant [Secretary-General of the United Nations] to do something about it very quickly" (CY, p. 164).

Nkrumah's theory (what he writes) and his practice (what he does, what he says before an audience, whom he sees, and who he talks with) make it imperative for him "to be secretive until I am damn sure and certain about everything. I cannot take chances. The time of calculated risk is past" (CY, p. 186). Secrecy was the watchword, for evidence of spying was all around him. Milne records that in November of 1967, Nkrumah's "exercise book for notes of ideas and reflections and for questions he particularly liked or wanted to remember … was subsequently 'lost' after he had spent a night at Sékou Touré's palace" (CY, footnote, p. 194). Interference and delays with Nkrumah's post continues, and on November 24, 1967, he writes a "trial letter" to June Milne to see if it would be tampered with: sure enough, there is "the tampering of these two letters" which makes him state that "we are going to be more careful" (CY, pp. 198–199).

The most serious incident of 1967, one which may be thought to shed light on Nkrumah's own death, is the death of his cook. Milne writes of her alarm when in May 1967 Nkrumah "suffered a further shock when his cook Amoah was taken to hospital in Conakry with 'liver trouble'" (CY, p. 109). The cook "seemed in excellent health" in March and "he was the only cook Nkrumah had employed for the past sixteen years. He travelled everywhere with him, and was with him on the Hanoi mission". Nkrumah's efforts to get Amoah to Moscow for treatment came of no avail, for he "was told Amoah's illness was too far advanced for a cure" (CY, p. 109). Amoah died on July 20, 1967. If Nkrumah had any doubts before then that he himself was in personal danger, the death of his cook and friend would have removed them. After Amoah's death, it would have been easier "to get at Nkrumah" via what he ate. Milne writes, "I realized the hopelessness of ever being one hundred per cent certain that his food was safe. Apart from the [new] cook, there were so many men working there [Villa Syli, Conakry], and others, wandering in and out all the time. … After Amoah's death … Nkrumah occasionally seemed to suffer from digestive trouble" (p. 109). Prior to Amoah's death, Nkrumah wrote to June: "I feel very fit. Health really excellent" (February 11, 1967: CY, p. 121). However, he did have one recorded health problem, a stomach upset, which he blamed on "a bad fish-head" (to Milne, June 26, 1967: CY, p. 159). Nkrumah's health would worsen in the succeeding years, increasing in tandem with his criticism of neo-colonialism, his call for armed struggle against colonial and neo-colonial regimes, and his worldwide (in particular, his African Diasporan) reputation.

1968

On October 5, 1968, Nkrumah writes to Reba Lewis pinpointing three distinct growth periods in his life: "My autobiography, *Ghana*, ended at Ghana's independence March 6, 1957; this was a decade (1945–57). Since then a lot has happened. My views on many things have changed. Another decade began ending in the coup in Ghana. We have entered a new decade … it is a decade of the armed phase of the African Revolution" (CY, p. 263). Nkrumah had learned a lot and grown a lot since the decade when *Ghana* was written. As a consequence, his vision was much clearer, especially on the nature of capitalism. This understanding causes him to change tactics; now he sees that armed struggle is the only sure way to defeat the manifestation of capitalism in Africa, neo-colonialism. And this tactic in turn makes him a danger to the lifeline of neo-colonialism, especially as Nkrumah writes in this same letter that he has "not accomplished even one-third of what I want to accomplish".

His clear vision on capitalist politics enables him to write to Milne, on March 31, 1968, that "I don't see any difference between Johnson and Kennedy. It does not matter who enters the White House. They are all under the stiff manipulation and the pressing thumb of big business and the Pentagon" (CY, p. 230). Nkrumah understood clearly that the political administration of a country is merely an arm of its economic system. If the economic system is corrupt, it corrupts everything connected to it—including politics. As Nkrumah's philosophical consciencism avows, matter is primary. And the essential matter in any society is its economic system because to survive one must have one's fundamental needs met: food, clothing, and shelter. Since nature does not provide these things ready-made, they can only be provided through an economic system. A capitalist economic system—one designed to enrich only a small portion of the population who own, control, and distribute the goods and services that all need to survive while the rest of the population works—benefits the owners.

Earlier in 1968, when he learns of Jomo Kenyatta's "puppet regime in Nairobi" in casting out Asian immigrants, instead of organizing "all the Asians there to do some real productive service and enterprise", he writes that sending them away will "weaken Afro-Asian solidarity. Why not send all the Europeans and Americans from that country. Why don't they send away the white settlers?" (to Milne, February 27, 1968: CY, p. 225). The USA comes up again, this time in connection with the ambassador who was instrumental in Nkrumah's overthrow: "I also hear that the negro [the term is used by Nkrumah as an insult] ambassador in Ghana is leaving Ghana for good. He himself announced this in Ghana and said that only Ghanaians can help themselves. Saying this after … the Ghana coup!" (to Milne, April 1, 1968: CY, p. 230). Nkrumah's criticism is not just against capitalist countries like the USA. On September 7, 1968, he criticizes "Soviet revisionism" that has caused problems in countries like Czechoslovakia. Nkrumah writes that this revisionism "allows the West to infiltrate into the Eastern democracies … . Let us hope that the

Soviet Union will revise her revisionist policies and do more to help the liberation movements" (JMC, Box 154-5, #57).

Two additional points need to be made concerning Nkrumah's increasing understanding of the nature of revolution. First, in a letter to James and Grace Boggs dated December 6, 1968, he discusses the necessity of a "leader" or "personality" of a revolutionary movement as proven by history. Therefore,

> there should be no running away from 'personality'. ... The leader of a revolutionary socialist movement is the personification of the people's struggle—no more and no less. He should not be seen in isolation from the masses, but as inseparable from them. ... where would the Soviet Union have been without Lenin, Stalin and Trotsky? Can the Chinese Revolution be seen in isolation from Mao Tse-Tung, Chou En-Lai, Lin Piao? (CY, p. 270)

From his perspective, the notion of the "personality cult" is not only nonsense but it is a ploy of the revisionists, since "throughout the ages, all revolutions and major political and social changes have been achieved under some unifying symbol—a personification of the movement. This is one of the fundamental laws of history and of nature" (CY, p. 270). Why is this discussion on revolutionary leadership and personality so important? It is Nkrumah actually describing himself in the context of history and revolution. It is Nkrumah to whom the youth of the world, especially the African world, look for guidance and leadership, for he is "the personification of his people's struggle—no more and no less".

The second point of significance in regard to Nkrumah's clear thinking in 1968 is his position on exporting revolution. The strategy and tactics of the African Revolution have changed. They are neither pulled out of thin air, nor determined based on idealism. Rather, they are determined by the material conditions that the socialist revolution confronts. Thus, on his fifty-ninth birthday, September 18, 1968, Nkrumah writes the following to Pat Sloan:

> Again, I disagree with you when you say that the Czechoslovakia crisis is 'in violation of such principles as "revolution is not for export", "non-interference", "each country to find its own way to socialism" etc.'. But if 'revolution is not for export' then what else is? I see socialism as an international event. The capitalists, imperialists and neo-colonialists, with USA-CIA as the spearhead, are exporting counter-revolutions all over the world, causing havoc and destroying socialist paths everywhere. (CY, p. 257-258)

In 1968, his conviction that only armed struggle can defeat neo-colonialism does not waver. In fact, he continues to get new ideas about how it should be waged. Before *Handbook of Revolutionary Warfare* is published, he continually adds new information. In a January 6, 1968 letter to June Milne, he writes:

> Excuse my referring to the *Handbook* again. You know one thing we left out? That which concerns the 'enemy within' during the armed phase of the African revolution. I categorise them as follows: 1) the liberal sympathisers; 2) the mis-educated left-wing sympathiser; 3) the subversive agent; 4) the ill-disciplined revolutionary agent. We shall talk about these when you come. (CY, p. 216)

Seeing a role for women in the armed phase of the African Revolution, Nkrumah, on February 9, 1968, writes to Milne seeking information about "women's organizations, and their militia, in Cuba" (CY, pp. 223–224). On February 16, 1968, he relates to Milne that he has "been collecting information, and studying the tactics and strategy applied by both sides involved in the Vietnam War" because these studies will be helpful in the shaping of AAPRA and the AAPRP. Most significant is that when both of these units are "shipshape for action" in "three to four years, perhaps less", then launched, "it will be exciting demolishing those puppet regimes in Africa" (p. 224). Ultimately, worldwide, "guerilla warfare will triumph over imperialism and neo-colonialism" (June 3, 1968; JMC Box 154–5, #57).

Nkrumah's worldwide reputation continues to grow. Outside of Africa, he is in communication with progressive forces. On February 27, 1968, Nkrumah writes to Milne: "The Vietnamese ambassador came to see me yesterday. He has just arrived from Hanoi and brought me a personal message of greeting from Ho Chi Minh. I autographed a copy of *Neo-colonialism* and asked the ambassador to send it to him" (CY, p. 225).

Regarding Africa, Nkrumah has something to say about Tanzania, Senegal, Somalia, and South Africa, or something to say to the leaders of these states. On February 24, 1968, two years after the Ghana coup, he writes: "Julius Nyerere was here. He came to see me in my villa. I had a serious talk with him about Africa. I was a little suspicious because he agreed with me about everything I said, and promised his cooperation" (CY, p. 225). Nyerere agreed on the necessity of armed force to execute the African Revolution, perhaps because he wanted Nkrumah's help. Evidently, it was Nyerere's belief that Nkrumah had influence over "rebellious" or "guerilla groups" in Africa: "He wants me to do what I can to soften Oscar Kambona. ... I jokingly told him that, if I am not in Ghana by Easter, I would go to Dar es Salaam and make that place my base in order to organise the freedom fighters and guerrillas into one formidable army of African liberation. He agreed and said I could come" (p. 225).

Indeed, Nyerere's conviction of Nkrumah's influence is correct. Nkrumah is being contacted by those both inside and outside of Africa who are interested in change, especially the youth. He receives letters from Somalia that he requests Milne to keep for him. He, in fact, sends many documents, including letters, to her for "safe-keeping"; before sending them, he makes "copies of some of them, but not all" (June 22, 1968; CY, p. 243). On May 12, 1968, for example, Nkrumah writes to Milne: "Enclosed you find *Zimbabwe News*. The guerrillas are fighting under difficulties. Imagine what they could do if they were backed by an All-African Front organisation" (p. 234). Those organized guerilla groups in the most developed country in Africa, South Africa, had to be critically important to both the neo-colonialists and to Nkrumah. A liberated South Africa, with its wealth of natural resources, would serve as a major contribution, a major spark for a united Africa. One letter comes from Potlako K. Leballo (Acting President of the Pan Africanist Congress) to Nkrumah on October 14, 1968: "We are eagerly awaiting your review of the basic documents of the Pan Africanist Congress so that after the necessary consultation these could be reproduced for circulation inside Azania [South Africa]" (pp. 264–265). Overall, Nkrumah was impressed with the youth movements in 1968. On May 12, 1968, Nkrumah writes to Milne: "I am happy about students' actions in Paris and West Germany. The future is in the hands of the youth; and they must act now before the stupid old men ruin everything" (p. 234). In fact, we learn once again that Ghana has been a training ground for freedom fighters. In a March 31, 1968 letter, Nkrumah writes: "Have you heard that Spain is going to give independence to Fernando Po and Rio Muni? It is going to be a bogus independence. And the men we trained in Ghana from these places—freedom fighters—have contacted me. They are coming to see me to plan what to do in case independence is handed to lackeys" (to Milne: CY, p. 230).

In a letter of April 6, 1968, just after the assassination of Martin Luther King, Nkrumah writes to Milne that he mourns for King, "even though I disagree with him on some of his non-violence views" (CY, p. 231)". And he continued prophetically, "Yesterday it was Malcolm X. Today Luther King. Tomorrow, fire all over the United States" (CY, p. 231).

In fact, Nkrumah is becoming more and more interested in the Africans born outside of Africa. His contact with Malcolm X, Julia Wright, American activists Grace and James Boggs, Stokely Carmichael, and Obi Egbuna (who led a Black Power Movement in Britain) helps him to see more clearly the relationship between the Diasporan Africans and Africa. Since he is already convinced that African people, wherever they are born in the world, are Africans and belong to Africa, he begins to think more quantitatively and qualitatively of the role they must play in the African Revolution. In his letters from July 1968 to December 1968, he evidences his thinking on both. And he begins to read more about the theory and practice of those living outside of the homeland. His contacts with these people outside of Africa and his study of the Revolution lead to the writing of both "The Spectre of Black Power" and "Message to the Black People of Britain". In a letter to Charles Howard (African-American lawyer and journalist) on July 1, 1968, he writes: "Please, if you can, send me copies of *Mohammed Speaks* [Islamic Newspaper published in the United States] regularly by airmail". While earlier he had shown reluctance in "getting involved" in the Black Power struggle in the USA, now he seems anxious to establish ties with it: "I count on you to keep the black community in the United States informed, so that they will not be unprepared for developments" (CY, p. 245). On July 6, 1968, he writes to Reba Lewis that "Ralph [Rap] Brown is right and Stokely [Carmichael] wrong. Black Power is anti-racism. Whoever is with us is a friend, regardless of colour. To me Black Power represents the power of the four-fifths of the world population which has been systematically damned into a state of undevelopment by colonialism and neo-colonialism" (CY, p. 246).

Nkrumah wants to get the "color" out of Black Power, to make 'Black Power' equal 'People Power' since with the destruction of capitalism comes the destruction of racism—eventually. The destruction of neo-colonialism in Africa and its socialist unification, in fact, will speed up the destruction of racism. Indeed, he spends a lot of his time trying to correct the Diasporan African's idea of Black Power: "They all seem to have woolly ideas about Black Power, and I school them when I get hold of them. I am giving Egbuna [in Great Britain] a few lectures as I did the Boggs" (to Milne, July 6, 1968; CY, p. 246). According to Nkrumah, "Black Power is a movement for survival. It is not a racist ideology" (CY, p. 246). On July 13, 1968, he writes to Milne:

> How I wish there were no race problems in the world and that all human beings could be brothers and sisters in the same human family. I am trying to give Black Power a universal concept. I hope there's no trace of racism in the message. (CY, p. 247)

It's a dialectical relationship, the relationship between Nkrumah and Diasporan Africans. Nkrumah "schools" them and the Diasporan Africans "school" him. On July 13, 1968, he writes: "I learnt a lot from [the Boggs] and I think they learnt a lot from me also. They are linking the Black Power revolution in America with the African Revolution" (to Milne: CY, p. 247). Of course, the reverse was true as well. On August 27, 1968, he writes to Christine Johnson that "I do keep in contact with all that is happening in America, and especially with the role that Black American brothers and sisters—Americans of African descent—are playing in the Black Power revolution going on in the States" (CY,

p. 253). The emphasis Nkrumah makes on the identity of Africans living in the USA signals his understanding that African people are one people, no matter where they happen to be born in the world. He goes on to write that "unless Afro-Americans think of themselves as black men and as people of African descent, they will never come up to their own. I am glad that they are now becoming conscious of their roots" (CY, p. 253).

Nkrumah again writes to Milne of Stokely Carmichael on September 24, 1968: "He said the 'little black book', that's what they call *Axioms* [*Axioms of Kwame Nkrumah*, 1967] in the USA, has been substituted for the red one by Mao. Everybody is looking forward to the *Handbook* and *Dark Days*" (CY, p. 260). By December of 1968, he is able to articulate a paradigm which includes Diasporan Africans. In a letter to James and Grace Boggs on December 6, 1968, Nkrumah writes:

> When you were here with me in Conakry, you agreed that there was no better unifying symbol for Africans and people of African descent everywhere, than the African Revolution—the goal of which is a united Africa under a socialist All-African Union Government and the emancipation of the entire black world. Until Africa is free and politically united, we are without power or status, and can only reach very limited objectives either in Africa or in the USA. (CY, p. 270)

Just three days later, on December 9, 1968, in an unpublished letter to the Boggs, Nkrumah writes that they "mentioned the need for a pamphlet to relate the African Revolution to the Black Revolution in the USA. This is an excellent idea, though it is not sufficient merely to 'relate' the two. They must be shown as indissolubly linked" (JMC, Box 154–2, #35).

Nkrumah connects the struggles of Africans everywhere outside of Africa with the African Revolution and calls in 1968 for "'Positive Action' in Ghana to overthrow the NLC" (CY, p. 211). Milne writes that Nkrumah "campaigned against the NLC through articles in *Africa and the World*, which were then published as Panaf pamphlets" (p. 211). For example, in his May 1968 "Ghana: The Way Out" (reprinted in *The Struggle Continues*, pp. 19–25; and in *Revolutionary Path*, pp. 414–420) Nkrumah wrote: "The terrible neglect which is now taking place in large areas of Ghana is a direct result of neo-colonialist policies and the abandonment of … socialist planning" and he called for a counter-coup (CY, p. 211). He is encouraged by a visit from the Soviet ambassador who assures Nkrumah that "his government [the Soviet government] is sure that I will be returning to Ghana soon" (CY, p. 239).

Such statements, which signal that Nkrumah not only approves of armed struggle, but encourages it because he sees it as the only solution to imperialism, are continually made in 1968. And he was fully aware of what might be the consequences. On May 12, 1968 to Reba Lewis, Nkrumah writes:

> History warns and urges me on, philosophy tells me to be cautious, but scientific socialism tells me to damn all and fight on, adding my quota to the eventual destruction of capitalism and imperialism and to the ushering in of man's total emancipation, where racial discrimination of any kind will be a criminal offence and those who practice racialism shall be considered madmen. We shall overcome. (CY, p. 234)

This determination to fight on is clear in a letter of September 24, 1968 in which he writes to Grace Boggs:

> The revolutionary fails only when he surrenders. As long as he continues the struggle—in whatever manner he can—he stretches himself towards the ultimate goal of Victory. Though he, the individual, die in the struggle, he has not failed. The sum total of all his endeavors, his aspirations, his efforts merge with the People who continue towards Victory. (CY, p. 261)

In a May 26, 1968 letter, he writes to Milne that "there's now a network of underground cells and organisations of the party all over Ghana, and these organisations are linked together, poised for action" (CY, p. 236); and shortly thereafter, "The human and material forces in Africa are poised. All that is needed is coordination and inspiration to spur them on to action" (June 10, 1968;, p. 239). In regard to the youth in particular, he continues to see them as playing a central role in "the armed phase of the African struggle. The whole question of urban and city guerilla warfare centres around students and local people" since "students are leading in the revolution because they are the most alienated" (p. 237).

Nkrumah's preparedness for and anxiousness to launch the armed phase of the African Revolution are clear. Every serious revolutionary group inside or outside of Africa seems to be waiting on Nkrumah's clarion call, for Africa's liberation, unification and socialist direction are what the immobilized world needs. He writes to Milne, "it is only in Africa that the situation is not frozen. The masses of Africa are simply waiting for the signal—the clarion call which must come from Ghana coinciding with our return. And [Stokely Carmichael] and others of the Black Panther Party are prepared and ready to answer the call" (September 24, 1968: CY, p. 261). Six days earlier, on his fifty-ninth birthday, Nkrumah writes to Pat Sloan: "What is happening in Africa is a grand rehearsal of the great armed revolution that will soon take place on that continent" (Unpublished letter, September 18, 1968, JMC Box 154–8, #38).

On October 1, 1968, Nkrumah writes to June Milne that Stokely Carmichael told him,

> ... whether I like it or not, I was chosen leader of the black people of the world and that the Black Panther Party is preparing, or is ready behind me, for the armed phase of the struggle. I asked him whether they were prepared for all the sacrifices, and he said 'yes'. I asked them to wait for my return. Without a base we can do nothing. (CY, p. 261)

In an unpublished letter to Pat Sloan, dated June 17, 1968, Nkrumah writes: "I shall again be in a free Ghana before I die!" (JMC, Box 154–8, #38). In the meantime, Nkrumah advises those involved in the Black Power movement to "organise scientifically through a vanguard Party" (to Milne, December 9, 1968: CY, p. 272). In his earlier letter of December 6, 1968 to James and Grace Boggs, he writes: "What is needed is a militant, well-organised vanguard Party, linked with the vanguard revolutionary Party of the African Revolution, not with a view to providing a President for the USA, but in order to unite and give direction, strength and leadership to the struggle" (to Milne: CY, p. 270). In that same letter, Nkrumah offers a four-point strategy for the African Diaspora in the United States:

> 1. Strive to improve by all means the conditions of black people in the USA;
> 2. Embarrass the US power structure, and so help to weaken its oppression and exploitation overseas;
> 3. Volunteer for active participation in the armed phase of the African Revolution, on African soil. This presupposes my return to Ghana, and its use as a base;
> 4. Equip themselves, through work at community level, in schools, study groups etc., so that each individual becomes a centre of organisation, and ideologically impregnable. (CY, p. 272)

In an unpublished section of the September 24, 1968 letter to Grace and James Boggs, Nkrumah writes that "a base to give political direction, perspection and to exercise discipline" is a necessity. He also adds that the increased consciousness of "the masses of black peoples is exerting pressures all along the line. Imperialist and neo-colonialist structures tremble under the repeated impact of black power" (JMC, Box 154–2, #35).

Always Osagyefo, the teacher, Nkrumah also writes to Grace and James Boggs that a nation and political power go hand in hand:

> How can there be a nation without political power? … . It is totally unrealistic to think that a 'Black Nation' can be created on American soil, since no Black Power movement can possibly succeed in seizing political control of the present white power structure in the USA. The African American will truly acquire nationality only through the successful completion of the African Revolution. He will then become like, for example, the Italians, the Germans, the Chinese, or any other foreign nationals absorbed into the USA—an American citizen, but with clear attachment to his parent nation overseas, and the status which that entails. Hence the great importance I attach to the identification of the Black Power Revolutionary Movement in the USA with the African Revolution. (CY, p. 271)

To help him to teach when he returns to Ghana, Nkrumah envisions a weekly newspaper: "*The African World*, which would make *West Africa* look silly and out of place. It would not regionalise Africa but look at Africa as one unit, one country" (to Milne, November 12, 1968: CY, p. 270). And he can use it to educate, mobilize, and organize Africans for the armed phase of the Revolution. In an unpublished letter to Reba Lewis, dated December 23, 1968, Nkrumah writes that this African armed "revolution began in 1967 and 1969 will put it on its course until this decade (i.e. 1967–77) completes the victory of the revolution … . Everything is mapped out and history marches on" (JMC, Box 154-4, #57).

Nkrumah is convinced of the rightness of the path he and others took in Ghana: "We have made no mistakes and we make no apologies. After all what we went through was a socialist effort to arrive at socialism without a revolution" (Unpublished letter of July 1, 1968 to Sloan, Box 154-8, #38). And he is just as convinced of the rightness of the armed phase of the African Revolution. In an unpublished letter of November 11, 1968 to Reba Lewis, Nkrumah writes: "There is a new world coming and that new world is going to come from Africa" (JMC, Box 154-5, #57).

Nkrumah's health declines during 1968. In *The Conakry Years*, Milne writes that Nkrumah's "health was not as good as before" and "he could not conceal" this fact. She continues, "he occasionally suffered symptoms which may have been stress-related, or which might have been early warning indications of [a] more serious illness: symptoms of digestive trouble, or a rapid, erratic pulse and pain in his back" (CY, p. 215). In November 26–December 11, 1968, she records: " … KN not very well. He had felt queer as he was getting up this morning. His heart was beating very fast and irregularly. I felt his pulse and was frightened … . He told me he had two previous experiences of similar turns" while in Ghana (CY, p. 274). Apart from Nkrumah's health issues at this time, other physical dangers were evident, although Nkrumah was resilient in the face of them. In Milne's notebook of July 31–August 21, 1968, she writes of a "bomb attempt at Kulungugu" that "made no impression on him. Walked calmly away from the scene and didn't even know he had been hit by bomb fragments until he entered his car and felt blood trickling down his legs from the many (about 13) pieces of shrapnel which penetrated his back" (CY, p. 250).

1969

By 1969, Nkrumah can no longer hide his failing health or the threat to his life in general. Nevertheless, he forges ahead, unmasking the machinations of capitalism and neo-colonialism and advocating armed revolution as the only recourse. Meanwhile, his worldwide reputation continues to grow.

Since 1966, there is clear evidence that Nkrumah knows the risks he takes in pursuing a socialist path of economic development and of criticizing neo-colonialism. Why would someone risk his life? Milne, in her notebook of November 21–December 9, 1969, provides the answer: "KN so obviously happy to be in the village. He loves the ordinary people with a great passion, particularly women and children. It hurts him deeply when he sees suffering" (CY, p. 346). In her notebook of August 6–12, 1969, Milne writes: "His gentle eyes. The kindest man I have ever known. Deep compassion for every living thing. Makes no attempt to kill cockroaches, or the little mice which scurry between his room and Nyamikeh's [nephew and personal attendant]" (p. 324).

Nkrumah's love for African people is symbolized by his love for Ghana. Milne recalls Nkrumah saying that "he and Ghana were like a man and a woman. The man had a beautiful wife and one day robbers came and tied his hands, then raped his wife 'before his very eyes'" (CY, pp. 323–324). On March 25, 1969, he writes to Milne: "Poor Africa! The international finance moneychangers and blood-suckers won't leave her alone. And the abuse they heap upon her and her people!" (p. 229). One day, he avows, "the history of Africa should be written viewing Africa as one country" (p. 336). On July 19, 1969, Nkrumah writes that the backwards direction of Ghana is not just being mapped out by the puppet NLC leadership: "We are dealing with the whole combination of American, British, West German, Israeli Intelligence organisations which are afraid of my return to Ghana, and are therefore doing all they can to stop me" (CY, pp. 320–321).

Nkrumah's clarity in regard to the enemy is reflected now in all of his correspondence and in all of his actions. On July 14, 1969, he writes to Reba Lewis: "Neo-colonialism is running amuck" (JMC, Box 154–5, #58). The most important thing, however, is that it should not run unobserved. On

April 13, 1969, Nkrumah writes: "The imperialists and neo-colonialists must know that we are not asleep. We know they are our enemies and we must prepare to face them anyhow, in whatever way we choose. The important thing is that we must make them know that we know them. Know the enemy, and prepare to confront him" (JMC, Unpublished letter to Reba Lewis; Box 154–5, #57).

Even in his letters to June Milne—a person deeply knowledgeable of, sympathetic to and supportive of Nkrumaism—he takes time to point the way to a future free from the exploitation and oppression of the people:

> You are wrong in saying that the 'socialist states have not been able to demonstrate that socialism can provide a higher standard of living for all than that enjoyed by the masses of capitalist states.' How many people in capitalist states can really afford to buy the goods and services in the capitalist stores? Higher standard of living in a capitalist state is only for the few. Poverty in the midst of plenty. Remember the socialist movement is not even 100 years old. Let there be a transformation of the machines of production in the USA, Britain, France, West Germany, etc. to socialist production and distribution and watch the result. Higher standard of living for the *whole* of the people—not the few. (January 19, 1969: CY, pp. 287–288)

Nkrumah's vision is unlimited. In the above passage, he has moved beyond the confines of Africa and other parts of the developing world. People of the developed world must awaken also to the benefits that will accrue for all under a socialist economic system.

Despite his socialist stance, Nkrumah is not naïve about the practice of socialism, however. In fact, he is puzzled by what he sometimes calls the revisionist practices of the Soviet Union. On April 28, 1969, he writes a letter to Reba Lewis: "Sometimes Soviet politics intrigues and flabbergasts me. Why they are in Nigeria helping one side to kill the other side, I do not know. Why they sometimes get softer with the West, I do not know and cannot understand" (CY, p. 305).

The neo-colonialists are the enemy, but also their African cohorts—those individual and organizational puppets that enrich and/or empower themselves at the expense of their people. Of the African puppets, Nkrumah writes on December 23, 1969 that *Class Struggle in Africa* "exposes this bastard African bourgeoisie" (JMC Unpublished Letter, Box 154–5). In another unpublished letter, dated February 3, 1969, Nkrumah's understanding of the African bourgeoisie is clearer: "Even though I do not like the way this whole Asian business is being handled in Kenya and other parts of East Africa, I sometimes cannot help but understand the root cause of what is going on there. The trouble there, however, is that they are trying to throw the Asian capitalists out and substitute them with African capitalists. Worse!" (Box 154–4, #57). From Dudley Thompson in Jamaica, Nkrumah receives the following: "It must be galling to you to watch the puppets strutting about in the States of Africa. Perhaps one day we shall raise a man of your calibre who will really seriously begin the task of unification" (JMC Unpublished letter; Box 154–8, #66).

One thing is certain. Nkrumah is not confused by the bourgeois politics of the OAU [Organisation of African Unity]. In a letter to Idris Cox, dated August 16, 1969, Nkrumah writes: "The OAU has become a puppet organisation in the hands of neo-colonialists and imperialists, and has neither the organisational machinery nor the will to conduct a revolutionary war … Certainly, imperialists and neo-colonialists and indigenous reactionary forces welcome platforms of protest such as the OAU" (CY, p. 326).

Additionally, Nkrumah has revised his position on non-alignment and crystallized his thinking in regard to other concepts. On October 23, 1969, he writes to Milne that he would like to include a chapter in *Class Struggle in Africa* entitled, 'Forward to Scientific Socialism': "In this chapter I can criticise and expose the fallacies of 'Third World', 'national democracy', 'non-capitalist road', 'non-alignment' etc. as vague concepts and illusions" (CY, p. 340).

"As a state of war already exists throughout Africa", fallacies like those above need to be exposed and discarded to usher in the armed phase of the African Revolution. Nkrumah is "convinced more than ever before of the need for centralised political and military direction" (to Idris Cox, August 16, 1969: CY, p. 327). There is no other way out of the stranglehold that the colonialists and neo-colonialists have on Africa: "there can be no peaceful solution to the problems posed by neo-colonialism. There's only one solution, armed struggle" (to Milne, April 8, 1969: CY, p. 302). Different time periods call for different strategies. Two previous stages called for non-violent, positive action. However, those stages have passed. In a letter of February 9, 1969, Nkrumah writes: "Now the third stage: Ghana's independence and its repercussions in Africa; the various independence movements—their successes and failures etc; the fight for the political unification of the continent, leading to the armed revolutionary phase, and the throwing overboard of constitutional forms of struggle. The theoretical weapon for this phase is the *Handbook*. So the struggle continues" (p. 293). On September 23, 1969, he writes to Reba Lewis: "At this stage of the armed phase of the African Revolution, cultural conferences are meaningless. It is around the revolutionary struggle of the African people that African culture can take on substance; it cannot take substance around songs, poems, folklore and dances" (p. 335). Nothing can proceed in the African world until the African's survival is ensured. There can be no business as usual. Time is of the essence because human lives are at stake.

The armed phase will sweep away bankrupt organizations and puppet leaders and bring revolutionary organizations and leadership to Africa. In fact, Nkrumah is convinced that it will bring him back to power in Ghana: "Luckily enough, it is the army, officers and men, who are supporting my early return. It is they who are going to act" (to Milne, January 27, 1969: CY, p. 290). And when he returns, the African Revolution will really surge, beginning with a call for "the 'Conference of all Black Movements in the World' to Accra!". The impact of the conference will mean that "the whole concept of Black Power will change, and a new world revolutionary movement will emerge" (to Milne, February 7, 1969: CY, pp. 291–292). What a difference to the African, as well as to the capitalist, world this conference would have made! It is the first on Nkrumah's agenda because it is the unity of African people worldwide in a fight for a unified, socialist Africa that will quickly and permanently solve the global problems of African people.

Nkrumah sees 1970 as "beginning the decade of the armed phase of the African socialist revolution. The next ten years are going to be crucial in Africa's history. And CS [*Class Struggle in Africa*] is going to lay down the historical and practical foundation for the struggle" (to Milne, December 23, 1969: CY, p. 350). Only one hurdle needs to be jumped: Nkrumah's return to Ghana.

Meanwhile, as he waits to return to Ghana, Nkrumah teaches about the inevitability of armed struggle. Several letters focus on socialist countries such as the Soviet Union. On January 25, 1969, in an unpublished section of a letter which appears in *Conakry Years*, Nkrumah writes: "If Lenin and Trotsky had not backed Marx's pen with armed revolution the writings of Marx would still have been in some dingy old museums waiting for researches to be made on them. Yes, Marx and Engels wrote but they also preached armed revolutions to support their writings. So you see, the success of the pen depends upon the gun" (JMC, Box 154–5, #57). In an unpublished letter to Reba Lewis on June 14, 1969, Nkrumah writes: "We need a *new Lenin* in the Soviet Union" (JMC, Box 154–5, #58). Still on revolution, Nkrumah writes to Lewis on July 14, 1969: "Why the socialist and communist parties in Europe today are afraid of socialist revolution and armed revolutionary warfare astounds me. Those who are for socialist revolution in Europe are being isolated by the very socialist and communist parties which should support them" (JMC, Box 154–5, #58).

Other letters concern armed struggle in general. In a letter to Reba Lewis on January 6, 1969, Nkrumah writes: "The gun without the pen is useless, but the pen without the gun is even worse; more useless than nothing" (JMC, Box 154–5). In a powerful letter regarding the importance of armed warfare, dated March 29, 1969, Nkrumah writes: "You cannot fight for freedom under capitalism because capitalism negates freedom" (JMC, Box 154-7, #83). He continues:

> Christ was the first socialist and even the first communist of the last two thousand years. I hope you remember how he took the whip, beat and drove the capitalist-money-changers from the Temple. Do not laugh at this because it is true today as it was in the days of Jesus, except that the problems are more complicated with the advance of science and technology ... . I am an African nationalist but at the same time I am an internationalist. The emancipation of man regardless of colour, creed or religion is my concern and if in this life I can do my little bit towards the achievement of that goal, I have done the best I can". (Box 154-7, #83)

In 1969 Nkrumah's worldwide reputation is steadily rising among the revolutionary sector of the world, especially the African world and the spark of that world, the youth. In an unpublished letter dated August 25, 1969, Reba Lewis writes: "We have heard your name often this week on BBC radio. One announcement said that posters with your name had sprung up over Jamestown! Another said that (Stokely) Carmichael was in Congo Brazzaville speaking for you and saying that you alone of the African leaders believed in a united Africa and had fought for this cause. It was very thrilling to hear the name of Nkrumah over the air" (JMC, Box 154-5, #58). On September 23, 1969, Nkrumah writes to Milne: "Revolutionary letters have been pouring in to me from various quarters. Something is possessing the youth of Africa ... . The youth of Africa are determined, and I seem to be their inspiration. How I wish we could have a base *now*. I am working hard" (CY, p. 335).

He is also an inspiration to African leaders. On September 6, 1969, he writes that President Kenneth Kaunda of Zambia "paid us a visit here and spent some time with us. I gave him a lot of advice and I hope he will abide by them. I do not like his 'nationalisation' plan because what he did was not 'nationalisation', it was what I call 'participation', and 'participation' always leads to neo-colonialism" (to Reba Lewis; JMC Box 154-5). He is especially an inspiration to Sékou Touré. In a letter of May 9, 1969, he writes: "I have just had a word with S.T. He wants me to be with him at the Palais du Peuple. He is having a big conference there ... . I have decided to go. He likes me to be by his side" (to Milne: CY, p. 307). Amilcar Cabral, President of PAIGC (African Party for the Independence of Guinea and Cape Verde) and actively engaged in armed struggle against the Portuguese in what will become Guinea Bissau, also seeks Nkrumah's counsel. Cabral visits Nkrumah numerous times while Nkrumah is in Conakry; one of these occasions is on July 9, 1969. In a letter of that date, Nkrumah writes: "I am meeting Cabral today". He also indicates that Black Power advocates in the U.S. seek his counsel: "I will give [Cabral] the addresses of Rogers and Boggs, and also Dan Aldridge so that he can send them materials and information about the struggle in 'Portuguese' Guinea" (to Milne, CY, p. 317). In her notebook of November 21–December 9, 1969, Milne describes Cabral as "a smallish, dynamic figure" and writes that he gave Nkrumah and her "copies of the latest PAIGC bulletins" (CY, p. 344).

Africans born in the USA and involved in the struggle there are anxious and thirsty for the words of Nkrumah. According to his June 10, 1969 letter to Milne, the "Nkrumah Book Service" is being set up in Detroit and Milne "will be sending 3,000 [copies of] *Axioms* to the big distributors in Philadelphia". The *Axioms* are quite a hit in the US, and Nkrumah writes that "the 'little Black Book' is not doing badly at all. If our distribution system is planned well and goes well, it will supplant Mao's red book in the USA, Africa, the Caribbean and other areas of the world where there are Africans and people of African descent" (to Milne: CY, p. 312).

Those in the Caribbean are just as thirsty. And Nkrumah has a brilliant proposition for the health and well-being of the peoples of Caribbean countries. In a letter to Dudley Thompson, dated April 8, 1969, Nkrumah writes: "The same way that I have been talking about African Unity for the African Continent, it is the same way that I would like to see the political unification of the Caribbean islands under black hegemony. If the African revolution succeeds its repercussions in the Caribbean will be felt ten-fold" (JMC, Box 154–8, #66). Earlier (7 June, 1962), in a letter to the West Indian Heads of Government (*The Nkrumaist*, 1985), Nkrumah wrote:

> I hope you will forgive the liberty I am taking in making this earnest appeal to you from the distance of Africa on the burning issue of the Federation of the West Indies and Guiana. My excuse for making this appeal is the sincere conviction I hold that success in the establishment of a powerful West Indian nation would substantially assist the efforts we are making in Africa to redeem Africa's reputation in world affairs and to re-establish the personality of the African and people of African descent everywhere ... . unless this can be done from the very threshold of independence, the islands will be torn apart by disunity and fall an easy prey to far greater dangers than the evils which they suffered under imperialism and colonialism.

Outside of the African world, Nkrumah is in touch with revolutionary governments that will prove helpful, economically and militarily, when he is re-installed as President of Ghana. In a letter of January 12, 1969, Nkrumah writes to Milne: "I autographed the book for Castro, and left it there for the Ambassador to send to him. I think Cuba wants to experiment with growing cocoa in Cuba in addition to sugar. Good luck to them. They helped us to grow sugar in Ghana" (CY, p. 286). On July 5, 1969, Nkrumah writes: "The Vietnamese visited me yesterday and brought some books and 'Perfume Tea' from Ho Chi Minh, with an encouraging message" (CY, p. 317). In a letter of February 3, 1969 he writes to Reba Lewis:

> National capitalism and international finance capitalism is what is smothering India and Pakistan; and so long as they allow these vultures of evil to remain with them, India and Pakistan will be wrecking from one rock to another until communism sets in to save them. Only forthright socialism can turn the scale in those two countries. Sometimes I wonder whether some parts of Asia and South-east Asia are not in a greater mess than the mess in which Africa is now—neo-colonialism enstranglement. (Box 154-5, #57)

Nkrumah is also in touch with the UN Secretary-General, U Thant. In a confidential letter, he writes to U Thant on May 4, 1969, not to ask for the UN's help to re-install him, but to offer his advice on three "hot spots" or "hot issues" in the world: the most effective way to run the UN, the Israeli-Arab conflict in the Middle East, and the Vietnam War. On the first "hot issue", Nkrumah begins: "I have been giving much thought to the problem of the Secretary-Generalship of the United Nations. It seems to me that the best solution would be for the post to be filled in rotation by a representative from each of the different areas of the world—Asia, Africa, Europe, Latin America, etc.—each Secretary-General serving a four-year term. Such a solution would prevent the post of UN Secretary-General from becoming a pawn in world power politics". On the matter of the Middle East, he writes "that the only hope for a lasting solution to the conflict between the Israelis and the Arabs, lies in the creation of an independent Palestinian state. Such a state could be formed from territory yielded by both Jordan and Israel". On the third matter, he writes: "In Vietnam, the solution lies as it has always done, in total American withdrawal, and I am glad to observe that events seem to be moving rapidly in this direction" (CY, p. 307). Nkrumah sends U Thant copies of *Dark Days in Ghana* and *Handbook of Revolutionary Warfare*. He receives a letter nine days later in which U Thant thanks him for his suggestions.

Nkrumah's worldwide reputation can also be measured by the passing references to him in newspapers and other publications. In an unpublished letter dated March 18, 1969, Reba Lewis writes: "Sunday, there was a review in the Times of Dr. [Eric] Williams new book *Inward Hunger*. The review is very snide and snobbish and ends by saying that if being in power {Eric Williams, Prime Minister of Trinidad and Tobago] has become a "little humourless and self-opinioniated [sic]", it doesn't matter because "if he has become neither a

Castro nor a Nkrumah he has to be congratulated". So you see everyone still thinks of you. The impact you made on world political though[t] has not diminished. You are still the greatest" (JMC, Box 154–5, #57).

Despite the encouragement provided by such communications, 1969 revealed a decline in Nkrumah's health and spirit. Milne writes that Nkrumah by now "was steadily losing weight, and weighed barely ten stone [140 lbs]. He had weighed well over eleven stone when he arrived in Conakry three years before. On each of the four times I visited Conakry during 1969 I noticed signs of deteriorating health" (CY, p. 280). Meanwhile, Nkrumah "kept insisting that he was 'fit and well'" and resorted to increased amounts of "health foods, vitamins and medicines" that he asked Milne to either send or to bring (p. 280). Add to this, the "further signs of the Villa Syli being run down"; and "More important, the morale of some members of the entourage appeared to be low" (p. 280). Finally, the Guinean government of Sékou Touré seemed to be endangered. For one thing, "Guinean exiles based in Paris were constantly reported to be making plans for an armed invasion of Guinea … [and] it was widely reported that mercenaries were beginning to assemble and train in nearby countries, namely in Portuguese Guinea, Ivory Coast, the Gambia and Senegal" (CY, p. 281).

An anti-Nkrumah, anti-Sékou Touré western media campaign also seemed to be mounting, according to Milne. This media campaign accused Touré of "dictatorship, mismanagement of the economy and the barbaric treatment of thousands of political prisoners languishing in Guinean jails" (CY, p. 281). Milne writes that a similar campaign was launched against Nkrumah in 1965 which "focused international attention on Ghana preparatory to the coup of February 1966" (p. 282). There were rumors spread as well of friction between Touré and Nkrumah ; one such rumor in a British newspaper stated that "Sékou Touré had banished Nkrumah to an off-shore island". Milne writes that "by the end of 1969, clouds were massing all around Guinea, generating the ominous, highly charged atmosphere typical before the onset of a tropical storm" (p. 282).

On September 8, 1969, Nkrumah writes to Milne that Africa need not pay attention to the puppet leaders in Africa. Sweep them aside and unite Africa:

> I am convinced that an African Union Government can be established at the same time as AAPRP and AAPRA. Such a government could be established over the heads of the Independent African States. Membership or citizenship of the Union will be based on individuals, and not on states. And the government doesn't have to seek diplomatic recognition. It will work through its individual citizen membership. Its main job is to work with AAPRA and AAPRP, and to boost up the

political unification of Africa. Such a Union Government will cut across the confusion and pandemonium reigning in Africa, since it will function independently of the African states, which the Union Government will consider as zones. Don't think this is impossible. It can be worked out. Africa must keep on challenging the world! (CY, pp. 331–332)

By 1969, Nkrumah believed that the people themselves must organize and snatch the power away from the puppets. This new piece of the Nkrumaist line works not only for neo-colonial Africa, but also for people worldwide who suffer under capitalist regimes. On October 14, 1969, Nkrumah writes that when Africa explodes against neo-colonialism "human beings, white, black, yellow etc. shall realize and appreciate the unity and the humanity of all the races of mankind. It is only then that love will chase out hate. But right now, in this sordid world, we must hate in order to love. This is the paradox of our age" (to Milne: CY, p. 338).

Other close associates of Nkrumah also see the coming storm. Dudley Thompson writes from Jamaica on January 24, 1969: "I have often pointed out to my friends that no one who knew so much about the serpentine interlockings of international big business could have been tolerated as an African Leader" (JMC Unpublished letter; Box 154–8, #66). In another unpublished letter from Reba Lewis, dated March 18, 1969, she writes: "Dearest, dearest Osagyefo, For sending me your latest work, *Revolutionary Warfare*, a thousand thanks. I shall read it this week and then write again. My first reaction is one of fear for you if the book is sold. I am always worried about your safety. It is a thought which never leaves me" (JMC, Box 154–5, #57).

Nkrumah himself sees the storm approaching. On January 27, 1969, he writes to Milne of "tightened security [in Guinea], and everybody is on the alert … . I have warned Sékou Touré about risks, and I think he understands" (CY, p. 290). In her notebook of March 4–19, 1969, Milne writes that there was an attempted coup in Guinea: "Planned by civilians and a group of army officers. Plan to capture and kill Sékou Touré and his leading ministers as they visit Labé. Then Guinea to be invaded by mercenaries standing by in Mali and Ivory Coast. Ghana to send ships in support of the plotters" (CY, p. 297). Milne also writes that Nkrumah "called twice on S. Touré and urged a thorough 'cleaning up', and no leniency" (p. 297). Weeks later, on April 1, 1969, Nkrumah writes that the arrests were "still going on" and that "they are more after me than Sékou Touré, but they know that if they got S.T. then they know they have got me" (p. 300). Still, Nkrumah is unmoved. He writes: "These fools! Those who plan in accordance with basic historical conditions eventually win. Do these blighters think that, even if they get me, they will be able to alter the course of the African Revolution?" (to Milne: CY, p. 300). Not if he continues to awaken, i.e. politically educate, the African masses. And he is determined to do so, despite the amassing clouds.

Earlier, on March 25, 1969, he wrote to Reba Lewis: "I know you will be worried but something has got to be done. The fact must be faced and imperialism and neo-colonialism must be challenged despite the cost. A man lives but once" (CY, p. 299). He writes to her again on April 13, 1969: "Do not worry about me. Everything here is under control. I am glad you have read m *Handbook of Revolutionary Warfare*. You are right, there is no use being afraid; and why should one be afraid at all? The secret of life is to have no fear". Once again, he indicates that he knows that his real enemy, the real power behind neo-colonialism, is the US: "You see, now that the Americans are pulling out from Vietnam, they might be planning for Africa. So we must let them know that we know them and we have plans to face them, and that we shall be ready for them" (CY, pp. 302–303).

In an unpublished letter of May 13, 1969, Reba Lewis writes " ... be vigilant and be careful. These are very dangerous and trying times all over the world" (Box 154–5, #57). Nkrumah replies on May 22, 1969:

> Please forgive me for being as irregular in my correspondence during the last few weeks. The fact is we have been occupied with so many things, indescribably busy: comploteurs in Guinea and the chaos in Ghana. These have pre-occupied me. With regard to Guinea all is quiet now and everything is under full control. The comploteurs have been dealt with according to 'law'. ... The coup here engineered by America and France, aided and abetted by West Germany, I hear, was aimed at me but could not succeed until they had got rid of Sékou Touré. The imperialists and neo- colonialists will never stop at anything! (JMC, Box 154–5, #57)

On June 29, 1969, Nkrumah writes to Milne about another attempted attack:

> I thought he [a person in the crowd] was one of those party fanatics who in his enthusiasm had come to hail us. But he jumped straight at S.T., who was standing between me and [Kenneth] Kaunda, and knocked him with a heavy blow of his hand. If he had had an implement in his hand, he would have hurt S.T. Somehow, suddenly I realized that the chap was serious, so I knocked him with my elbow right to his stomach. I am sure it got his guts because he fell from the car. (CY, p. 316)

On August 25, 1969, Reba Lewis writes to Nkrumah: "We have heard your name often this week on BBC radio ... . It was very thrilling to hear the name of Nkrumah over the air. But be careful. Be vigilant. Remember your enemies are strong and powerful and you must never be careless about your personal safety. This I beg of you as they say in Ghana" (Unpublished letter; JMC Box 154–5, #58).

On October 2, 1969, Nkrumah writes to June Milne: "On the 30th September I went to discuss security matters with [Sékou Touré]. In the discussion he said to me: 'So long as you are here in Guinea no harm will come to me.' Somehow he has that faith. I only told him that god helps those who help themselves" (CY, p. 336).

It is possible to conjecture that if a Guinean coup d'état was unsuccessful, other measures might be resorted to in order to get rid of Nkrumah. His physical health was deteriorating and poisoning might be thought the cause of the ill health. On January 16, 1969, he writes to Milne: "Don't worry about me. I am now as fit as a fiddle. But I am in total agreement with you. I must go to the Soviet Union for a little rest and a complete medical check up" (CY, p. 336). On October 6, 1969, he writes to her again: "I have stopped taking the black treacle. I think it is the cause of gas in my stomach. It just doesn't agree with me. But I am consuming a lot of honey" (CY, p. 337). Because of his deteriorating health, Nkrumah even begins to think of preparing a will and writes to Milne concerning it:

> Contact the lawyer who is preparing your Will and ask him to prepare one for me also ... . Mine is a simple one: just say that if anything were to happen to me, the whole of my shares in Panaf Books Ltd automatically goes to you, or to Peter as your next of kin. And also that all the money with my bank in London, whatever the amount, goes to you". (CY, pp. 339–340)

In a cable of December 31, 1969, Nkrumah reveals that his condition has worsened: "Had malaria attack but better now" (to Milne: CY, p. 351).

1970–1972

Nkrumah's correspondence from 1970 to 1972 was not as voluminous as that in previous years, perhaps as a result of the physical pain he was now enduring. However, his mind remained clear throughout this time.

On January 15, 1970, Nkrumah writes to Milne: "Until the guerilla struggle in Africa is united and centralised, I can see no hope for total victory for the liberation forces" (CY, p. 260). Neo-colonialist forces could easily beat down a small grassroots, revolutionary organization within a single territory. However, a coalition of grassroots organizations would be nearly impossible to defeat. Six months later, he writes to Christine Johnson: "No great revolutionary struggles have been won without high cost in suffering and sacrifice, and the violent struggles at present taking place throughout the world are an inevitable phase in the progress towards total liberation" (July 28, 1970, JMC Box 154–5, #5).

Nkrumah's determination to link the struggles of Diasporan Africans with the struggle in Africa is unshakeable: "The Black Power movement in the U.S.A. and the African Revolution are one and the same, and nothing can prevent their ultimate fulfillment" (July 28, 1970, JMC Box 154–5, #5). There is no Nkrumaist tenet more potentially powerful to the African Revolution than this one. Showing that Africans no matter where they were born in the world are part and parcel of the African Revolution, Nkrumah strengthens, empowers, and ensures the success of the African Revolution. Diasporan Africans can aid the Revolution in countless ways: by offering their technical skills to Africa, by enlisting in the AAPRA, by serving as doctors and nurses during the armed struggle, by lobbying their governments on behalf of Africa, by donating cash to the African Revolution, and/or by simply politically educating people in their part of the world about the African Revolution.

The African Revolution is always uppermost in his mind. Even those "petty" squabbles between bourgeois Africans fighting among themselves to fulfill the role of capitalist prostitute are problems that must be solved by the African Revolution. In fact, this two-year period marks Nkrumah's clearest understanding of the enemy. The first and primary obstacle to the African Revolution, in regard to the enemy, is the puppet leadership of Africa. In *Class Struggle in Africa* (1970), Nkrumah calls this leadership the "true enemy" of African people. Thus, he devotes much of his time to exposing it. On February 2, 1970, Nkrumah discussed the violent struggles occurring in Africa in an unpublished letter to Reba Lewis: "You know my view on the Nigerian situation—it is a national bourgeois conflict. One national bourgeoisie fighting another national bourgeoisie to see who could be the proper puppet for neo-colonialism. Until the workers and peasants arise in revolution, I take no sides. If they do rise, I am on their side" (JMC, Box 154–5). This is another powerful unpublished letter, evidence of the change in the political line of the Revolution. In his early years as president of Ghana, Nkrumah thought that there was some hope for the national bourgeoisie, that they could play a role in solving the problems of Africa. That is why he was so vehement about erecting the OAU.

Thus, puppet governments outside of Africa, as well as inside, command Nkrumah's attention. In an unpublished letter to Reba Lewis on January 5, 1970, he asks, "As for Indonesia, what can we do with a puppet neo-colonialist government? These puppets seem to be die-hard, inverterate [sic] enemies of socialism" (JMC, Box 154–5). What other choice is there for the healthful survival of Africa and other developing areas of the world, Nkrumah implies, than for everyday people of the world to build grassroots movements to liberate themselves? On October 23, 1970, he writes to Milne: "These capitalists are real rogues" (CY, p. 383). But Nkrumah is particularly concerned to expose the puppets of the capitalists: "The OAU is as dead as a door nail", he writes on January 15, 1970 (to Milne: CY, p. 360). On June 10, 1971, he asks, "Can you imagine me having anything to do now with those crypto-colonial states which now constitute the OAU?" (to Milne, CY, p. 410). On January 5, 1970, in an unpublished letter to Reba Lewis, Nkrumah shows why one must expose the puppets of the capitalists and engage in class struggle: "Imagine talking of African 'aliens' in Africa" (JMC, Box 154–5). Every African belongs to all of Africa. Nkrumah is alert, astute, and forthright. He has no time to lose. In order to unify the struggle of Africans at home and abroad; that is, in order to conduct the African Revolution, class struggle among African people must be waged. Much of the last two years of Nkrumah's life is devoted to highlighting this class struggle. Since the balkanized states, created during colonialism, are artificial and alien, the people of Africa should be able to move from South Africa to Algeria as citizens of a united country, just as citizens in the United States move freely from California to New York. And, according to Nkrumah, this citizenship should not be based on race. Speaking to Seydour Keita (Guinean Ambassador to Europe) in Bucharest a few months before his death, Nkrumah said: "It is not the colour of the skin. The solution is the political unification of Africa. When Africa is a united strong power everyone will respect Africans, and Africans will respect themselves" (October 12–16, 1971: CY, p. 406). On an earlier occasion, in a letter to Reba Lewis on July 13, 1970, Nkrumah writes: "When I leave Guinea my destination will be a bee-line to Accra—non-stop. And I am not going to leave Africa either. It is the base area for the struggle of her unification and emancipation" (CY, pp. 376–377). A unification and emancipation that is based on class, not race, struggle. And in order to successfully wage this class struggle, there must be a base, a land base from which to struggle: Africa.

That the base for the African Revolution is Africa and that the African Revolution primarily is based on class, not race are points that Nkrumah reiterates in a letter of October 23, 1970 to Milne. Of the "black man" in the USA, Nkrumah writes: "There is no solution unless they base their struggle on the class struggle. For the black Americans the only way open to them is the African Revolution and class struggle" (CY, p. 383). Nkrumah emphasizes that class struggle is primary, not race or gender struggle, while reading Bobby Seale's *Seize the Time*: "These Black Panthers are along the right lines. The class struggle is the main issue, and the sooner this is realised the better for the black revolution" (to Milne, November 6, 1970: CY, p. 384). For this reason, he is compelled to write a book devoted to explaining it. That work is *Class Struggle in Africa* (1970). In it Nkrumah points out that a backwards economic system like capitalism gives rise to race oppression. Therefore, no matter that racism has become concomitant with class exploitation, the enemy to attack is the economic system of capitalism—in all of its forms. Socialism is the answer. On the first day of 1970, Nkrumah writes to Milne: "In Vietnam, the village is organised on modern lines with a socialist base. And this, in future, we must do in Africa. Modern Africa can learn a lot from the modern village commune of North Vietnam" (CY, p. 359). And while we are working to establish a socialist Africa and even once we organize Africa along these lines, we must watch out for idealism: "Too much idealism and too much religion retard a nation's progress. These sometimes weaken the guts for direct practical action" (to Milne, CY, p. 360).

Some of these points (i.e. some parts of the Nkrumaist line)—elements of the African Revolution—are not new. Some, like the tactic of armed struggle, are. By 1970, Nkrumah had developed the entire political line of the African Revolution.

1. Identity = Africans born inside and outside of Africa are Africans and belong to the African nation
2. Enemy = Capitalism (in all of its forms, including colonialism, neo-colonialism and settler-colonialism)
3. Solution = A union of African states under a scientific socialist economic system
4. Strategy = Grass roots revolutionary organizations in Africa (and throughout the world) in which all African people play a role, no matter where they live in the world
5. Tactics = Armed Struggle via an All African People's Revolutionary Army (AAPRA).

From 1970 to 1972 Nkrumah iterates and re-iterates the Nkrumaist line so that it reaches as many ears as possible and so that there is absolutely no chance of its being misunderstood. Worldwide, and in Africa particularly, Nkrumah's reputation is at its zenith. Several unpublished letters (or unpublished sections of letters) from young people such as Etop J. Usoroh at the University of Lagos, Nigeria are written to Nkrumah from July 1970 through August 1971. They are important in reflecting the stature that Nkrumah held, particularly among politically-conscious youths of African descent. These youths comprise the most progressive and revolutionary sector of the world. A letter of July 31, 1970 is addressed: "Nkrumah of Africa". In the letter, Usoroh writes: "Some of us in Nigeria are totally fed up with the complacent attitude of the African leaders and public over the important question of the political and economic emancipation of Africa ... . we are looking up to you as the 'patron-in-chief' of the African revolution".

On October 15, 1970, Usoroh writes: "It has been proposed that a group of patriotic, dedicated, well-informed young Nigerians should work underground for some years to form what will be called the peoples army in our part of Africa ... For this reason, we have decided that all movements with the aim of combating neo-colonialism should come under a single directive with you as the patron" (JMC, Box 159-9, #12). Nkrumah sends Usoroh a copy of *Class Struggle in Africa*, the receipt of which the latter acknowledges in a letter dated April 26, 1971: "It makes a very interesting reading especially as my country presents itself as a model of almost all the chapters discussed in the book. I have been making contacts with some Guinean students in our university here" (Box 159-9, #12). In the last letter in Usoroh's file, dated August 7, 1971, Usoroh writes: "My dear Dr. Kwame Nkrumah, I hope that you are in perfect health. We in Nigeria have not heard much about you for the last few months, especially after Guinea was invaded by the Pirates of Portugal. Look at the copy of our daily paper "Daily Times" May 26, 1971. This is the wish of all comrades in our country. Will you give this some consideration?"

Young people living in the US were also looking to Nkrumah for inspiration and leadership. Lamin Jangha—born in the Gambia, once a member of Nkrumah's Young Pioneers, a former central committee member of the All-African People's Revolutionary Party, and a co-founder of the Pan-African Revolutionary Socialist Party—writes to Nkrumah in 1970 and 1971. On December 13, 1970, Lamin writes:

> This country (US) is becoming more and more racist. The white establishment is using every means to divide the African people over here. There are a whole lot of black people here who are yearning for a base to relate to. Many of them have talents and skills they want to use in the service of Africa. But they have no real base on the continent. This goes further to demonstrate how urgent and absolutely incumbent it is for you to go back to Ghana, so that we can at least have a starting point in the fight. (CY, pp. 385)

On April 27, 1971, Lamin writes: "My stay in the US so far has taught me a whole lot of things, in the sense that I've been able to observe how our people have been dehumanised and miseducated under this die-hard capitalist system. I would therefore like to come back immediately if you deem it necessary, and carry out any project. I'm of the belief that the first priority in the African Revolution is to see that you are back in Ghana" (CY, p. 398). On August 31, 1971, the Political Committee of the Malcolm X Liberation University in the USA sends a cable to Nkrumah: "Heard reports that you are ill.

Hopefully these reports are not true. If so we wish you a speedy recovery. We shall hold high the banner of Revolutionary Panafricanism and socialism" (CY, p. 391). On behalf of the brothers of Morehouse College, Edgar Thomas writes a letter to Nkrumah on December 12, 1970:

> The brothers of Morehouse College have formed a Pan-African Congress, and we are concerned about the struggle in the motherland and the safety of our leaders. We were more than overjoyed to know that the people of the Republic of Guinea were able to drive the Portuguese and their black lackeys into the sea. We understand the position of Africans in the struggle for national liberation and the unification of the African continent. We, your brothers colonised in America, are with you 100% in the liberation of Africa. (CY, p. 385)

Those most ideologically clear on the continent, Amilcar Cabral and Sékou Touré, understood and appreciated the importance of Nkrumah to the African Revolution; they also relied on the connection they had with him. As noted by Milne (CY, footnote, p. 360), on the title page of his book *Revolution in Guinea*, Amilcar Cabral wrote in his own hand: "*Au pionnier de la libération et de l'unité Africaine—Dr Kwame Nkrumah dont la solidarite et l'exemple nous ont toujours encourage—ce de notre admiration et amitié militante.* Amilcar Cabral, January 1970". Nkrumah also understood that those like Cabral were invaluable in helping him to think clearly about the African Revolution. Cabral and the people of Guinea Bissau, for instance, were in the throes of armed struggle against the Portuguese. Nkrumah understood and wrote about the theory of armed struggle, but the people of Guinea Bissau were practising armed struggle daily. On January 15, 1970, Nkrumah writes to Milne of the book: "I have not been able to read through carefully but I have gone through the Chapter on 'Brief Analysis of the Social Structure of Guinea', page 46. I want you to read it and test it with *CS* [*Class Struggle in Africa*] and see if there's anything we have left out" (CY, p. 360).

Perhaps one most inspired and reliant on Nkrumah was Sékou Touré. On January 1, 1970, Nkrumah writes to Milne: "It is exactly 1, p.m. and I have just returned from a short visit to ST and his wife, just to say to them: 'Bonne année'. I thanked them for all they have done for me. ST was so happy to see me, he wouldn't let go of my hand. He was holding tightly on to it as if to get hope and inspiration from it. He guarded me, as it were, walking with me with my hand still in his, down the stairs" (CY, p. 358). Touré also presented Nkrumah with a collection of documents which related to the invasion of Guinea, *L'Agression Portugaise contre la République le Guinée*. According to Milne, "handwritten by Sékou Touré on the title page are the words: '*A mon ami et cher frËre president Kwame Nkrumah—Avec l'assurance de ma fidele amitié revolutionnaire au service de la Patrie Africaine*. Ahmed Sékou Touré 18–1–71'" (CY, p. 389fn).

Nkrumah's contribution, inspiration, and value to the African Revolution is clear. What is not so clear are the circumstances surrounding his death. Julie Medlock writes on February 1, 1970: "Lord knows, *something* must be protecting you!" (Unpublished letter, JMC Box 154–6, #39). That protection did not last, however. Everyone familiar with the theory and practice of Kwame Nkrumah was in fear for his safety. Mary Winters had good reason to write the following: "All I can think about is you, your friends, and their safety and well-being. My thoughts are with you. May you all be guarded and guided" (Unpublished letter dated November 23, 1970; Box 154–9, #26).

That physical danger surrounded him is evidenced in the many coup attempts, invasions of Guinea, the suspected death by poison of his faithful cook, phone taps—Milne writes that when she received a call from Nkrumah on August 17, 1971, she "had good reason to think that my telephone was being tapped" (CY, pp. 390–391)—and the tampering with his mail. Milne writes that "Nkrumah wrote fewer and briefer letters" due to his health, but also due to "the interference with the mail which almost undoubtedly was taking place in Conakry" (CY, p. 356).

Nkrumah too must have felt that his days were numbered. On January 13, 1971, he writes: "You should not bother about the complete silence in the press about me. You know my policy about press and radio reports. It is me they want and they cannot get me without getting ST" (CY, p. 394). Nkrumah was referring to the attempted coup in Guinea. Milne writes that only three months after the publication of *Class Struggle in Africa* (August 1970), "the invasion of Guinea [22 November, 1970] and the involvement of reactionary elements within Guinea in the attempt to overthrow Sékou Touré's government, confirmed Nkrumah's exposure of the class struggle in Africa" (CY, p. 356). As Milne relates, "for 24 hours, the fate of the PDG government, and with it, the safety of Nkrumah, hung in the balance" (CY, p. 355). More than that, the attack confirmed to those concerned about Nkrumah that the neocolonialists would not rest until Nkrumah was dead.

Beginning in the summer of 1970, it was clear that Nkrumah was seriously ill. Milne writes that Nkrumah "could no longer conceal the fact that his health was deteriorating. He was losing weight fast and suffering from acute back pain. It became worse with the rainy season when he suffered what was diagnosed by a Russian doctor as acute lumbago" (CY, p. 355). Milne writes that one night between July 24–August 4, 1970, she "found KN in great distress, severe lumbago. He couldn't move and was lying on his bed at a very awkward angle" (378). In August, he was still suffering severe back pain and was examined by the Russian doctor who "gave him a painkilling injection, and remarked that the whole of Conakry seemed to be suffering from rheumatism of one kind or another" (CY, p. 355).

It seems that Nkrumah himself may at first have believed that he was suffering from rheumatism. In a letter to Reba Lewis dated October 19, 1970, Nkrumah related that he "had a very bad hit of lumbago" (Unpublished letter, Box 154–5, #58). To Reba Lewis again on June 17, 1971, he writes: "I have not been very well and the trouble is rheumatism and sciatica, with pains which came on and off" (CY, p. 402). But by August 1971, Nkrumah thinks it is cancer. In a letter dated August 30, 1971, Dudley Thompson writes saying he was sorry to hear that Nkrumah was "very seriously ill with cancer" (Unpublished letter, Box 154–8, #66). By then, Nkrumah was in Bucharest, Romania. There he stayed, in excruciating pain, until his death on April 27, 1972.

What exactly was the cause of Nkrumah's death? Some letters indicate it was cancer. If that is the case, then one wonders why he was left untreated or treated inappropriately. Dr. Francis Nkrumah, Kwame Nkrumah's son, stated in December 1972: "There was inexplicable medical bungling in Guinea" (CY, p. 410fn). Certainly, knowing the threat Nkrumah posed to the forces of capitalism and neo-colonialism everywhere, suspicions of foul play are unavoidable. And it is undeniable too that the untimely death of Nkrumah marked one of the unluckiest moments in the history of the African Revolution.

~ ~ ~ ~ ~

Part Two

Nkrumah's Practical Contribution to the African Revolution

3

The Cabinet Minutes

While the term "theory" is used in this work to refer to Nkrumah's philosophy in regard to the African Revolution as presented in published works, the term "practice" here refers to *actions* taken by Nkrumah on behalf of the African Revolution. Newspaper articles, for example, document the practical steps taken in regard to Pan-Africanism. Too, speeches are included in this section on practice because delivering a speech to an audience is an act; in other words, while the speech itself as written is the theory, the delivery of it to an audience is an act. Cabinet and Parliamentary decisions are, as well, included because they represent past actions taken or future actions that will be taken.

    Nkrumah's practical efforts to erect a Union of Socialist African States are documented in the decisions made by his administration as reflected in the Cabinet minutes. These decisions were principally proposed by Nkrumah. From 1959 through 1964, there is ample evidence, recorded in the minutes, of what can be called the "unity" and "socialist" practice of Kwame Nkrumah. Organizing the documentation from the Cabinet minutes into five topic areas allows for the ease of discussion as well as for an effective measurement of Nkrumah's commitment to the African Revolution. These five topic areas are as follows: 1) Nkrumah's struggle to build a unified Africa; 2) Ghana's struggle to build socialism; 3) Ghana's struggle to equalize the status of women; 4) Ghana's struggle to make education available for all youths and to incorporate political education into the Ghana school curriculum; and 5) Nkrumah's struggle to contribute to world socialism.

The Struggle to Build a Unified Africa

In regard to Ghana's struggle to build a unified Africa, on March 10, 1959, "the Cabinet considered a memorandum by the Minister of Education, and approved the institution of a scheme under which scholarships could be awarded exclusively to peoples from African states and territories to undertake courses of study in institutions of higher learning in Ghana" (Ghana National Archives [GNA] 13/1/28, Jan-Dec 1959, Item 6, p. 4). Even at this early time in his leadership, Nkrumah is thinking of Africa as one united land base. What would facilitate the growth of Ghanaians, according to him, should be made available to all Africans since identifying oneself as Ghanaian or Gambian or Ethiopian is accepting the boundaries of Africa as set out by European colonizers. Three days later, "the Cabinet also decided that Mr. George Padmore, Adviser on African Affairs to the Prime Minister … . should also be invited to lecture once a week to the students of the Ghana School of Journalism on African affairs" (GNA 13/1/28, Other Business ii). Padmore was born in Trinidad and studied in Great Britain where he first met Nkrumah. Nkrumah's belief that all people of African descent belong to the African nation is reflected in Padmore's appointment as adviser to Nkrumah on African affairs. It is also a gesture that reflects Nkrumah's respect for Padmore's expertise on African affairs. On December 8, 1959, item 16 (GNA 13/1/28, Other Business iv) concerns the establishment of the Bureau of African Affairs, an absolute necessity if Nkrumah is serious about building Pan-Africanism. For the ultimate objective is a liberated, united, socialist Africa, not just a liberated, socialist Ghana. In fact, without the former, the latter cannot be realized. The only item on the agenda for the February 13, 1960 Cabinet meeting was "French Nuclear Tests in the Sahara" (GNA 13/1/29 Jan–Dec 1960). (Soon after this testing, an earthquake occurs in Agadir, Morocco. On March 4, 1960, this earthquake disaster appears in the Cabinet minutes: "the Cabinet decided that a sum of £25,000 should be sent immediately to the Government of Morocco" (GNA 13/1/29, Other Business iv). These early Cabinet actions reflect Nkrumah's early practical contributions to the African Revolution. As the following decisions reflect, Nkrumah will continue to take practical steps to erect Pan-Africanism in the years leading up to his overthrow.

Opening prayers for the Parliament of the Republic of Ghana was an agenda item for the meeting of June 3, 1960. Two prayers are recorded in the Cabinet minutes, the second of which ends as follows: "Inspire and strengthen our people that they may give time, thought and sacrifice to speed the day of the coming beauty of Ghana and the total liberation of Africa. Amen" (GNA 13/1/29, Other Business ii). The importance of these minutes is that they reflect Nkrumah's influence in getting his Cabinet to act on behalf of all of Africa; in this case, simply by articulating a prayer for African unity. On June 10, 1960, the Cabinet minutes reflect that an agenda item was the "Implementation of Proposals in Respect of the Ghana-Guinea Union" (GNA 13/1/29, Other Business iv). On August 2, 1960, a practical step was taken in regard to this Union in that the Cabinet considered the idea of a common currency between Ghana and Guinea. Then on July 22, 1960, there were resolutions in regard to the

Second Conference of Independent African States. At this same meeting, "the Cabinet also agreed that, with effect from the 1st of August, 1960, the Government of Ghana should start an official and total boycott of South Africa in protest against the policy of apartheid and racial discrimination of the Government of the Union of South Africa" (GNA 13/1/29, Item 2). Nkrumah is already acting as if Africa is united. And Nkrumah is acting quickly. All of these agreements, resolutions, and proposals are made in the summer of 1960.

Even more than South Africa, the Congo reflects Nkrumah's continental approach to matters affecting a Union of African States. Events in the Congo required much Cabinet time beginning on July 28, 1960 when "the situation in the Congo" (GNA 13/1/29, Item 1) was reported on by Major General H. T. Alexander at the request of Nkrumah. On August 8, 1960, the Congo situation was the only item on the agenda: "The President gave the Cabinet background information to the Joint-Communiqué which had been issued earlier that morning in connection with the visit to Ghana of His Excellency Patrice Lumumba, the Prime Minister of the Congo" (*ibid.*). Nkrumah also contacted the Heads of Independent African States and the governments of the United Kingdom and the United States of America in regard to the Congo. On August 9, 1960, the practical matter of assistance to the Congo Republic commanded the attention of the Cabinet (GNA 13/1/29, Item 12, Other Business v).

Another matter related to unity was considered on August 26, 1960: "Economic Co-operation with Neighbouring West African Countries" (GNA 13/1/29, Item 17, Other Business v). In the discussion of this cooperation, the following was stated: "It was appreciated that this type of co-operation was essential, but the view was also held that it must be based on a clear definition of the political relationship between participating countries. Until such a definition had been made, there could be no question of economic co-operation in which Ghana should participate" (*ibid.*). This statement, of course, is a reflection of Nkrumah's belief that political unity must precede economic unity. While no action was taken, the criterion for action was laid.

Once again, on December 30, 1960, the Cabinet had to address "French Nuclear Tests in the Sahara": "The view was expressed that the explosion of the French Third Atomic Bomb in the Sahara in opposition to the wishes of the African Peoples raised grave political issues. It was AGREED that the Government should seek the agreement of other African States for joint action in taking stern measures against France" (GNA 13/1/29, Item 1). France's acts are unconscionable, exposing African people to the dangers of nuclear waste. Nkrumah's concern for all of Africa demands that he and his cabinet take action. What were the actions proposed? The same as any united sovereign state's would be: "(1) Breaking of Diplomatic Relations with France; (2) Introduction of trade boycott against France; (3) All French assets should be frozen;

(4) All French assets should be seized; (5) All French Firms should be nationalised; and (6) There should be no transfer of currency from Ghana to any area outside Ghana by the French Firms" (*ibid.*). In addition, "it was also AGREED that Ghana should raise the matter in the UN General Assembly and that, in consultation with the United Arab Republic and Ceylon, the matter should also be raised in the Security Council" (*ibid.*). Finally, "it was DECIDED that no announcement about these decisions should be made until after the other Independent African States had been consulted at the Rabat Conference" (*ibid.*).

First, these decisions can only be made if an African, born and raised in Ghana, sees himself as an African, not merely a product of an artificially carved out territory called Ghana. Second, they can only be made if an African anywhere in Africa or throughout the African world sees an injury to any part of Africa as an injury to himself. And, third, they can only be made if Africa is seen as one undivided, sovereign nation. All of these prerequisites must play a critical role in understanding the following Cabinet minutes when Cabinet members came together at 7, p.m. on Monday, February 13, 1961 for an emergency meeting regarding the murder of Patrice Lumumba. The minutes of this meeting record that "(3) A Note should be sent to the Casablanca Powers, excluding Ceylon, strongly recommending a meeting in Accra of their Foreign Ministers or accredited representatives to consider common action. It was agreed that the 18th of February should be suggested for this meeting" (GNA 13/1/30). Further, "(4) The Government of Ghana should offer to provide education in Ghana for the children of Mr. Lumumba" (*ibid.*).

A statement was made on "Angola-Portuguese West Africa" in an informal Cabinet meeting held on February 17, 1961: "The President referred to the situation in Angola, Portuguese West Africa, and stated that it was most undesirable that Ghana should remain a silent spectator to events of the last few weeks in that country. He suggested and it was AGREED that the stand of Ghana in this matter should be made unequivocally clear to the world. He directed therefore that a statement should be prepared for consideration by the Cabinet" (GNA 13/1/30). Nkrumah is once again serving as an acting prime minister of a continent, a nation, yet to be consolidated.

South Africa's racist apartheid practices drew the attention of the Cabinet on April 18, 1961: "The Cabinet considered a memorandum by the Minister of State for Foreign Affairs, and APPROVED the proposal that at the 45th Session of the I.L.O. [International Labour Organisation] Conference in July, 1961 Ghana should seek the expulsion of the Union of South Africa from the International Labour Organisation" (GNA 13/1/30, Item 2). Once again, the status of the Union of South Africa commanded the attention of the Cabinet on two days in May 1961, the 30th and 31st: "The President informed the Cabinet that as from 31st May, 1961, the Union of South Africa had ceased to exist and a so-called Republic had purported to have been established in its place. Osagyefo proposed and the Cabinet AGREED that Ghana cannot recognise the so-called Republican Government of South Africa as possessing any legal authority" (GNA 13/1/30, Item 28, Other Business xi). Also recorded in the same minutes:

> "The Government of Ghana has further taken note that no Independent State on the African Continent intends to establish or continue diplomatic relations with the so-called Republic in South Africa as at present constituted … . [T]hose persons voting in favour of a Republic constituted scarcely one-tenth of the potential voters in South Africa if the voters list had been compiled on the basis of one man one vote … . The Government considers that this action is in accordance with the decisions of the All African People's Conference held in Accra in 1958".

Once again, the Cabinet responds to the exploitive and oppressive policies of the colonial regime of Portugal. Because of the vicious exploitation and oppression of "Angola and other territories in Africa at present under domination of Portugal" (GNA 13/1/30, Item 1) sanctions were instituted against Portugal at an emergency meeting of the Cabinet held on June 1, 1961. Some of the sanctions include the following (*ibid.*):

> (a) To close all Ghanaian sea and airports to Portuguese shipping and aeroplanes, and no vessels flying the Portuguese flag will be permitted to enter any Ghanaian Harbour and anchorage, except in cases of distress. (b) To withdraw the existing open and general licences to import goods from Portugal.

Another step was taken to consolidate the emergence of a united states of Africa on June 30, 1961 at an informal meeting of the Cabinet. At that meeting, an information paper circulated detailing "arrangements that had been made for Osagyefo the President to speak to his Presidential colleagues, President Sékou Toure and President Modibo Keita at 11 a.m. and 12.00 noon respectively, on Saturday, 1st July, 1961 in connection with the inauguration of radio communication between the capitals of the Union States of Ghana-Guinea-Mali" (GNA 13/1/30, Item 4).

On the first anniversary of the death of Patrice Lumumba, February 6, 1962, the Cabinet "APPROVED the issue of a commemorative stamp in honour of the death of the late Premier Patrice Lumumba … to be issued on 30th June, 1962, Congo Republic Day" (GNA 13/1/31, Item 8).

In another effort to unify Africa, the Cabinet ratified a treaty establishing the African Common Market at its July 24, 1962 meeting. This treaty represents Nkrumah's struggle to build Pan-Africanism any way he could, even by setting up continental apparatus for a common market prior to the existence of a ratified constitution unifying all the states of Africa (GNA 13/1/31, Item 2). Also, on October 16, 1962, in a show of support and unification, and in an attempt to further build cooperation among African States, "the Cabinet had before it a memorandum circulated by the African Affairs Secretariat, and DECIDED that, until further notice, the outstanding interest on the loans made by the Government of Ghana to the Governments of Guinea, Mali and the Upper Volta should be paid in the currencies of these countries" (GNA 13/1/31, Item 17). On November 6, 1962, the Cabinet approved a memorandum authorizing that "(1) A Conference of Union of African Local Government Councils should be held in Accra between 20th and 25th March, 1963 and Local Government Council Associations and other similar bodies in independent and self-governing African States should be invited to be represented at the Conference by three delegates in respect of each country. (2) The Government of Ghana should bear all the expenses" (GNA 13/1/31, Item 3).

On November 20, 1962, the Cabinet considered a proposal for the formation of a West African Commonwealth Airline, but declined to approve it. Instead, "the Cabinet directed that the Ghana Airways Corporation should intensify its arrangements to extend its services to as many African States as possible, as this would be a more practicable and effective contribution to the achievement of African continental unity" (GNA 13/1/31, Item 2). Although in 1945 he was amenable to the idea as a first step toward continental unity (see *Towards Colonial Freedom*), regional unity anywhere in Africa was now anathema to Nkrumah. By 1962, Nkrumah's theory and practice were geared toward full continental unity.

Since unity is the goal of Nkrumah and the CPP, it is noteworthy that Nkrumah invites and introduces to the Cabinet two representatives of the states that make up the Ghana-Guinea-Mali union: "Mr. Paul Louis Faber, newly appointed Guinea Resident Minister in Ghana, Mr. Senenta Kalsoum, Charge d'Affaires of the Mali Embassy". Also, on June 4, 1963, the "Cabinet ... APPROVED the proposal that Ghana should play host to the first meeting of the Union of African News Agencies scheduled to be held in December 1963" (GNA 13/1/32, Item 21). Then, on July 2, 1963, the Cabinet "AGREED that the decisions of the Casablanca Powers on the establishment of the African Common Market would be implemented in the context of the Charter of African Unity" (GNA 13/1/32, Item 17). The Casablanca Powers or Group was comprised of the so-called "radical" states in Africa, including Egypt, Ghana, and Guinea. They were stalwart Pan-Africanists, believing that African states, in order to survive, must unite and must embrace socialism.

The February 18, 1964 Cabinet meeting addressed an Ethiopia-Somalia border dispute. In building Pan-Africanism, Nkrumah knew that one of the tasks that needed resolution was that involving territorial disputes. Until such time as an African union was established, however, he took on this task himself, as he did many others, rather than allowing discord to reign. Therefore, "Osagyefo The President proposed, and the Cabinet AGREED, that in addition to the letters already addressed by Osagyefo to Emperor Haile Selassie of Ethiopia and President Abdullah Osman of Somalia, advising them to adhere to the ceasefire arrangements, another appeal for cessation of hostilities should be made to the two Heads of States" (GNA 13/1/30, Item 20). Also, the Cabinet "AGREED that Osagyefo should send a Goodwill Mission to Ethiopia and Somalia to submit to the two Heads of States Osagyefo's proposals for resolving the crisis" (*ibid.*).

Two significant acts by the Cabinet took place on August 4, 1964. It "APPROVED the appointment of … 18 committees for the organisation and arrangements for the Conference of Heads of State and Government scheduled to take place in Accra in September next year" (GNA 13/1/30, Item 19: State Enterprises). Nkrumah was determined to persuade his counterparts of the necessity of Pan-Africanism and coordinating and hosting conferences was one way to do so. It was one of the most effective actions taken to ensure that his political beliefs, clearly in service to the continent, were dominant. In preparation for this Conference, the first committee approved was the "General Political Committee" of which Mr. Kojo Botsio was the chairman. The duties of this committee were those in regard to unification: "(a) Continental Union Government of Africa" (GNA 13/1/30, Item 7).

Ghana's Struggle to Build Socialism

Ghana's efforts to build socialism are also documented in the Cabinet minutes. One of the challenges of any state's efforts to establish socialism is to harness the nation's wealth in order to secure the well being of its people. Nkrumah knew that a socialist economic system was best for Ghanaians and Africans in general (indeed all of humanity), and also that a socialist Ghana would serve as a role model for the rest of Africa. The one item on the Cabinet's agenda of February 6, 1961 was "Take over by the Government of Five Gold Mining Companies": "it was DECIDED in principle that the Government should take over all the existing Gold Mines in Ghana, except those of the Ashanti Goldfields Corporation and the Konongo Gold Mines Limited" (GNA 13/1/30, Item 1), since private property, at least that which was vital to the survival of the society, must be taken out of the hands of private companies and made public.

At the June 26, 1962 Cabinet meeting, there were three items of interest that reflect Nkrumah's attempt to build socialism in Ghana. First, "the Cabinet discussed the running and management of Gold Mines throughout the country, and AGREED that the operation of these mines was not in the best interest of the country. It was considered that the time had come for the existing gold mines to be acquired by the State" (GNA 13/1/31, Item 12: Other Business v). Likewise, in an effort to correct the undue emphasis "some Ministers and High Party Officials" seemed to be placing on the "Private Sector" of business organization in Ghana, the minutes reflect that "the Government has recognized 5 sectors, all operating side by side in the nation's economy" (GNA 13/1/31, Item 12: Other Business vii). The five sectors include: 1. State Enterprise; 2. Enterprise owned by Foreign Interests; 3. Enterprise jointly owned by the State and Foreign Private Interest; 4. Co-operatives; 5. Small Scale Ghanaian Private Enterprise. As these sectors make clear, private property is still present in a socialist society. However, this is not private ownership of the major means of production—that is, of companies which manufacture products that the citizens of the country rely on for their survival. The minutes on this re-organization of businesses within the Ghana economy, and Nkrumah's commitment to it, conclude: "The Government's programme of socialization is well known and is being prosecuted as fast as circumstances will allow. In the meantime, however, the pattern of organisation as laid down by the Government will continue and in public statements one sector should not be emphasised as being more or less important than the others" (*ibid.*).

Nkrumah's efforts to "accelerate the socialist transformation of Ghana" are reflected in the July 17, 1962 Cabinet minutes during which "the means of bringing all classes of people together and providing all people with ever-increasing social benefits and every-widening opportunities for the enjoyment of leisure" (GNA 13/1/31, Item 26: Other Business ix) were discussed. Since the people are the end, not the means to the end, Nkrumah believed that the speediest process to the highest health and welfare of the people must be implemented. Thus, this decision and agreement reflect Nkrumah's efforts to break down class divisions. Therefore, it was "DECIDED that in future invitations to State Functions should not be restricted to very important persons, as at present, but that people from all walks of life should be invited to State Functions" (*ibid.*) Furthermore, "it was also AGREED that at State Functions, Ministers and other very important persons need not always sit according to the table of precedence but that they should as often as possible mix with the people and identify themselves with the masses" (*ibid.*). Also on July 17th, the Cabinet addresses the economic socialist transformation of Ghana:

The Cabinet NOTED that all the former Agricultural Experimental Stations had been converted into State Farms and that all the former Agricultural Development corporation agricultural projects had been taken over by the State Farms.

The Cabinet DECIDED that State Farms should be organised on a very large scale and that they should be devoted to the cultivation and the production of foodstuffs which were in great demand by the people and not to minor food items like pawpaw.

Osagyefo informed the Cabinet that he had given instructions for the recruitment from the U.S.S.R. of an Agricultural expert well versed in the establishment and management of big State Farms to train Ghana's State Farm personnel. The Cabinet ENDORSED this arrangement. (GNA 13/1/31, Item 26: Other Business xvi)

The Cabinet ended the year by returning to the matter of State Farms on December 18, 1962. At this meeting, "it was noted, in the present initial stage, the cost of establishing State Farms throughout the country was borne by the Government and that the personnel now working on the State Farms were paid employees of the State". The Cabinet "AGREED that these arrangements could not continue and that, ultimately, the State Farms should become fully economic, self-supporting and self-financing units operated by the workers of each farm for themselves" (GNA 13/1/31, Item 14 Other Business vi). Furthermore, "the cost of running the Farms should be met out of their profits, and, subject to the payment of an agreed proportion to the State, the workers on each farm should be entitled to the amount realised from the sale of their crops" (*ibid.*). Since the economic system is primary in shaping the political and social realities of a society, Nkrumah wasted no time in nationalizing the major sectors of Ghana's economy, including farms, so that the profits from these sectors could be used for the needs of all Ghanaians.

Early the next year, Nkrumah's struggle to build socialism was once again evident at the Cabinet meeting of February 7, 1963 when the only item for discussion was the "Construction and Organisation of the Trades Union Congress" (GNA 13/1/32, Item 1). As the minutes reflect, "it was considered that the leadership of the Trades Union Movement had failed to reorientate itself completely to the socialist ideals of the party and the Government, in that it continued to function like Trades Union Movements in countries where the workers were always in conflict with their Capitalists employers" (*ibid.*). The second point recorded in the minutes is one regarding how the Union should operate: "In the State Owned Sector of the Economy, and throughout the State Owned Enterprises, there should be no antagonistic relationship between workers and employers such as exists in capitalists countries; therefore, the aim of the TUC, as one of the integral wings of the Party, should be to maximise by every possible means the productivity of all the workers" (*ibid.*).

At its informal meeting of March 1, 1963, the Cabinet again took up the struggle to build socialism . This time the focus was on the "efficiency and security of State-owned enterprises" (GNA 13/1/32, Item 3) as role models for the building of socialism in Africa and throughout the world. The discussion included the following point: "In view of the special role of Ghana in the African revolution and in World affairs generally, the highest standards of efficiency and integrity should be exacted in the administration and operation of every sphere of our economic and industrial development" (*ibid.*) As always, Nkrumah is thinking of all of Africa: if Ghana could provide a positive socialist role model for the whole of Africa and if, other African States modeled themselves after Ghana, then progress towards continental unity would be accelerated.

On November 19, 1963, "the participation of workers in the management of State Enterprises was discussed. It was AGREED that a beginning should be made in selected industrial projects and State Farms, and that the selected industries should be handed over to the workers engaged in them, to operate and manage" (GNA 13/1/32, Item 16: Other Business v). This agreement, of course, goes beyond state ownership. It gets to the roots of socialism: that those who work, control and that those who control, work. At its December 12, 1963 meeting, the Cabinet continued to approve policies that directly relate to building socialism. The Ghanaian Constitution was amended: "In conformity with the interests, welfare and aspirations of the people, and in order to develop the organisational initiative and political activity of the people, provision shall be made by Law for the establishment of one national party which shall be the vanguard of the people in their struggle to build a socialist society and which shall be the leading core of all organisations of the people" (GNA 13/1/32, Item 2). This Cabinet meeting was labeled "secret". With the neo-colonialists' maneuverings to penetrate newly independent states, and with their particular interests in thwarting socialism on the African continent, Nkrumah was convinced that a one-party state was a necessity. He knew that the rationale behind the neo-colonialists' push for a two-party state was simple: to prop up an opposition group to feed dissension in order to collapse the state.

Two significant acts by the Cabinet took place on August 4, 1964, one of which concerned the building of a socialist state. The Cabinet was informed of twenty-three State enterprises and eight joint State/private enterprises "already in operation" (GNA 13/1/30, Item 19). Efforts to build socialism in Ghana were evident too in the minutes of the August 11, 1964 Cabinet: "Item 2. Report of the Cabinet Committee on the Re-organisation of the Co-operative Movements in Ghana" (GNA 13/1/30). Item Points 9 and 10 of the Report are of interest as well: "(9) The Fishermen should be organised into a new Co-operative Union outside the United Ghana Farmers' Co-operatives Council. (10) Government's policy should lead ultimately to the organisation of all farmers into Co-operative Societies within the United Ghana Farmers' Co-operatives Council" (*ibid.*). Thus co-operatives were being formed and the predominance of private property was being whittled away.

Ghana's Struggle to Equalize the Status of Women

Nkrumah stated that "The degree of a country's revolutionary awareness may be measured by the political maturity of its women" (*Handbook of Revolutionary Warfare*, p. 91). The underlying principles of socialism include egalitarianism in regard to women, and should be transparent and reflected in every sector of the state. One of the first series of actions that the Ghanaian government took, therefore, was to put into effect legislation aimed at achieving equality between men and women. On February 19, 1959, item 6 on the Cabinet agenda was equal employment of civil service women. On September 22, 1959, item 2 dealt with "providing for the election of the women Members of Parliament either from amongst the members of the electoral colleges or from outside them" (GNA 13/1/28, Item 2). A "Conference for Women of Africa and African Descent" was a part of the "Other Business" of the Cabinet on June 24, 1960 (GNA 13/1/29, Item 10: Other Business vii). And on November 17, 1964, "The Cabinet had before it a memorandum by the Minister of Defence, and APPROVED in principle the proposals ... for the formation of a Women's Auxiliary Corps in the Ghana Armed Forces" (GNA 13/1/30, Item 3). Again, on December 15, 1964, the Cabinet made "recommendations regarding [the] composition of Boards for State Corporations" as affecting women. According to the minutes, "out of 24 corporations listed, 12 women were recommended as board chairmans and some in capacities that are not typically thought of as 'woman's' work" (GNA 13/1/30, Item 18: Other Business i). Some examples are the State Marble Works Corporation, the State Fishing Corporation, the State Electronic Products Corporation, and the State Telecommunications Corporation.

Ghana's Struggle to Educate its Youth

In *Handbook of Revolutionary Warfare*, Nkrumah writes: "On our youth depends the future of Africa and the continent's total liberation and unity" (HRW, p. 88). He always knew that young people are the spark for the African Revolution, and thus he made sure that his government addressed their education—their political education, in particular. To this end, he established the Young Pioneer Movement, modeled after the youth movement in the USSR.

Several of the Cabinet minute items concerned youths. On August 4, 1959, "the Cabinet had before it a memorandum circulated by the Prime Minister, and approved in principle the establishment of a movement to be called the Young Pioneers" (GNA 13/1/28, Item viii). Then, there was a financial provision for Young Pioneers considered by the Cabinet on June 17, 1960 (GNA 13/1/29, Item 2). And, at its September 2, 1960 meeting, "the Cabinet AGREED that a Ghana Young Pioneer Authority (GYPA) should be established to which all youth organisations in Ghana should be required to affiliate" (GNA 13/1/29, Item 3). At its September 3, 1963 meeting, "the Cabinet discussed Party Education with particular reference to the youth. It was AGREED in discussion that more concerted efforts should be made in the Educational Institutions to give sound Party Education for citizenship to their pupils. It was DECIDED accordingly that specific responsibility should be arranged to selected persons of Ministerial rank for the dissemination of Party Education throughout all Educational Institutions" (GNA 13/1/32, Item 17: Other Business ix). To help disseminate this education, the Cabinet DECIDED at its February 11, 1964 meeting to establish a "Working Committee of the Young Pioneers" in each region of Ghana in order "to be responsible for the organisation and the administration of the Young Pioneer Movement in the Region" (GNA 13/1/30, Item 49, Other Business vii). Finally, on December 8, 1964, the Cabinet "AGREED that Ghana should accept the invitation extended by the All-China Youth Federation to the Ghana Young Pioneer Movement to send a 10–member youth delegation to undertake a three-month study tour of the People's Republic of China under the Youth Exchange Programme between the Ghana Young Pioneers and the All-China Youth Federation" (GNA 13/1/30, Item 21). Ten Young Pioneers were chosen "to undertake the study tour".

Nkrumah's Contribution to Worldwide Socialism

Finally, in Ghana's Cabinet minutes, decisions concerning world affairs are reflected. Such decisions are important to note because Nkrumah's concept of the African Revolution reflected a threefold plan: the achievement of socialism in Ghana, the liberation and unification of Africa under socialism, and the contribution to world socialism. In regard to the latter, Ghana, and Nkrumah in particular, played an instrumental role in world affairs. The minutes of April 28, 1960, for instance, reveal that, after an invitation from Cuba, Ghana sent a delegation to Cuba to attend a conference "on the Economy of Underdeveloped Countries" (GNA 13/1/29: Item: Ghana Delegation to Cuba). Four months later, on August 19, 1960, item 8 of the Cabinet minutes referred to a "Visit to Viet-nam of the Ghana Delegation to the 49th Inter-Parliamentary Conference" (GNA 13/1/29, Item 8): "The Cabinet ... agreed that the invitation from the National Assembly of the Republic of Viet-Nam for the Ghana Delegation to the Tokyo Conference to visit Viet-Nam after the Conference should be accepted" (*ibid.*). The USSR offered development assistance to Ghana, and on November 1, 1960 the Cabinet agreed with Nkrumah that a Ghana delegation should "liaise with the delegation of experts from the Union of Soviet Socialist Republics at present visiting Ghana on the selection of projects on which assistance would be needed" (GNA 13/1/29, Item 37).

An informal Cabinet meeting was held on February 15, 1961 to discuss the proposed visit of Brezhnev to Ghana: "The President informed the Cabinet that he had invited President L. I. Brezhnev, chairman of the Proesidium of the Supreme Soviet of the U.S.S.R. who is now on a visit to Guinea, to pay a short visit to Ghana and it was expected that the President would be arriving in Ghana on Thursday, 16th February, 1961" (GNA 13/1/30, Item 10). On July 8, 1962, the Cabinet had an informal meeting during which a Soviet Technical Aid Agreement (State Farms) for rice and maize and a Ghana-Soviet Technical Assistance-Development project for rubber farms in Ghana were noted.

As testament to Nkrumah's contribution to worldwide socialism, the "Award of the 1961 Lenin Peace Prize to Osagyefo the President" was mentioned in the notes of an informal Cabinet meeting held on May 5, 1962, at Flagstaff House (GNA 13/1/30, Item 3). On May 8, 1962, "The Cabinet DECIDED that an appropriate letter should be sent in the name of Osagyefo The President to the Lenin Peace Prize Committee. ... It was AGREED that the letter should convey an expression of Osagyefo's thanks and sincere appreciation for the award of the Peace Prize, and indicate that the people of Ghana consider the award not only as an honour to Osagyefo and to Ghana but also as an honour to the whole of Africa" (*ibid.*).

Nkrumah's ongoing efforts to forge relationships with socialist governments in the world are reflected in the "Other Business" section of the May 22, 1962 Cabinet minutes: "Trade and Payments Agreement with the Revolutionary Government of the Republic of Cuba". Agreements with both the USSR and China were forged on October 15, 1963 and October 22, 1963. On the 15th, Ghana and the USSR agreed to "Economic and Technical Co-operation: Contract No. 8406 on Complex of Fishing Industries" in the Tema Harbour area (GNA 13/1/32, Item 2). On October 22nd, "the Cabinet had before it a memorandum by the Cabinet Secretariat, and APPROVED the proposals set out in the memorandum for the implementation of projects under the Ghana-China Economic and Technical Agreement" (*op. cit.*, Item 14).

There are two ways to build Pan-Africanism: 1) legislation enacted by Africa's leaders, declaring that a union of African states will be in effect as of a certain date and, following the legislation, erecting the necessary unifying structures (theory first, then practice); 2) erecting unifying structures first and then passing legislation declaring in effect a Union of African states (practice first, then theory). Nkrumah tried both ways. Once much of the African leadership showed reluctance to move toward Pan-Africanism, he began the building process on his own, erecting the necessary structures and depending on young progressive activists inside and outside of Africa to support him. As these Cabinet Minutes document, Nkrumah was determined to put into practice his theory for the African Revolution.

~ ~ ~ ~ ~

4

Nkrumah's Parliament Speeches

Kwame Nkrumah's Presidential addresses to Ghana's Parliament are significant in providing another measure of his practice, for they convey the acts that he had already taken or was about to take regarding the economic, political and social development of Ghana; the development of the African Revolution; and the development of world peace. These addresses are, for the most part, informational sessions similar to 'state of the union' addresses delivered by presidents in the western world. The Parliament listens, sometimes responding by voicing the comment "Hear, Hear". Once the address is delivered, Nkrumah departs and the Parliament discusses, proposes, and votes. For the purpose of this study, the following discussion focuses primarily on the acts taken, or those about to be taken, as a result of the ideas of and presentations by Nkrumah to the Parliament.

By concentrating on nine of the Parliamentary addresses delivered from 1957 to 1966, the growing stature of Nkrumah as Ghana's first President, as the architect of the African Revolution, and as a prominent, progressive world leader can be charted.

The first two speeches examined below reflect Nkrumah's need to consolidate his power as leader of the first independent sub-Saharan African country in a hostile, colonial and burgeoning neo-colonial environment. On August 29, 1957, the speech was entitled, "Ghana's Policy at Home and Abroad". As an early address, just five short months after Ghana had achieved its independence, the content unsurprisingly reflects Nkrumah's naïveté about several issues, including foreign relations with capitalist countries and class struggle. However, there is political astuteness here as well. For example, Nkrumah recognized at this early juncture that non-alignment should define Ghana's relationship to the rest of the world, and as a result this policy of non-alignment was pursued: "We [intend] to adopt policies, as necessary, which would best suit our national interest" (29 Aug. 1957, p. 1). Later in the speech, he writes:

We of Ghana feel, therefore, that at this stage our country should not be committed in any respect of its foreign policy and that it should not be aligned with any particular group of powers or political bloc. But at the same time, our new State does not intend to follow a neutralist policy in its foreign relations. It is our intention to preserve our independence and to act as we see best at any particular time. (29 Aug. 1957, p. 3)

Also, he was clear on the question of peace, national sovereignty, and freedom: "My Government intends to pursue a policy of exerting our influence on the side of peace, respect for the independence of other nations, the rights of all people to decide for themselves their own government and the protection of the right of all men to lead their own lives in freedom and without fear" (29 Aug. 1957, p. 3).

Nkrumah's lack of development in regard to foreign relations with capitalist countries is demonstrated by his early willingness to engage in a relationship with Israel, as he noted: "Recently a ministerial delegation returned to Ghana after a very successful visit to Israel" (29 Aug. 1957, p. 1). Later, Nkrumah will cut ties with Israel.

In regard to Africa, Nkrumah makes two important points. First, he gives us a glimpse of what will later become a part of the ideology of Nkrumaism, the idea that Africa must extract the positive from its experience and become a new Africa with a new African Personality. He states: "We cannot make a distinctive contribution to African development if we merely mechanically adopt Western ideas. We can only make our contribution significant if we succeed in showing how an African society can be transformed without losing its essentially African character. We must seek methods by which the old and the new can be blended" (29 Aug. 1957, p. 10). Secondly, Nkrumah places Ghana in the position of welcoming Africans who are fleeing oppressive conditions: "It is the policy of my Government that Ghana shall afford an asylum or refuge for all Africans who suffer from religious, racial or political persecution and intolerance" (29 Aug. 1957, p. 11). To become the new Africa that Nkrumah envisioned, the artificial borders forced on Africa by the West must be eradicated. Later, Nkrumah will ask how can there be an African refugee anywhere in Africa. Africa belongs to all Africans.

Most of this 1957 speech, however, is devoted to Ghana's domestic policy. Since Ghana was just emerging from the throes of colonialism, the economic development of Ghana commands Nkrumah's utmost attention at this early stage of state consolidation, especially "the attainment of greater agricultural productivity" (29 Aug. 1957, p. 4). Of especial significance will be the "Volta River Project" since it "would provide the best means of diversifying and strengthening the national economy" (p. 4). Also, Ghana must solve the problems surrounding its dependency on one single crop, a colonial legacy: cocoa. The whole economy of Ghana is being held hostage by the vulnerability of this one crop due to the "appreciable drop in the world price" (p. 4). Also, on his mind are the need for a Central Bank, securing aid from the United States and the United Kingdom, the inauguration of "a Shipping Line to be known as the 'Black Star Line'" (p. 6), Ghana's educational program ("our desire to improve our social services, and to increase the possibilities of employment") (p. 6), the establishment of a "national Builder's Brigade", and "a system of compulsory National Service for Ghana" (p. 7). Nkrumah has to try as expeditiously as possible to help Ghana develop—not only for the sake of the people of Ghana, but also for the sake of the people of all of Africa and the rest of the world.

Commanding most of the speech is the question of Ghana's civil service. Inherited from the British colonial regime, it was in 1957 dominated by Europeans, who as a part of the former colonial structure, felt superior, but powerless, fearful, and revengeful as a result of Ghana's independence. The matter of the civil service must be one of the first matters of concern in architecting an independent African State. The seriousness of the issue is revealed in the following comment: "It is to be observed that no government can tolerate disloyalty from its civil servants and in a democracy such as ours the only step open to any civil servant who feels out of sympathy with the policies of the Government of the day and finds himself unable to carry them out is to resign or retire" (29 Aug. 1957, p. 12). In the case of sabotage or attempted sabotage, "the Government is determined that strong disciplinary action will be taken against any civil servant who openly or secretly indulges in disloyal, subversive and political activities" (p. 12). In light of planned acts of internal and external sabotage, Nkrumah plans for a Ghanaian intelligence agency: a "provision has been made for the cost of organising an Intelligence Service. This Service, which the Government intends to establish as a matter of urgency, will be under the Ministry of Defence and External Affairs and will form part of the Foreign Service organisation of Ghana".

Even in this early presidential address to Ghana's Parliament, Nkrumah's understanding of the dialectical relationship between Ghana's development, as the first independent sub-Saharan African country, and Africa's development is clear: Ghana's interest is in "achieving the goal which we have set ourselves of being the prototype of the new free nations which will emerge in Africa" (29 Aug. 1957, p. 8). Moreover, his understanding of the necessity for a liberated Africa and its relationship to the rest of the world seems clear: "People all over the world are interested in us because they see exemplified in Ghana the struggle for the freedom of the African Continent" (p. 8). It is Nkrumah's intent that Ghana should serve as a role model for building socialism, as a base for building Pan-Africanism, and as a major contributor to worldwide peace and socialism. Too, Ghana's independence has not blurred his vision of the enemy, for he knows the enemy is simply morphing into a new colonialism, ready to sabotage any efforts at *true* independence: "It is also flattering to us that our enemies should have taken so much note of events in Ghana. This too is a measure of the importance of our influence which is, as I have said, far greater than our political experience and economic strength would justify" (p. 8)

On December 16, 1959, Nkrumah places before Parliament a motion to approve the Government's foreign policy. Nkrumah sets forth the rationale for the timing of this motion by stating that "we should take stock of our performance and achievements in our relations with other nations and peoples, and to re-assess and re-state our policy in the light of the changing circumstances in present-day international relations and the events taking place around us" (16 Dec. 1959, p. 626). This motion portends Nkrumah's future role as world statesman. Ghana, under Nkrumah, will not just be concerned with Ghana. Ghana is a part of Africa and it is a part of the world. In fact, Nkrumah's point has always been that Ghana's independence is "meaningless unless we are able to use the freedom that goes with it to help other African peoples to be free and independent, to liberate the entire Continent of Africa from foreign domination, and ultimately to establish a Union of African States" (16 Dec., 1959, p. 628). Accordingly, as his record demonstrates, Nkrumah from the moment he steps into office is a Ghanaian, an African, and a world spokesman. The following statement underscores this point: "The United Nations Charter ... recognises that disarmament matters are of world-wide interest and concern to all nations and peoples, and that they are not the exclusive preserve of the Great Powers" (16 Dec. 1959, p. 627).

Nkrumah cites the conflict between India and China: "In this connection [disarmament] we would call upon our friends in India and China to resolve their differences by peaceful negotiation". He continues by reminding his listeners of the Bandung Conference of 1955 during which disarmament was discussed: "The ideals of Panchsheel, so convincingly promulgated at Bandung, and the bonds of traditional friendship and the common culture that unite the peoples of Asia and Africa would indeed become a hollow mockery, if we allow ourselves to drift into open hostility" (16 Dec. 1959, p. 628). He reminds his listeners too that the division and domination of Africa—a division and domination still present throughout much of Africa—were successful due to "the sheer force of superior arms". On this question, Nkrumah notes that not to disarm completely jeopardizes "the continued existence of humanity". Consequently, all foreign domination in Africa must be eradicated. Therefore, Nkrumah states that "in the interest of peace and security in Africa and in the world [the two are symbiotically connected], we call upon the colonial powers to grant independence to all the African countries at present under their control" (*ibid.*). Moreover, Nkrumah appeals "to all peace-loving nations and peoples of the world who believe in the ideals of democracy, freedom and justice, to support us in our efforts to secure unity among the African peoples" (*ibid.*).

A final point to make here is that Nkrumah afforded himself the opportunity, with the introduction of this motion, to review Ghana's record since 1957 in taking "concrete steps to implement our policy of independence and unity among the African peoples" (16 Dec. 1959, p. 628). Beginning with the Conference of Independent African States held in Accra in April 1958, it is a sterling record, one that demonstrates Nkrumah's early understanding of the relationship between Ghana, Africa, and the world.

Two speeches before Ghana's Parliament in June of 1963 and one in October of that year are significant in illustrating Nkrumah's push for a united Africa. Nkrumah is wasting no time. Fresh from the May 1963 founding conference of the Organization of African Unity (OAU), Nkrumah, on June 21, 1963, gives an address on the charter of the OAU. He begins: "I am here to invite you to ratify the Charter of African Unity adopted by the Addis Ababa Conference" (21 June 1963, p. 74). The purpose of the OAU is simple:

> [to] fight against imperialism and its twin instruments of colonialism and neo-colonialism. Our combined effort and our combined strength are to be placed at the service of our brothers waging an all-out struggle against oppressive colonialism in all those parts of our continent still under alien domination. We have covenanted together to co-ordinate and harmonise our general policies in the sphere of our poltical, diplomatic, economic, educational, cultural, health, scientific and technical activities, as well as in the sphere of defence and security. (*ibid.*)

Of all these spheres, the political must precede all others. To struggle for the welfare of *all* the people, not the profit of a few is a political decision that shapes the economic, the education, the social and the cultural spheres of the State. That is why Nkrumah states that "when we talk of African Unity, we are thinking of a political arrangement which will enable us collectively to provide solutions for our problems in Africa" (21 June 1963, p. 87). Nkrumah tells Parliament that "the Charter of African Unity must be regarded as the last but one step on the road to a Continental Union" (p. 74). Already, a "Provisional Secretariat" had been set up with its headquarters in Addis Ababa and also a Co-ordinating Committee, "responsible for regulating the assistance from African States and for managing the special fund" contributed by the independent African Governments, was set up with its headquarters in Dar-Es-Salaam, Tanganyika (p. 75).

Always thinking of Africa and its people as one, Nkrumah states that the first and most important task of the OAU is to ensure that other colonial territories gain their independence. For this to happen, independent African countries must come to their aid. It is a task that would not only benefit the colonies, but also the independent states, securing their safety: "Apart from the sense of oneness and unity which impels us to go to the aid of our suffering compatriots in Angola, Mozambique, Southern Rhodesia, South Africa, and other parts of Africa still under colonial rule, we know that none of the Independent African States is safe so long as a single colonial ruler remains on African soil" (21 June 1963, p. 75).

Since all "the signatories to the Charter of African Unity solemnly pledged themselves to fight colonialism, neo-colonialism and imperialism in all its forms" (p. 76), independent African countries have a double duty to perform. They must aid those struggling against colonialism and they must aid those struggling against a new form of colonialism, one that slithered in on the heels of the old retreating colonialism. Thus, Nkrumah identifies two types of freedom fighters:

> ... those fighting in colonial territories for the overthrow of exploitation and oppression by foreign governments; and those who consider that they have a duty to fight in order to strengthen the independence of their countries where colonial rule has been overthrown, but where it is still necessary to create conditions for the welfare of the people and for the elimination of neo-colonialist interference and influence. (p. 75)
>
> ... the Governments of such countries are a menace, not only to their own states but also to the safety and security of our entire continent" (p. 76).

In the wake of these "menaces", independent countries like Ghana have no other choice but to open their doors/arms to freedom fighters fleeing the retribution of neo-colonial and colonial governments:

> "We did not invite them here, but they naturally felt that they could enjoy sanctuary and be given the necessary protection in Ghana which has for the past six years since her attainment of independence and sovereignty played host to Freedom Fighters from all over the continent … . The African Affairs Centre in Accra is a symbol of this determination" (p. 76).

There are conditions for asylum, however. These conditions, enumerated by Nkrumah, include respect for the Government and institutions that they are fleeing, self-reliance (Ghana will not provide material assistance), and the promise not to engage in subversive acts against their governments while in Ghana (p. 77).

Nkrumah uses some of his speech to discuss the most vicious colonizers in Africa—Portugal and South Africa. In regard to the former, he states: "The arms which the Portuguese colonialists use in Angola and Mozambique, the bombs which they drop in Senegal, were not manufactured in Portugal, nor were they paid for by Portugal. Portugal is the poorest State in Europe and the average Ghanaian, as our statistics show, is now wealthier than the average citizen of Portugal" (p. 77). Of South Africa, Nkrumah states: "South Africa is probably the biggest impediment to the liberation and unity of the African continent" (p. 80). The vicious acts of genocide perpetuated by these two colonizers impelled the signers of the OAU charter to break off "diplomatic and consular relations between all the African States and the Governments of Portugal and South Africa. They call for an effective boycott of foreign trade with the two countries" (p. 81).

Non-alignment was a commitment made by Nkrumah since becoming president of Ghana, and so it was not surprising that the "States of the Organization of African Unity have, in Article three of the Charter, solemnly affirmed and declared their adherence to the principle of a non-aligned policy" (p. 82). As a consequence of this policy, no state should allow foreign military bases on their soil. In fact, to secure "the defence and protection of our established independence, then it goes without saying that all such [existing] bases and all such [military] pacts need to be annulled" (*ibid.*). Indeed, Nkrumah believed that all offers of military help should be seen as suspect, knowing that the imperialists are only looking out for their own self-interests: a way to slither back into Africa to enrich themselves.

Nkrumah discusses additional ways to build African unity, including "co-ordination of our political and diplomatic policies, harmonisation of our economic, educational and cultural activities, collaboration in health, sanitation and nutritional matters, co-ordination in scientific and technical fields, [and] co-operation for defence and security" (21 June 1963, p. 83). Of keen interest to Nkrumah as well is student exchange, for he knew that students are the spark of revolution and that all youth of Africa had to become politically educated in order to contribute to the African Revolution. Accordingly, Nkrumah states that he is "setting on foot immediately plans for the exchange of students and for the provision at the University of Ghana of a course of studies in African Affairs and in History, Economics and Politics generally, which may be of value to other States who do not as yet possess universities" (*ibid.*). These students will become future leaders and, as such, must learn the part they are destined to play in the African Revolution. So too the workers of Africa—farmers and peasants included—must be harmonized in order to play a decisive role in this struggle. The All-African Trade Union Federation is the unifying link for workers. It "must therefore be in a position to mobilise the exploited masses of Africa for the final onslaught in the battle against imperialism and neo-colonialism" (21 June 1963, p. 84).

In this June 21, 1963 speech Nkrumah comments on world affairs since the world affects Africa and Africa affects the world. A united Africa, he states, will contribute to world peace: "one of our great hopes in pursuing the goal of total African liberation and unity is the vista of world peace that it opens up" by driving colonialism and neo-colonialism from Africa's shores (p. 88). In regard to Africans born in the US, Nkrumah states that "racism is a blot on the conscience of mankind, and the sooner, it is removed the greater the prospects of world peace will be" (p. 85). Because the African in the Diaspora did not voluntarily enter the "New World", "the U.S. has therefore a moral duty to accept the essential humanity of the Afro-American" (p. 86). On the Middle East and the arms race, Nkrumah states: "In the interests of world peace a way must therefore be found quickly to end the dangerous arms race between Israel and Egypt which could easily lead to disaster for Africa, the Middle East and the world" (p. 86). Unlike in 1959 when Nkrumah unabashedly announced an agreement with Israel, not mentioning the colonization of the Arab people on their own land, on this occasion Nkrumah makes sure to voice his position on the Arab position in Israel and to link it with the arms race: "I have repeatedly called for a nuclear moratorium in the Middle East, for the creation of an Arab State for the refugees and for the permanent delimitation of the State of Israel" (p. 86). On Cuba, Nkrumah states: "Whatever the causes of disagreement may be, the United States and Cuba must find a way to co-exist". And since Cuba has indicated an amenability to come to some agreement with the US, Nkrumah thinks it is "reasonable ... for the United States which, in size, economic and military power, is far greater than Cuba, to express her greatness in an equal—if not greater—gesture of goodwill, magnanimity and statesmanship" (p. 86).

One additional point must be noted. As mentioned earlier, a liberated, unified Africa, without a socialist economic system, would be nothing but a continental neo-colony, operating as a satellite state for the capitalists and African bourgeoisie. Thus Nkrumah puts forward what is the heart of Pan-Africanism:

> It is our earnest hope and belief that our own [Ghana's] example in the creation of a Socialist pattern of Society, in which the free development of each is a condition for the free development of all is bound to have a striking impact on reactionary regimes in Africa in which the wealth and resources of the people are concentrated in the hands of neo-colonialists and their agents. (p. 77)

Nkrumah's final comment to Parliament is this:

> Time is everything in our march. We must in Africa crowd into a generation the experience and achievements attained through centuries of trial and error by the older nations of the world. ... we do not wish to see Africa set on a course in which her nations grow in different, separate and competing directions until they develop into a confused and disorderly economic tangle of 'Sixes and Sevens'" (p. 89).

This will be Nkrumah's clarion call until his death: Africa must unite as quickly as possible.

One of the strategies that becomes more and more pronounced in Nkrumah's ideology is educating, mobilizing, and organizing African youth. In that regard, the "Private Members' Motions" section of the Parliamentary Debates of June 25, 1963 are highly significant for they are focused on the Ghana Young Pioneer Movement. These motions by members of Parliament reflect the sentiment of Nkrumah in regard to the role of the youths in general and Ghana's Young Pioneer Movement in particular. The following comment by J. K. Twum is a case in point:

> Inspired by a deep sense of patriotism and selfless devotion to duty not only to Ghana, but to the entire continent of Africa, and by his sincere desire to turn his dreams into reality, Osagyefo Dr. Kwame Nkrumah founded the Ghana Young Pioneers on 14th June, 1960, and charged the movement with the training of the youth on the socialist pattern, and with the development of the innate qualities of the youth in order to provide them with a new progressive and dynamic impulse for the solution of the economic and social problems created through many years of colonial neglect and domination. (25 June, 1963, p. 150)

Modeled after the Soviet Union's Pioneer Movement, the Ghana Young Pioneers got its start in 1960 with an initial membership of fifty-one. That nucleus grew. By the time of this parliamentary meeting, the membership had exceeded one million and Nkrumah's aim was to make "every child of school going age a member of the Young Pioneer Movement" (p. 164).

Nkrumah's speech before the Ghana Parliament on October 15, 1963 is once again on the need for Africa to unite: "The tempo of development in Africa, since Addis Ababa [where the OAU ratified the Charter of African Unity], has been such that this Charter is already being overtaken by events. It has become clear that we must move forward quickly, with a united voice, to a Union Government of Africa" (p. 2). The events that threatened the effectiveness of a charter devoid of any operative, practical apparatus or machinery that puts in place a Union government include the Congo crisis, the crises in the various Portuguese colonies and other colonial territories in Africa, and the nuclear arms race. Of the Congo, he states:

> Now that the United Nations troops are about to be withdrawn from the Congo, the African States have an opportunity and an obligation to set an example of African self-help by going to the aid of a sister State. [Hear, hear.]. By so doing, we would have eliminated the rivalries of neo-colonialist and imperialist powers from the Congo. I have accordingly proposed to the Government of the Congo, to the Secretary-General of the United Nations and to the Heads of the Independent African States and Governments, that an all-African force should take over from the United Nations well in advance of its withdrawal from the Congo. [Hear, hear.] Although this proposal was acceptable in principle, it could not be carried out because the African States, in spite of our resolutions at Addis Ababa, had not provided an effective machinery for such united action. The longer we delay action for a continental Government of Africa, the greater will be our troubles and confusion. (15 October, 1963, p. 2)

For those still exploited and oppressed by colonialism, Nkrumah states: "African unity is the only solution to the vast problems facing our oppressed brothers and the Freedom Fighters in the Rhodesias, South Africa, Mozambique, Angola, South West Africa, Bechuanaland, Basutoland and Swaziland" (p. 3). The colonialists must go. If not on their own accord, then it is clear that "we shall in our unity compel them to do so. The struggle is not against race; it is against a system. The racialists and imperialists must quit Africa now" (p. 3).

Once again, Nkrumah concerns himself with the state of the world, for "our struggles in Africa will have no meaning except in the context of world peace" (15 Oct. 1963, p. 4). In this regard, Nkrumah revisits the topic of the nuclear arms race: "the government of Ghana has welcomed and has become a party to the partial Test Ban Treaty recently adopted in Moscow by the nuclear powers" (*ibid.*). This treaty "is only a small step towards the abolition of nuclear warfare"; other steps must be taken, including the destruction "of the stocks and production facilities of nuclear, chemical, biological and other weapons of mass destruction" (*ibid.*). Although "only a small step" toward a world free of nuclear warfare, this act on the part of Nkrumah is quite significant. Ghana's signature adds weight to a worldwide movement against the imperialists' motions.

The other major focus of this speech is Ghana's progress toward socialism. A review of the progress reveals startling accomplishments: "factories and industrial plants are springing up in Ghana with speed and ease" (p. 5);

university education is free—in fact, "the Government of Ghana spends more on education in relation to our national income than any other country in the world" (p. 6)! This fact of course is phenomenal when one makes note of the "anachronistic", western-biased education system left in place by the colonial regime, a system only "designed to produce those persons best suited to serve the interest of a colonial power" (p. 6). Employment for all is another goal Ghana struggled to achieve (p. 7). The training of doctors is a priority in securing the health and welfare of all Ghanaians: "In future, all newly-qualified doctors, whether in Government service or intended for private practice, will be required to work initially for the State for at least two years". Furthermore, "during this period, they will be posted to the rural areas to get first-hand experience in the treatment of tropical diseases" (p. 8). After receiving free training, why shouldn't young doctors give back to those who are needy? Committed to socialism, Nkrumah believed that the purpose of education is "to lead" humanity out of the problems it faces, not to profit from them. Improvement in agriculture must also be achieved: "Why import rice? Why import corn? And why import oranges?" (p. 9). These are all struggles and achievements in line with building a socialist state. In fact, socialism "is our only insurance against privation and want. We aim to create a society in which the maxim from each according to his ability and to each according to his work, shall apply, and in which the condition for the development of each shall be the condition for the development of all" (p. 7).

Moreover, all must contribute to building socialism, not just the peasants and the industrial laborers: "Members of Parliament should put their specialized skill and knowledge at the disposal of the Nation. Many of you in this House are teachers; some are pharmacists, university graduates, doctors, ministers of religion, surveyors, or hold qualifications in many other fields. You can participate actively in the building of our Nation" (15 Oct. 1963, p. 13). If not, Ghana will just remain a stratified society, with those more educated, powerful, and wealthy on top, and those with little education, power and wealth on the bottom. Also, "in accordance with our socialist principles, those who are relatively well-to-do must contribute more for the well-being of all" (*ibid.*). Everyone must work; everyone must sacrifice to make socialism a reality in Ghana, and Ghana must become a model for all of Africa.

The next selection of speeches before the Ghana Parliament reflect a more forthright Nkrumah, one who feels neo-colonialism nipping at his heels and one whose reaction to it is a greater determination than ever to build socialism. On May 25, 1965, he states:

> Our aim is to ensure that all persons living in Ghana shall have adequate means to provide themselves with enough food to eat, clothing

> to wear, a house to live in and free education for their children and dependents. This means hard work. They shall also have access to free medical treatment. Finally, it is very important, that is why you must work hard—it is our aim to ensure that every citizen of Ghana will have full social security throughout his working life and will enjoy a pension on retirement from active work. All our socialist policies have been geared to this end. (p. 299)

Africa, Ghana, can afford to waste no time. The speedy bankruptcy of the OAU and the re-entry of colonialism into Africa under a new guise, the Government corruption scandals, the imperialist verbal attacks on Nkrumah, and the attempted assassinations have all proven that time is of the essence. Thus the struggle for socialism must be accelerated:

> We must be prepared to accept a sterner discipline at all levels, and among all our Party functionaries, public officers and all sections of our society. Only in this way, can we wipe out those anti-social and anti-socialist practices and other forces which militate against our national reconstruction, our progress and aspirations. The Party and the Government will therefore take such steps as will lead to a tightening up and enforcement of discipline, and to ensure the strict observance of the objectives of our socialist revolution and construction. (p. 299)

Nkrumah's concern and commitment for all of Africa is demonstrated in everything he says and in everything he does. It does not supercede his commitment to Ghana; rather, it reflects his clear understanding of the relationship between the two. Ghana's health and security are dependent on Africa's health and security. Unless Africa unites, "independent" states will perish one by one at the hands of the neo-Colonialists.

In his January 12, 1965 speech before Parliament, Nkrumah addresses the question of the role of Ghana's armed forces, which " ... continues to be: to defend the territorial integrity of Ghana from external aggression and internal subversion, and to assist in ensuring the security of the African continent within the context of the Charter of the Organisation of African Unity" (12 Jan. 1965, p. 21). The Congo debacle showed the impotency of the UN to effect meaningful protection. NATO's forces are the instruments of the very enemy Africa is battling. Nkrumah has two choices: do nothing and let Africa sink back into the throes of imperialism, or fight. Instead of diminishing his will, imperialist aggression in Africa in particular and the world in general feeds and strengthens Nkrumah's will and clarified his thinking. Now it forces him to reevaluate the role of women in the African Revolution. Earlier in his administration, he thought women would play a minor, contributory role in the African Revolution. For example, in his July 18, 1960 speech at the Conference of Ghana Women and Women of African Descent, Nkrumah had stated: "Not only can you carry back this message to the men of your respective countries..., you can also bring your feminine influence to bear in persuading you brothers, husbands and friends of the importance of African Unity as the only salvation for Africa" (p. 112). Five years later, in this speech before Parliament, he sees women playing a major, active role: "at the moment, some of our women are undergoing Pilot Training at the Ghana Air Force Training School at Takoradi" (January 12, 1965, p. 21); and states, "We have also established a Women's Auxiliary Corps which will enable our young women to work shoulder to shoulder with the men in the service and development of our country" (p. 21). Women, in this long, arduous struggle for the health and welfare of all African people, cannot be marginalized; they must play an equal part in the liberation process.

Of Parliament itself Nkrumah avowed that it "will be enlarged, and will continue to be a forum for the expression of views fully reflecting the spirit of our socialist revolution and of the new age in Africa" (12 Jan. 1965, p. 22). As stated earlier, Nkrumah was speaking much more openly of socialism in the last few years of his administration. As if he knew that time was not on his side, he pounds the ideas of liberation, unity, and socialism in Africa. He ends his address with the following commitment: "Ghana will, therefore, continue to give maximum support and assistance to the freedom fighters and liberation movements in Africa for the final and total liquidation of imperialism and colonialism from Africa" (*ibid.*). Neither the OAU nor much of the African leadership was proving its commitment to Pan-Africanism, the first step of which is the liberation of all states. But that inaction did not mean that Nkrumah and Ghana need sit idly by watching Africans suffer and die.

Nkrumah opened his August 24, 1965 address to Ghana's Parliament in a spectacular, unequivocal manner:

> This Session marks, as it were, the watershed in our strivings to consolidate the gains we have made since Independence. From now on, we must devote all our energies to the pursuit of a unifying and progressive ideology, and dynamic but flexible economic policy, a positive and constructive role in the African Revolution, and a balanced relationship with the rest of the world. Above all, we must devote our energies to the establishment of a strong and prosperous socialist society, which can fulfil the aims and aspirations of our people. (24 Aug. 1965, p. 15)

It is a long and critical speech, touching on matters of national, continental and world concern: socialism, one-party systems, African unity and world peace, the enemy, Vietnam, the OAU, Ghana's role in the African Revolution, and Ghana's economic and social development. Of Ghana's socialist path, Nkrumah states: "In a socialist democracy, the people should be the final repository of political power; the people are the ultimate sanction of authority. It is therefore of the utmost importance that the Party through democratic means should always explain its intentions and actions to the people, so as to gain their confidence and support" (24 Aug. 1965, p. 16). Although there were those critical of one-party political systems, Nkrumah argued that there are clearly some moments in history when they are necessary, most notably when your enemy attempts to foment dissension in an effort to overthrow a progressive, non-capitalist government; in other words, when you have a leadership that struggles to place the interests of its citizens before the profit of a few greedy individuals. These were the conditions existing in Ghana in 1965. Thus, Nkrumah could tout the one-party system: "Ours is a House united by one Party, one ideology, one aim, one destiny. One of the fundamental aims of our National Assembly is to assist in the building of a Socialist society" (p. 16).

Once again, he is adamant on the role Ghana must play on the continent and in the world:

> Mr. Speaker, in international affairs, we are concerned at the moment not only with the liberation and unification of Africa but also with the struggle for world peace and security. We must keep a vigilant eye on the explosive areas of the world today ....
>
> From its first day of independence, Ghana has been concerned with world peace as a priority both for its own development and for humanity's survival. In this nuclear age it will avail us nothing to seek refuge in geographical remoteness from the main centres of the world tension, or in creating an illusory shell or cocoon for our own industrial, agricultural and cultural progress. The peace of world events and the triumphs of technology will no longer permit us to live in isolation. We must either learn to live together now, or together perish. (pp. 16–17)

Nkrumah knew that Africa's success at becoming a unified, socialist nation would be a success for unity and socialism everywhere and its defeat would be a defeat for unity and socialism everywhere, and a victory for balkanization and capitalist/imperialist forces. In fact, always the teacher, Osagyefo takes the time in this speech to remind his listeners of the devices of imperialism:

> Until the economic, political and military and financial aggressions of imperialism are ended in every part of the world, and until neo-colonialism has been unmasked and driven out everywhere, we cannot retire from the struggle against imperialism. It is foolhardiness to think that we can buy security by coming to terms with imperialism or neo-colonialism. Nor can we find security, even if we were prepared to pay that price. (p. 17)

Indeed, Ghana was an example for the world in its attempts to thwart imperialism and to achieve world peace:

> This Parliament should reach new heights in its support for every effort we are making to attain general and complete disarmament; to strengthen the authority of the United Nations as a peace-keeping body; to achieve the solidarity of the nations of Africa, Asia and Latin America against imperialism; to liberate the rest of Africa still in chains; to cleanse the world of imperialism and war, so that Ghana together with other nations can devote her energies and resources to the promotion of peace, progress, and the welfare of mankind. (24 Aug. 1965, p. 17)

As host of the forthcoming OAU Summit Conference on October 21, 1965, Nkrumah hoped that Ghana more particularly would serve as an example for the continent and planned once again to drive home the message "that the independence of Ghana is meaningless unless it is linked up with the total liberation of Africa. The progress we have so far gives renewed confidence and inspiration to our Government to work harder towards this goal and the destiny of Africa" (24 Aug. 1965, p. 20).

Nkrumah was relentless in his quest for a free, liberated, united and socialist Africa:

> So long as our brothers in Angola, the so-called Portuguese and Spanish Guineas, Mozambique, Bechuanaland, Basutoland, Swaziland, South West Africa and all the islands surrounding our Continent remain under the yoke of imperialism, so long as the minority of settlers continue to dominate our brothers in South Africa and Southern Rhodesia, so long shall we continue to give all the help that is within our power to all those who are fighting to overthrow oppression; so long shall we strive to regain Africa's inalienable right, and restore her dignity and heritage. (p. 21)

In the workers of Africa lay Nkrumah's hope for Pan-Africanism:

> My faith in the trade unions as instruments for building socialism has never wavered. The workers of Africa know and have felt the effects of exploitation. Our struggle to build socialism is first and foremost in the interest of the workers and peasants of our continent. That is why we must give them all aid and assistance, in fulfilling their organisational and educational role in the struggle for the unification of Africa. (p. 23)

Although heretofore Nkrumah has devoted his speech primarily to the problems of Africa and the world, he assures Parliament of his equal concern and commitment to national issues; for if Nkrumah can show Africa and the rest of the world the benefits that will accrue from a socialist Ghana, he is convinced that others will struggle for Pan-Africanism: "In spite of our necessary preoccupation with international affairs and in spite of our efforts for the unification of Africa, we are nevertheless giving full attention to our domestic problems" (p. 24). He highlights the cardinal goals of Ghana's Seven-Year Development Plan. Some of these goals include the following: a "high standard of living for each citizen based on gainful employment; income "utilized for socially purposeful ends, such as education, welfare, and health services for our people", and production "designed as to enable Ghana to play her full part in a Pan-African economic community" (pp. 26–27). Since independence, Nkrumah reports that there has been "an impressive industrial advancement in Ghana. Cocoa processing factories, cement clinker mills, textile mills, a jute bag factory, the paint factory" (p. 31). Nearing completion are "two sugar mills at Akuse and Komenda, the glass factory and gold refinery at Tarkwa and Aboso" (31). Next on the agenda will be "a complex of wood industries" and "a Paper and Pulp Factory" (p. 32). In fact, "no less than fifty-two State Corporations" had been established at the time of the speech (p. 33). Other accomplishments include a Ministry of Cooperatives to foster and encourage a co-operative movement; the implementation of the Social Security Act of 1965; the Ministry of Pensions and National Insurance in order to devise "plans for a comprehensive pensions and national insurance or social security programme under which every citizen of Ghana will benefit" (p. 36); free education through middle school; a new medical school in addition to the other university institutions; the Kwame Nkrumah University of Science and Technology; "a College for the training of teachers for the Deaf and Dumb" (p. 40); "in furtherance of African Unity, our institutions of higher education will continue to open their doors to eligible students from other African States" (*ibid.*); "the construction of an International Airport Terminal in Accra" to service Ghana Airways, but also eventually "for the establishment of a West and Equatorial African Airline" that "will lead to the creation of a Pan African

Airways" (p. 42); the "Ghana Nautical College is stepping up its training of Ghanaians to man the Black Star Line ships" (*ibid.*). All these accomplishments and more, Nkrumah could claim by 1965.

Concluding this speech, Nkrumah calls on the Parliament to study, for:

> ... socialist planning, socialist vigilance, morality and dynamism can only spring from a sound socialist ideology. To make sure of this, the Party decided on the revolutionary step of insisting that all Ministers in the first Cabinet of the first Socialist Parliament of Ghana should attend a course of ideological study and self-examination at Winneba. This is obviously such a correct step of a Socialist State that I hope the practice will continue. (pp. 42–43)

Nkrumah has never used the term "socialism" and "socialist" more in any other single speech to Parliament. In fact, he uses every speaking opportunity as if it were his last. Consider the following passage:

> The Ideological Institute at Winneba carries a great responsibility for the diffusion of our Party's ideology. Our socialist ideology contains the great truths and realities of our age. We must know what we are doing, and why we are doing it, in every phase of our efforts and endeavours—intellectual, cultural, moral and physical. The Party organisation must meet new trends, challenges and realities in order to give expression to the democratic nature of our society. This Parliament must help to consolidate our gains and assist in the building of socialism on the foundations which we have laid. We are thankful for the past, bound by the needs of the present, and inspired by the vision of the future. (p. 43)

As can be seen from his August 24, 1965 address to Parliament, Nkrumah wasted no time in constructing an air-tight case in support of a united, socialist Africa. This quickened pace—demonstrated by the tone of the speech and the repetition of key words, none more key than socialism—is due to the empirical observation that Nkrumah had made in regard to capitalist maneuvers. Thus in the September 3, 1965 speech to Parliament Nkrumah minced no words in sharing what he knew and what he believed was correct for Africa, her people, and worldwide peace. This is a speech on International Affairs and one of Nkrumah's main topics is the United Nations. Like the OAU, Nkrumah believed that the United Nations was a bankrupt institution. The fact of the UN's motions, or lack thereof, in Africa made that clear: "We in Africa have experienced to our cost the ineffectiveness of the United Nations in the Congo; in regard to Southern Rhodesia and South Africa, and in our struggle for the eradication from our continent of imperialism with its concomitants, colonialism and neo-colonialism" (3 Sep. 1965, p. 415). According to Nkrumah, no one was to blame for this ineffectiveness except the African leadership, for if it were united, its power would resonate in the UN. But since the leadership was disunited, it was weak and thus had no influence on the UN: "This failure of the United Nations to deal with these problems is largely our own fault. If Africa had a solid political front and was able to speak with a united voice, there is no doubt in my mind that our problems would have been solved in the best interest of our people, and with the interests of our continent primarily in mind" (p. 415). Nkrumah's point is so clear. So, why did the African leadership fail in its historic responsibility to Africa, its people, and the world? The quest to hold onto colonial-made nationalities? The quest to enrich themselves from the crumbs of neo-colonialism at the expense of their own people? The lack of understanding of the dire need for Africa to unite? One or more of these reasons influenced the leadership of most of the newly independent African countries.

Today, no one can deny that Africa has paid the price for the failure of its leadership. This is why Nkrumah "over and over again called for a united Africa which would enable the independent African States to stand together and to mobilise all our resources for the development of the continent" (3 Sep. 1965, p. 415). One can almost feel Nkrumah's pain in this speech, but one also can gauge his relentlessness, steadfastness, determination to win in the face of imperialism. Africa is rich, he reminds his Parliament, but its riches are not owned and controlled by Africans:

> Only a united Africa can redeem its past glory and renew and reinforce its strength for the realisation of its destiny. We are today the richest and yet the poorest of continents, but in unity our continent could smile in a new era of prosperity and power. What is the promise of this plenty we dream about today? The facts are sufficient evidence of a future greatness that should propel us forward to unity. Africa produces the major proportion of the world's cocoa, sisal, barley, cotton and maize. Our continent also has 98 per cent of the gem diamonds, 69 per cent cobalt, 63 per cent gold and many other minerals. Africa has the greatest but the least-developed hydroelectric potential of any continent in the world. It has immense reserves of iron ore, coal, mineral oil and natural gas. [If] we stop the political interference of foreign powers who seek to prevent our unity, and bring an end to their economic exploitation of our resources we shall regain our dignity, and we shall see a great power emerge from our continent which will become a bulwark of world peace. (p. 416)

A united Africa would not only benefit Africa, but also first world people everywhere. For example, Africa would "join with the people of Asia in the fight to restore the lost glory and dignity of the Afro-Asian world. Asia and Africa, the oldest of the continents, must continue to stand together for progress and world peace" (3 Sep. 1965, p. 416). When this bi-continental unity occurs, the enemies of both, watch out: "Let the ramparts and parapets of imperialism and neo-colonialism in Africa, Asia and Latin America resound with the echoes of our united assault upon them" (pp. 416–17). And when this unity of continents occur, the United Nations will be in a much better position to service all of the peoples of the world (not just its present few), making "effective use of its noble principles for the preservation of world peace" (p. 417) and thus realizing "the objectives set out in its Charter" (p. 418).

The February 1, 1966 speech to Parliament prefigures Nkrumah's overthrow. He begins by reporting on the current reality of Africa: "All over our continent, we are beset by forces created by neo-colonialism, forces which must be faced, fought and vanquished" (p. 1). What are these forces? One of the tricks of the neo-colonialists is to find or to create an opposition group, legitimize it, and then tell it what to do (in exchange for a very small portion of the profit once the neo-colonialists begin to run things). The way to prop up this opportunistic group and legitimize it in the quickest possible time is to choose a military representative to govern. Nkrumah warned the Parliament of what happens when an army governs:

> Normally, the duty of the armed forces is to defend and support the Civil Government, and not to overthrow it. It is not the duty of the army to rule or govern, because it has no political mandate and its duty is not to seek a political mandate. The army only operates under the mandate of the civil government. If the national interest compels the armed forces to intervene then immediately after the intervention the army must hand over to a new civil government elected by the people and enjoying the people's mandate under a constitution accepted by them. If the army does not do this then the position of the army becomes dubious and anomalous and involves a betrayal of the people and the national interest. The substitute of a military regime or dictatorship is no solution to the neo-colonialist problem. (p. 2)

It was as if Nkrumah had felt the "winds of change" at his back. He, himself, had experienced assassination attempts; he had witnessed the murders of Patrice Lumumba and Modibo Keita, and he had seen successful coups d'état. Too, he had most certainly caught a wind emanating from within Ghana itself:

> What therefore has led to the military intrusions and interference and violence which we are now witnessing? Why is it that the armies of certain African States have been forced to take the steps which they have taken? ... . Their root cause can be found not in the life and traditions of the African people, but in the manoeuvres of neo-colonialism. (p. 2)

Because neo-colonialism was so entrenched in Africa and because it seriously threatened the stability of any independent State, Nkrumah was compelled to begin his "State Opening" to Parliament with dire warnings and exposés of puppet African leadership:

> In a neo-colonial State, the leaders of the Government allow themselves to be used and manipulated by foreign states and financial interests. The whole regime of a neo-colonial state is therefore subject to remote control. In other words, the rulers and governors of the neo-colonialist regime are teleguided from afar. These foreign powers and interests seek to maintain the exploitation and oppression of the people even after independence. Corruption, bribery, nepotism, shameless and riotous and ostentatious living become rife among the leaders of the neo-colonialist regime. This brings untold suffering on the workers and people as a whole. (1 Feb. 1966, p. 2)

Nkrumah now states that the people must take matters in their own hands:

> Even though disillusioned and frustrated, the masses are once again mobilised even more militantly to remove the neo-colonialist and client regime, knowing full well that the regime, supported by the neo-colonialists, will not hesitate to use the army to crush them. If the masses persist in their protest, they are sure to come in conflict with the army, and civil war results. The masses of the people have then no where to turn for redress. They therefore have no choice but to organise to isolate the army from the corrupt regime, if the army itself is free from the taint of corruption. But if the Army itself is corrupt or if it proves impossible to detach it from the corrupt regime, then the people have no choice but to take up arms against the neo-colonialist regime. The people's struggle for freedom and justice would have reached the phase of civil conflict which invariably takes the form of guerilla war, that is, people's war—a nationalist revolutionary war. (p. 3)

Not only must the people act, they must act via armed struggle. Non-violent, positive action, an earlier Nkrumah tactic, will not work. These directions to the masses of Ghana read almost like a blueprint for what the people should do in twenty-three days, on February 24, 1966, when Nkrumah' himself will become the victim of a successful coup. They must conduct a people's war. For those who might be duped by the neo-colonialist messages and propaganda—for example the neo-colonialist strategy of encouraging coups d'état and encouraging independent African States to model their constitutions "on an imitation of Western Parliamentary systems"—Nkrumah again justifies Ghana's adoption of a one-party state:

> As part of the neo-colonialist strategy, the independent African States are made to believe that their constitutions must be based on an imitation of Western Parliamentary systems. Before they quit the colonial power imposes a Constitution which is alien to the traditions and true aspirations of the people. It is this state of affairs which fosters the development of neo-colonialism and breeds discontent and frustration among the people. But the chaos, confusion, corruption, nepotism and misery engendered by such unreflecting imitation have exposed the futility and ineffectiveness of the Western Parliamentary system in Africa. (p. 3)

Though foreign to "Western Parliamentary Systems", the one-party system works in Africa. The one-party system is a strategy, not a principle, however. It can work only under particular conditions. First, it "is an effective and safe instrument only when it operates in a socialist society. In other words, it must be a political expression of the will of the masses working for the ultimate good and welfare of the people as a whole" (p. 4). It cannot work in a neo-colonialist state, however, for such a state will merely become a dictatorship.

All of the neo-colonialist maneuverings in Africa would not have been possible had Africa united in 1963 when the Charter of African Unity was first signed. Nkrumah warned that African States must unite or fall one by one. He reiterates this same warning before Parliament in meticulous detail:

> [1] Alone, few of the Independent African States have the markets, the raw materials for the capital to build even a single large scale modern industrial complex. United in a continental Union Government, we could plan the use of our rich natural resources, our markets, and our capital to build giant complexes, iron and steel industries, hydro- electric projects in key areas throughout the continent. Such projects, planned on a continental scale, could assist in our endeavours for continental economic reconstruction. [2] United, we could bargain more effectively with foreign investment and governments. Our united economies could provide large markets and would make large-scale efficient industries profitable for all

concerned. Together, we could borrow funds to finance our hydro-electric schemes, construction of essential transport, factories and infrastructure facilities to ensure the necessary specialisation and division of labour for continental economic growth. Together, in a mighty continent-wide political union, we could ensure the stability and resources necessary to guarantee that loans and investments were paid off at reasonable rates. Thus the potential of a new life can be provided for all Africa, if we establish a continent-wide Union Government. [3] A Union Government of Africa would be in a position to provide ready assistance on a continental scale to the independent African States, whose resources are inadequate to meet their expanding needs. It will also prevent them from seeking such help outside the African continent. The African States will thus be assisted in their efforts to safeguard their national independence and sovereignty against the pressures and plunder of foreign powers and foreign interests. Thus all the Independent African States, big or small, have everything and little to lose by a continental Union Government of Africa. (pp. 4–5, *enumeration added*)

Moreover, a Union Government with a centralized military in service to all of Africa could be able to come to the military aid of colonial territories in Africa under attack. The "Ian Smith illegal regime" in Rhodesia is a case in point. Nkrumah planned to "put forward concrete proposals for joint action when the OAU Council of Ministers meet in Addis Ababa on the 27th of this month" (p. 5). However, he was overthrown three days prior to this meeting.

It is impossible to imagine that Nkrumah would not have been conscious of the potential for a coup against his regime; this February 1, 1966 speech to Parliament, detailing the benefits of Pan-Africanism and the machinations of the neo-colonialists, prove this awareness. But he is steadfast and unwavering. No matter how often he had called for a united Africa, he called once again in this speech: "A Union Government for Africa is therefore a necessity, and a pre-requisite for Africa's economic progress and survival" (p. 6).

Nkrumah's vision is broad and all-encompassing. He is concerned about Africa and its people first and foremost. But, as a humanist, he is also concerned about world socialism and world peace. To argue convincingly that Pan-Africanism is the only solution for Africa and its people and to demonstrate his unwavering concern for and commitment to Africa and the rest of the world, he must show *practically* how peace and prosperity can co-exist for the benefit of the people. He does so by using Ghana as an example. Thus, most of Nkrumah's address is on the phenomenal domestic accomplishments made in Ghana since 1957:

Within the short span of eight years since independence, we have built some of the finest roads in the world; we have provided adequate medical and health services for the large majority of our people; we have built universities, secondary schools, training colleges and provided opportunities for free education for the great mass of the population. We have completed the gigantic Volta River Project one year ahead of schedule. (1 Feb. 1966, p. 7)

What does the future hold for Ghana's development? According to Nkrumah, in "the next five years a thousand rural industrial projects" will be established throughout Ghana (p. 9). In regard to the telephone and telecommunication services, "in Ghana alone there are over 35, 000 subscribers, more than double the position at independence in 1957" (p. 11). Moreover, by the end of 1966, "in keeping with our policy of forging close links with the Independent African States, direct telegraph and telephone communications between Accra and the capitals of African States will be completed" (*ibid*.). Other past accomplishments and future goals include the following [*enumeration added*]:

[1] "In one year we have almost doubled the number of teacher training colleges in Ghana". (p. 12)

[2] "Modern science laboratories for use by elementary schools have been built at Accra, Kumasi, Cape Coast, Sekondi and Ho". (p. 12)

[3] "The student intake at the University College of Science Education in Cape Coast is expected to reach 1, 400 in October this year and this College will attain full University status. When this happens, Cape Coast will be declared a University City". (p. 13)

[4] "The Ghana Medical School recently established will enter upon its first course of clinical studies in April this year". (p. 13)

[5] "Mr. Speaker, the welfare of women continues to engage our special attention. Quite apart from the several Mass Education Women's Groups operating in our towns and villages, we have established many Girls Vocational Training Centres throughout the country with the aim of catering for the training and welfare of the future mothers of Ghana". (p. 14)

[6] "It is our policy to abolish illiteracy entirely from Ghana. Much has already been done in this field that we are in sight of the complete abolition of illiteracy in Ghana. To this end, a mass assault on the remaining pockets of illiteracy in the country will soon be launched. The popularity of our television service is increasing daily. It is serving a useful role not only in entertainment but also in education and the fight against illiteracy". (p. 14)

[7] "Today, the All African trade Union Federation which is fighting in the forefront of the African revolution, has become a living reality. The workers of Africa cannot co-exist with the forces of colonialism and exploitation, they cannot co-exist with imperialism and neo-colonialism. Seeing poverty and exploitation around them and seeking a new way of life for themselves, they will continue to strive for a better life for all the people in Africa". (p.15)

At the end of this significant address, Nkrumah reiterates his goals. First, he expresses his confidence in the Ghana Parliament's "loyalty to the Party and Government" and pins his hope on its "sacrifice and devotion" in order to advance "national reconstruction and development" (p. 17). According to Nkrumah, it is only by accomplishing such an advancement that "we can justify the confidence placed in us by our people. Only thus can we promote the upliftment of Ghana, the redemption of Africa, and make our contribution to world peace and to the welfare and happiness of mankind" (p. 17).

On February 24, 1966, less than a month later, Nkrumah's government was overthrown. However, instead of silencing him, this act merely intensified his political development. He became clearer than ever before on the enemy's machinations and on the only tactic remaining, armed struggle, needed to launch Pan-Africanism.

~ ~ ~ ~ ~

5

Nkrumah's Conference Speeches

> I do not think that I have ever attended a single meeting or conference between African states where I have not warned against the dangers of delaying unification. It is not practical politics in Africa today to work for any other goal. There is not an African state which is secure, or which is free to develop its resources to the full for the benefit of its own people. All are economically weak, and all are politically unstable. Unless we unite there can be no progress, and the suffering of the African masses will continue. (*Revolutionary Path*, p. 140)

Nkrumah's sponsoring of conferences, as well as attending conferences, are indicative of his influence in the African world. At these events influential audiences would be in place, comprised of statespersons, future statespersons, or potential statespersons. Furthermore, by sponsoring conferences, Nkrumah ushered in the era of the practice of Pan-Africanism. Before 1958, Pan-Africanism, from its inception in 1900, was more a theory than a practical reality. Nkrumah "contributed significantly … to the sustenance of the Pan-African idea as conceived after the Manchester Pan-African Congress of 1945 … [and] was one of the driving forces at the Manchester Congress in 1945" (Thompson, *Africa and Unity*, p. 89). That theoretical contribution paved the way for the practice of Pan-Africanism. Once Ghana received its independence on March 6, 1957, Nkrumah, with unparalleled energy and commitment, began the practical work of building Pan-Africanism.

Nkrumah's influence on Africa and its descendants, even before the "active" years of Pan-Africanism, is important to note, for it was during this phase of the African Revolution that the idea of Pan-Africanism was planted and nurtured, largely through conferences or congresses. The first four Pan-African Congresses, according to Nkrumah, "were attended mainly by intellectual and other bourgeois elements of African descent living either in the USA or the Caribbean" (*Revolutionary Path*, p. 42).

Although these were, as Nkrumah notes, "bourgeois" conferences, the Fifth Congress was significantly different in that "there was strong worker and student participation, and most of the over two hundred delegates who attended came from Africa" (*Revolutionary Path*, p. 42). For this Fifth Pan-African Congress held in Manchester, England from October 15th-21st, 1945, Nkrumah was the joint secretary of the Organization Committee, along with George Padmore. Also instrumental in organizing the Congress was T. R. Makonnen, Peter Abrahams, and Jomo Kenyatta. As principal organizers for this event, this group of progressive Africans ensured that a more practical, African unity focused, anti-imperialist conference prevailed.

Nkrumah himself wrote the "Declaration for the Colonial Peoples of the World", approved and adopted in 1945 by the Fifth Pan-African Congress. In it, he wrote: "We believe in the rights of all peoples to govern themselves. We affirm the right of all colonial peoples to control their own destiny. All colonies must be free from foreign imperialist control, whether political or economic" (*Towards Colonial Freedom*, p. 44). Nkrumah here signaled his understanding of the enemy and his concern for African and other colonial peoples as early as 1945. Even earlier, as a student in the United States, Nkrumah demonstrated his interest in solving the problems of Africa, attending meetings of the Council on African Affairs, for example.

This Fifth Pan-African Congress was so well-organized that "where distance prevented organisations from sending representatives, they appointed local representatives in Britain to act on their behalf" (Thompson, p. 57). Commenting on the progressive nature of the congress, Thompson writes that the resolutions of the Congress, "had a common feature: anti-imperialism" (p. 58). Most important, however, was the inclusion of the idea of Pan-Africanism in the resolutions: "The West Indies, and the sovereign states of Haiti, Ethiopia, and Liberia were discussed and resolutions centered on the demand for freedom, the dismantling of colonialism, the repudiation of racism, and the call for unity under the banner of a socialist United States of Africa" (p. 58). Nkrumah and Padmore understood that socialism was integrally tied to unity as early as the 1940s. As both knew, without socialism a unified Africa would, as Nkrumah writes in *Towards Colonial Freedom*, offer colonialists and neocolonialists an easier method of exploitation. Even more revolutionary and powerful was the resolution concerning the unity of the West Indies. According to the *Manchester Guardian*, "two resolutions were passed … ; the first asked for the federation of all West Indian Islands, that federation to be followed by the grant of dominion status" (Thompson, p. 60). In 1962, Nkrumah, still convinced that a unified West Indies would contribute to a unified Africa, and vice versa, writes a letter to the heads of state in the West Indies urging them to unite their states. At the Conference of African Freedom Fighters held in Accra on June 4, 1962, Nkrumah stated: "The emergence of the Caribbean isles as united States, free and progressive, federated in strength and purpose, and contributing substantially to the total success of all our peoples" would be of help to Africa and her descendants (June 4, 1962, p. 6).

These Pan-African Congresses were important in their theoretical contribution to the African Revolution. But of even more significance in their practical contribution to Pan-Africanism were the conferences held between 1958 and 1965. These were all held in Ghana. The 1958 "Accra Conference of Independent African States was the first conference of its kind ever to be held, and it paved the way for a succession of other Pan-African conferences of various kinds" (*Revolutionary Path*, p. 126). Only eight African countries were independent at the time: Ghana, Ethiopia, Libya, Tunisia, Morocco, Egypt, Liberia and Sudan. All were represented at the conference, the purpose of which was to reactivate Pan-Africanism on the soil of Africa. At the end of his "Speech of Welcome to Representatives of Independent African States", Nkrumah states: "Today we are one. If in the past the Sahara divided us, now it unites us. And an injury to one is an injury to all of us. From this Conference must go out a new message: 'Hands off Africa! Africa must be free!'" (p. 129).

In December 1958, delegates from "62 nationalist organizations attended the All-African People's Conference in Accra, including Patrice Lumumba. Nkrumah writes: "The primary aim of the Conference was to encourage nationalist political movements in colonial areas as a means towards continental unity and a socialist transformation of society" (*Revolutionary Path*, p. 130). Again, Nkrumah was calling for a liberated, united, *socialist* Africa. And his call for a unity tied to an economic system designed to serve all of Africa's people was timely since he was speaking to the nationalist leaders of Africa. Nkrumah's definition of Pan-Africanism, unlike Garvey's, included the type of economic system best for Africa. Under Nkrumah, Pan-Africanism would mean "the total liberation and unification of Africa under scientific socialism". Planting the seed of Pan-Africanism prior to the independence of African colonies was indeed a way to speed up the stages of the African Revolution. In "A Call to Independence", a document available at the conference, appears the following: "This Conference will formulate and proclaim our African Personality based on the philosophy of Pan-African Socialism as the ideology of the African Non-Violent Revolution". The only element of this "Call" that Nkrumah later revises is "African Non-Violent Revolution". Just prior to his overthrow, he is convinced that the only way that Pan-Africanism will be realized is through armed struggle.

As a measure of the success of Nkrumah's organizing strategy of first calling conferences (specifically the 1958 conferences) and, second, not losing a moment to promote Pan-Africanism, Thompson attributes the subsequent increase in the liberation struggles in Africa. Now "Pan-Africanism moved from the realm of idealism and romanticism to that of practical politics. Liberation movements began to challenge the dependent states of the African continent" (Thompson, pp. 126–127). "Ghana's initiative in convening the first conference of independent African states and later a conference embracing all Africa, that is, the All African People's Conference, was an indication that Pan-Africanism had, at last, found a home on African soil" (Thompson, p. 129).

The All African People's Conference had a tremendous effect on the young militants present, of especial significance were those from the Congo and South Africa. Patrice Lumumba made a short speech which he ended with "Down with colonialism and imperialism. Down with racism and tribalism. Long live the Congolese nation, long live independent Africa" (Thompson, p. 130).

Clearly, the December 1958 conference was more radical than the earlier one comprised of Heads of State. Thompson writes that "the earlier Conference of Independent States pitched its tone low and made modest pronouncements, the later conference of All African Peoples expressed in unequivocal terms more radical views and passed resolutions in keeping with that radicalism" (Thompson, p. 134). The truth of this statement is reflected in the radicalism of the youth engaged in anti-colonial struggles throughout Africa. More militant than the heads of state who already had more to gain, personally, from the ex-colonial masters, those younger Africans like Lumumba were not as divorced from the people and saw, therefore, the interests of the people as their own interests.

The Second All African People's Conference in 1960 was just as, or even more, revolutionary as the first, for, according to Thompson, it "did stress African unity more than its predecessor" (p. 135). Held in Tunis between January 25 and January 30, it sought to establish an All African Federation of Trade Unions, distinct from other non-African trade unions. In Article II—Aims and Objects: Constitution of the All African people's Conference, objectives include "(e) The working for the emergences of a United States of Africa" (p. 135). Thompson writes that at this conference, "African trade unions were brought institutionally into the orbit of Pan-African activity" because of Ghana's initiative (p. 138). More than any other single act, this organizing effort on behalf of the workers of Africa took Pan-Africanism from the realm of the theoretical to that of the practical, by "encourag[ing] nationalist movements in other parts of Africa" (p. 138). Nkrumah later writes of developments after 1958:

> A first step towards the political unification of Africa was taken on November the 23rd, 1958, when Ghana and the Republic of Guinea united to form a nucleus for a Union of African States. The following

year, in July 1959, President Tubman of Liberia, President Sékou Touré and I met in Sanniquellie to discuss the whole question of African liberation and unity. At the end of our talks we issued a Declaration of Principles explaining the nature of the organization we agreed to form which was to be known as the Community of Independent African States. (*Revolutionary Path*, p. 135)

Of the ten principles enumerated, 5, 6, 9, and 10 demonstrate Nkrumah's persistent, consistent efforts to bring about Pan-Africanism (p. 141):

> 5. (a) The acts of states or federations which are members of the Community, shall be determined in relation to the essential objectives which are Freedom, Independence, Unity, the African Personality, as well as the interest of the African peoples. (b) Each member-state or federation shall, in its acts or policies, do nothing contrary to the spirit and objectives of the Community.
> 6. (a) The general policy of the Community shall be to build up a free and prosperous African Community for the benefit of its peoples and the peoples of the world and in the interest of international peace and security. (b) This policy shall be based essentially on the maintenance of diplomatic, economic and cultural relations, on the basis of equality and reciprocity, with all the states of the world which adopt a position compatible with African interests and African dignity. (c) Its main objective will be to help other African territories, subjected to domination, with a view to accelerating the end of their non-independent status. [...]
> 9. The Community shall have a flag and an anthem to be agreed upon at a later date.
> 10. The motto of the Community shall be: INDEPENDENCE AND UNITY.
> *Signed:*   W. V. S. Tubman, President of the Republic of Liberia
>   Sékou Touré, President of the Republic of Guinea
>   Kwame Nkrumah, Prime Minister of Ghana

Unlike the nucleus founded by Ghana and Guinea, and later Mali, this Community was not a political union of states; rather, it was "an economic, cultural and social organization designed to promote African unity by building up a 'free and prosperous African Community for the benefit of its peoples and the peoples of the world, and in the interest of international peace and security'" (*Revolutionary Path*, pp. 135–6). Nevertheless, it is significant that its main objective is "to help other African territories, subjected to domination". And, of course, the end objective would be for these newly independent territories to join the Community and to struggle for African unity.

All of these conferences were encouraged and shaped by Nkrumah. He not only promoted the African Revolution (Pan-Africanism, liberated countries, a united Africa and worldwide socialism), but also sought to offer history and current events lessons, warnings, and short term goals and strategies, especially for freedom fighters. But, of course, Pan-Africanism was the only guarantee of liberation. Therefore, having Africa's interests foremost in his mind, as the young African freedom fighters knew, Nkrumah always used the conferences to promote Pan-Africanism.

One of Nkrumah's key speeches in regard to the African Revolution was made on July 18, 1960, at the Conference of Ghana Women and Women of African Descent (Obeng, 1960, p. 110–115). While this speech does not represent Nkrumah's most progressive views on the role of women in the African Revolution, it does reflect his practice of using every occasion, every conference to share his views on the necessity of Pan-Africanism, a goal that will liberate and advance the cause of all Africans, including African women. Nkrumah begins: "Who would have thought that in this year of 1960 it would be possible to even hold a conference of all Ghanaian women, much less of women of all Africa and African descent!" (p. 110), and outlines the role African women must play in building Pan-Africanism:

> Your role in this direction is of great importance. Not only can you carry back this message to the men of your respective countries, but, if you are convinced that unity is the right answer, you can also bring your feminine influence to bear in persuading your brothers, husbands and friends of the importance of African unity as the only salvation for Africa. (p. 112)

Phrases such as "carry back this message to the men" and "bring your feminine influence to bear in persuading your brothers, husbands and friends" might seem to relegate women to the age-old position of being "helpmeets" to "their men". However, Nkrumah rescues and promotes the role of women from one of subservience to one of equality in the following passage:

> There is a great responsibility resting on the shoulders of all women of Africa and African descent. They must realise that the men alone cannot complete the gigantic task we have set ourselves. The time has come when the women of Africa and of African descent must rise up in their millions to join the African crusade for freedom. (p. 112)

Although he does not spell out the specific role women must play in the African Revolution as he will do in 1968, Nkrumah does continue to emphasize an active role for women:

> Sisters of the African Liberation Front, the last century was one of European occupation of Africa. This century-the twentieth century is one of African liberation. The year 1960 is the most challenging and significant year in this historic development. It is the year of the climate of the revolution in which Africa has rebelled against the shame and injustice which for so long has been meted out to her. The clarion command echoes across the mountains and the valleys, across the rivers and the lakes, across the oceans and the deserts. Hands off Africa! Hands off Africa! (p. 113)

This speech is also significant in prefiguring his watershed work, "The Spectre of Black Power", for Nkrumah advances the question of identity in regard to African people: "All artificial boundaries which separate brother from brother and sister from sister must be wiped out. Africa, so mighty, so rich, must be developed not only for the common good and prosperity of the African, but also for the peace and happiness of all mankind" (p. 113).

One final point regarding this speech is well-worth noting. Nkrumah does not end it before returning to neo-colonialism, the new disguise of capitalism in Africa:

> We in this Africa liberation movement are fully alert to this, new form of colonialism which is struggling to get a hold in our continent. To perpetuate imperialist interests in Africa, the colonial power now makes a point to grant fake independence. Chaos ensues and this enables the ex- colonial master to re-enter the territory on the pretext of maintaining law and order. Their idea is to grant independence with one had and to take it back with the other. (p. 114)

The Casablanca Conference, held from January 3–7, 1961, continued to illustrate Nkrumah's drive toward Pan-Africanism. This conference was attended by the "radical" African states of Ghana, Guinea, Mali, Libya, Egypt, Morocco, and by the Algerian revolutionary organization, the FLN. Either truly believing that economic cooperation should precede political unity or already corrupted by the "crumbs" that the neo-colonialists held out for them, the French-speaking independent African States refused to attend. Also, Tunisia, Nigeria and Liberia did not attend. The primary purpose of this conference was to find ways "to give political support to the liberation struggle" still being waged by occupied colonial territories (*Revolutionary Path*, p. 138). According to Nkrumah, "our unity of purpose was absolutely clear on this point and it was the liberation issue above all others which led to the calling of the Casablanca Conference" (p. 138). In particular, these leaders discussed "the situation in the Congo, the war in Algeria, and apartheid in South Africa" (*Revolutionary Path*, p. 138).

In his speech at the closing session of the Conference, Nkrumah once again warned African leaders of the absolute necessity for unity:

> I can see no security for African States unless African leaders, like ourselves, have realized beyond all doubt that salvation for Africa lies in unity ... for in unity lies strength, and as I see it, African States must unite or sell themselves out to imperialist and colonialist exploiters for a mess of pottage, or disintegrate individually. (p. 138)

At the Casablanca Conference and subsequently in Cairo on May 5, 1961 and in August of 1961, Nkrumah urged that the machinery was in place to make such a reality possible, for example, through:

1. an African Consultative Assembly
2. a Heads of State [or Heads of Progressive Organizations?] Committee
3. economic and cultural committees
4. a Joint African High Command and its Commandos (headquartered in Accra and a permanent Secretariat with its Secretary-General (headquartered in Bamako)
5. an Economic Customs Union and an Economic Council
6. an African Common Market
7. an African Economic Development Bank
8. an African Payments Union (to settle member States' accounts)
9. a postal and telecommunications union
10. a joint shipping company. (*Revolutionary Path*, p. 139)

Moreover, according to Nkrumah, "it was also decided that an agreement on economic and technical co-operation should be concluded between member states; that labour legislation in member countries should be gradually coordinated; and that members should conduct a joint foreign policy" (pp. 139–140).

In his address at the Conference of African Freedom Fighters in Accra, Ghana on June 4, 1962, "African Freedom and Unity", Nkrumah states the objective of the conference as follows: "to examine our position in the great struggle to rid Africa completely and forever of imperialism and its handmaidens, colonialism and neo-colonialism". Later, he adds that the real objective, the ultimate objective, is "the political unification of Africa" (p. 3). He adds, "it gives us the opportunity also to review our strength as well as that of the enemy, and to reorganize our forces and our strategy in order to carry the struggle forward to victory" (p. 3). Who is the enemy? Nkrumah is always clear on this question of the enemy: "The enemy is imperialism, which uses as its weapons colonialism and neo-colonialism". One of the ways in which colonialists and neo-colonialists seek to succeed is by fomenting tribal conflicts. He states that those freedom fighters "who are in the thick of the struggle in Angola, Mozambique, Portuguese Guinea and elsewhere know this game too well". He warns all of them, however, to "guard against it by forging a common united front against the enemy". While this statement does reflect Nkrumah's understanding of the importance of these revolutionary organizations unifying, it does not reflect his understanding that if progressive states forged a link with a continental revolutionary coalition of organizations the chances of building Pan-Africanism would have increased. For there is no evidence that Nkrumah forged a formal link between progressive states and progressive organizations in Africa as an alternative strategy for building Pan-Africanism.

The enemy is "formidable", Nkrumah states. "They are entrenched and powerful ... . They operate in world-wide combinations at all levels: political, economic, military, cultural, educational, social, and trade; and through intelligence, cultural and information services. They operate from European and African centres, using agents who, I am ashamed to say, are often unpatriotic sons of Africa, buying personal satisfactions with the betrayal of their countries' safety and integrity" (June 4, 1962, p. 4). Here, Nkrumah is unveiling the class struggle that exists among Africans. Class struggle is again highlighted later in the speech when Nkrumah states: "Some of the [African] leaders, it must be confessed, do not see the struggle of their brother Africans as part of their own struggle ... . Thus rifts are consciously created by the imperialists between Africans, which they can sit back and watch with sly satisfaction, as well as contempt for those who fail to see how they are being used against Africa's best interests" (p. 5). If the enemy is not forging rifts, they are "coming as Greeks bearing gifts": "How generous they can be, we have learned from our sad experience over a good long time ... . As long as it is possible to deal with us singly, we are at the mercy of the imperialists rather than their generosity ... . Those of us who cannot see through these implications can only be suffering from an intense myopia" (p. 5). Or, they can be selfishly pursuing their own individual self-interests at the expense of their people's interests.

What should be done to fight this formidable enemy, while marching toward the ultimate goal of unification? Once again, Nkrumah offers a blueprint. First, and "without delay, aim at the creation of a joint military command". Second, "set up in Africa a common economic planning organisation". Third, "devise a constitutional structure which will secure the objectives I have outlined and yet preserve the sovereignty of each of the countries joining the union". Fourth, the West Indies must unite: "The emergence of the Caribbean isles as united States, free and progressive, federated in strength and purpose, and contributing substantially to the total success of all our peoples" would be of help to Africa and her descendants. Besides, as with individual African states, "how can these little islands hope to stand by themselves in the future any better than they have done in the past?" (June 4, 1962, p. 6). As stated earlier, in the same year, 1962, he writes a "Letter to the West Indies" to the heads of state in the Caribbean. Fifth, the UN must be made to act as an "effective deterrent in connection with the more outrageous forms of colonial oppression" (p. 7). In fact, "Africa ... demands that a meeting of this year's United Nations session should be devoted to the problem of colonialism in Africa. Furthermore, the United Nations should make a firm declaration calling upon the colonial powers to quit Africa by the 31st December, 1962" (p. 4). The UN cannot again fail to act as it did in the case of the Congo (p. 8). Sixth, Africa must seek help from the people within imperialist countries like Great Britain and the US because "we must not overlook the struggle which some sections of the European working class and intelligentsia are bringing out into the open against colonial governments in Africa" (p. 7). (Later, he will recognize the significant role Africans in these imperialist countries can and will play in building Pan-Africanism.) The working class of the world must unite because "there is a definite link between our struggle and the working class battling for democratic rights and liberties against the metropolitan colonial governments" (*ibid.*). There are also forces in Africa, which when linked, are formidable: "the trade unions, the farmers and peasants associations, the co-operatives, the youth movements, the women's organisations, the political parties" *(ibid.)*.

Most important, the freedom fighters must not think that once they've have won national independence, all is well. They must not drop the quest for true liberation (via a united Africa) "for some token aid" (June 4, 1962, p. 5). Rather, they must prepare themselves for a long, arduous battle involving four stages:

(1) the attainment of freedom and independence;
(2) the consolidation of that freedom and independence;
(3) the creation of unity and community between the free African States;
(4) the economic and social reconstruction of Africa.

Of course, for Nkrumah, this latter point, "the economic and social reconstruction of Africa" is synonymous with socialism.

Pan-Africanism promised to enjoy a categorical leap in May 1963 with the establishment of the Organization of African Unity. In Addis Ababa on May 24, 1963, Nkrumah makes his historic "Unity Now" speech. All the essential arguments in favor of Pan-Africanism are once again articulated in this speech. First, the fundamental element of unity is established. However, in the wake of neo-colonialist maneuverings to convince African states only to seek economic unity—if any unity at all, Nkrumah clarifies that political unity takes precedence: "African Unity is, above all, a political kingdom which can only be gained by political means. The social and economic development of Africa will come only within the political kingdom, not the other way round" (*Revolutionary Path*, p. 235). In addition, Nkrumah speaks of the exigency, the speed at which this unity must occur. African countries are "fast learning that political independence is not enough to rid us of the consequence of colonial rule" (p. 236), and that the new form of colonialism "is covered up under the clothing of many agencies, which meddle in our domestic affairs, to foment dissention within our borders" (p. 236). The need for unity is urgent: otherwise, "we who are sitting here today shall tomorrow be the victims and martyrs of neo-colonialism" (p. 236). He warned the leaders not to become their "own executioners" (p. 236).

Second, Nkrumah reviews Africa's potentialities. Three essential points are made in this section. The first documents the rape of Africa's resources: "Fifty-two per cent of the gold in Fort Knox at this moment, where the U.S.A. stores its billion, is believed to have originated from our shores. Africa provides more than 60 per cent of the world's gold" (*Revolutionary Path*, p. 237). Moreover, "a great deal of uranium for nuclear power, of copper for electronics, of titanium for supersonic projectiles, of iron and steel for heavy industries, of other minerals and raw materials for lighter industries—the basic economic might of the foreign Powers—come from our continent" (p. 237). In other words, let us be clear: "it was our continent that helped the Western world to build up its accumulated wealth" (p. 237). Further, if the wealth that was being siphoned off were kept in a united Africa, Africa's potential as a formidable world power would be realized:

> It is only by uniting our productive capacity and the resultant production that we can amass capital. And once we start, the momentum will increase. With capital controlled by our own banks, harnessed to our own true industrial and agricultural development we shall make our advance. We shall accumulate machinery and establish steel works, iron foundries and factories; we shall link the various states of our continent with communications; we shall astound the world with our hydro-electric power; we shall drain marshes and swamps, clear

infested areas, feed the under-nourished, and rid our people of parasites and disease. It is within the possibility of science and technology to make even the Sahara bloom into a vast field with verdant vegetation for agricultural and industrial developments. We shall harness the radio, television, giant printing presses to lift our people from the dark recesses of illiteracy. (*Revolutionary Path*, p. 238)

Lastly, investors dealing with a united Africa will no longer have the opportunity to exploit. Moreover, to their advantage, "investors will no longer have to weigh with concern the risks of negotiating with governments in one period which may not exist in the very next period. Instead of dealing or negotiating with so many separate states at a time they will be dealing with one united government pursuing a harmonized continental policy" (*RP*, p. 239). But isn't this just the point? Nkrumah understood that the neo-colonialists preferred the risks of dealing with unstable governments than in negotiating with a harmonized, socialist continent. A small micro-territory would not have the power to negotiate fair trade policies. Of course, if one is speaking of a harmonized neo-colonial continent, this is the best of all scenarios since only one supreme puppet would be manipulated. That is why Nkrumah called for a united, *socialist* Africa.

In his "Unity Now" speech, Nkrumah highlights the problems of the peasantry who are at "the mercy of foreign cash crop markets" (*Revolutionary Path*, p. 239) and border disputes that affect almost all States since "hardly any African State [does not have] a frontier problem with its adjacent neighbours" (p. 239). What is the solution? According to Nkrumah, "by creating a political union … , we can tackle hopefully every emergency, every enemy, and every complexity" (p. 240) because Africa has "emerged in the age of science and technology in which poverty, ignorance and disease are no longer the masters, but the retreating foes of mankind. We have emerged in the age of socialized planning, when production and distribution are not governed by chaos, greed and self-interest, but by social needs" (p. 240). A unified, *socialist* Africa is the solution.

Regarding stability and security, one essential point of the speech stands out: "Without necessarily sacrificing our sovereignties, big or small, we can here and now forge a political union based on Defence, Foreign Affairs and Diplomacy, and a Common Citizenship, an African Currency, an African Monetary Zone and an African Central Bank … . We need a Common Defence System with an African High Command to ensure the stability and security of Africa" (*Revolutionary Path*, p. 240). Addressing continental policy, Nkrumah warns that "no independent African State today by itself has a chance to follow an independent course of economic development, and many of us who have tried to do this have been almost ruined or have had to return to the fold of the former colonial rulers. This position will not change unless we have a united policy working at the continental level" (p. 242).

Regarding unity and identity, and using the USA as an example. Nkrumah states:

> When the first Congress of the United States met many years ago at Philadelphia one of the delegates sounded the first chord of unity by declaring that they had met in "a state of nature". In other words, they were not in Philadelphia as Virginians, or Pen[n]sylvanians but simply as Americans. This reference to themselves as Americans was in those days a new and strange experience. May I dare to assert equally on this occasion, Your Excellencies, that we meet here today not as Ghanaians, Guineans, Egyptians, Algerians, Moroccans, Malians, Liberians, Congolese or Nigerians but as Africans. (*Revolutionary Path*, p. 245)

On the subject of unity Nkrumah articulates practical strategies, some of which can and should be implemented before the end of the summit. Some of these include a declaration of unifying principles, an All-African Committee of Foreign Ministers; the new Headquarters or Capital of our Union Government", a common market for Africa, an African currency, an African Monetary Zone, an African central bank, a continental communications system, a liberation Bureau for African Freedom Fighters [since "only a United Africa with central political direction can successfully give effective material and moral support to our freedom fighters"] (*Revolutionary Path*, p. 246). Nkrumah ends this speech, with the following message:

> Let us return to our people of Africa not with empty hands and with high-sounding resolutions, but with the firm hope and assurance that at long last African Unity has become a reality. We shall thus begin the triumphant march to the kingdom of the African personality, and to a continent of prosperity, and progress of equality and justice and of work and happiness. This shall be our victory—victory within a continental government of a Union of African States. This victory will give our voice greater force in world affairs and enable us to throw our weight more forcibly on the side of peace ... . Many of the world's present ills are to be found in the insecurity and fear engendered by the threat of nuclear war. Especially do the new nations need peace in order to make their way into a life of economic and social well-being amid an atmosphere of security and stability that will promote moral, cultural and spiritual fulfillment. (*Revolutionary Path*, p. 248)

The content of this speech holds the key to Africa's and her peoples' liberation even today.

On November 11, 1963, Nkrumah speaks at the "Opening of the Second Conference of African Journalists". His speech is unique in that it reveals his impatience with the leadership of Africa. The promise that the founding of the Organization of African Unity (OAU) once held was already proving to be empty. The categorical leap in regard to Africa's liberation did not look promising at all, especially in light of the reluctance of the regional Union Africaine et Malagache to disband in favor of a greater union, a united Africa (Thompson, pp. 191–2). Nkrumah believed that the people of Africa could not afford to wait on their leaders. Thus, this Conference of the African Journalists reflects Nkrumah's plan to begin to reach out to others who had the power to help him promulgate the African Revolution. Once conferring the power of unity on the heads of African states, Nkrumah now yanks back this power and gives it to each individual African, stating: "Every African is responsible to the African Revolution by the heritage of his birth and by his experience of colonialism and imperialism" (*Revolutionary Path*, p. 145). Nkrumah makes clear his plan from the very beginning of the speech: "It is not simply out of courtesy that I am here to open this Conference of African Journalists … . If we interpret journalism as the dissemination of news and the clarion to action, then journalism is certainly not new to Africa (*Revolutionary Path, p.* 140).

What then is this "clarion to action" that Nkrumah expects from the journalists? "The special significance of this gathering is that it is the first conference of African Journalists since the Organisation of African Unity was established at Addis Ababa in May this year. As such it can do nothing less than fulfil the purpose of a continental press conference on the Unity of Africa" (*Revolutionary Path*, p. 140).

After his intent is crystallized, Nkrumah methodically and clearly explains the nature of, the opportunities accrued from, and the role of the journalists in the African Revolution. He tackles the latter point first by distinguishing between types of journalists. His point is to isolate those journalists who are servicing colonialists and neo-colonialists from those who work on behalf of their people:

> In Africa today, three types of African journalists can be recognised on our continent. There are those who are purposefully and unreservedly devoted to the cause of the African Revolution. Such journalists are dedicated to African freedom, African progress and African unity.
> Then there are those who by their work serve only the interests of private capital. These journalists have no minds of their own, no devotion to their people or their continent. They carry out the dictates of their foreign employers operating in Africa; they gyrate in the effort

to anticipate their masters' wishes.

> Thirdly, there are those journalists who, unwittingly, or deliberately, serve the interests of foreign governments by their support of the client and puppet regimes that have been established in Africa. (*Revolutionary Path*, p. 144)

After politically educating the journalists about their sharing a common training, but not a common goal, Nkrumah concentrates on the role of the politically conscious journalists:

> Truth, we say, must be the watchword of our African journalists and facts must be his guide. These [tenets], however, must not excuse dullness in our newspapers and our journals. They must not be used as a cover for shoddy writing and ambiguous intentions. The African journalist is not only expected to communicate the facts and aims of our African Revolution, but to do so compellingly and without fear. He must continually and fearlessly expose neo-colonialist subterfuge. He must attain a proper understanding of the African Revolution, its purpose and its travails. He must acquire technical proficiency and literary skill. (*Revolutionary Path*, p. 146)

Nkrumah even discusses the particular way in which journalists must present the facts of the African Revolution, for, according to him, they must always be conscious of their competition-the capitalist, neo-colonialist media:

> We must make our publications attractive to the eye and easy to handle and read … .We have more genuine fare to offer, but we would be foolish to dismiss airily the blandishments that cover their [capitalists'/imperialists'] frivolities and poisonous intentions … [in] their determination to penetrate deeply into our midst and draw our people away from their own true interests. (*Revolutionary Path*, p. 146)

In this speech Nkrumah again focuses on exposing the insidious machinations of neo-colonialism:

> What is neo-colonialism? It is the situation we find in a country where a colonial power grants nominal political independence to a territory, but sees to it that the control of the economic arrangements of the territory are still in the hands of the ex-colonial power; which is thereby able to dominate its economy and, indirectly, the state apparatus. It is empire-building without the flag. And here is how it works:
>
> They see to it that the political power remains in the hands of indigenous reactionaries.

> They manoeuvre to control the Army, the Police and even the Intelligence Services.
>
> They see to it that the economic institutions of the country are in the hands of their agents, and that economic production is completely controlled by private foreign capital leaving only the less profitable infrastructure in the hands of the indigenous population.
>
> They divide the Trade Union and other popular movements. When they have gained full control, in this way, of a client or puppet state, with a client or puppet administration, then they are in a position to do what they like to the territory, its government and its people.
>
> If they cannot get their own way, then they engineer political and military coups, to overthrow the regimes and install new reactionary regimes which will carry out their orders.
>
> Some of us allow ourselves to be used as agents of such neo-colonialist and settler government espionage systems operating in Africa. Even the Fascist Regime of South Africa could have agents among us here. (*Revolutionary Path*, pp. 148–9)

Next, Nkrumah lists the "hot issues" that plague the continent-including the French testing of atom bombs in the Sahara, the Moroccan-Algerian border dispute, and the plight of the Congo-in an effort to urge the journalists to act quickly on behalf of the African Revolution, for "only a continental government of Africa will give reality and purpose to African Unity". Before ending his speech, Nkrumah shares his belief in the economic system he feels best suited to raise Africa from the mires of deprivation in the speediest possible manner, namely socialism:

> Unless Africa embraces socialism, it will move backward instead of forward. Under any other system our progress can only be slow. Our people will lose their patience. They want to see progress, and socialism is the only means that will bring it speedily. Congo Brazzavil[l]e and Dahomey are object lessons for us. The attempt to enforce a one-party system in a non-socialist environment can lead only to disaster. (p. 155)

Nkrumah's parting words to the African press demonstrate the importance he places on it, and all other sectors of the African population, to serve the African Revolution:

> If we are to banish colonialism completely from our continent, every African must be made aware of his part in the struggle. This is the kind of education which the African press can and must help to spread. ... You have a noble cause—I would say a holy cause: to work

unstintingly, unhesitatingly, and fearlessly for the equality of all our people in this continent for the universality of man's rights everywhere on this globe.

Yours is the responsibility to be ever on the alert for truth and to use it without fear or favour in the noble task of forwarding total independence in Africa. (156)

As Nkrumah's speech delivered at the Second Conference of Non-Aligned States held in Cairo, Egypt on October 7, 1964 demonstrates, by 1964 he was no longer proposing the idea of non-violence as a tactic of the African Revolution or the worldwide socialist revolution. In this speech entitled, "Peace and Progress", a speech which shows him as a world leader, Nkrumah states: "As we sit here, neo-colonialism has created a situation in Africa in which the only way it seems to fight and eradicate it is by armed revolution and armed struggle" (7 Oct. 1964, p. 2). To this conference, at which there were representatives of "as many as 46 participating and 10 observer countries", Nkrumah states, "We, who are assembled here, represent the vast majority of mankind in Europe, Africa, Asia and Latin America, and from the borders and shores of the Caribbean islands" (p. 2). It is the vast majority who live in these geopolitical areas throughout the world who "suffer most from the suffocating weight" of imperialist and neo-colonialist "intrigues and intervention", and who cannot find any other way to lift this burden than by armed struggle.

If you had these representatives of neo-colonies in front of you, what would you say to them? Of course, you must acquaint them with the most recent problems and solutions confronting Africa. But just as Nkrumah knew that Ghana's liberation meant little without the liberation and unity of a socialist Africa, so too he knew that Pan-Africanism means little in a world dominated by capitalism. More, as a humanist, he could not sit idly by in his "own kingdom", even if Africa were to become united and socialist, while the rest of the first world peoples suffered. So, first, Nkrumah reminds his audience who the enemy is: "To my mind, the overriding cause of tension in the world today lies .... in the difficulties placed in the path of development of the emergent and developing nations by the imperialist and neo-colonialist powers" (Oct. 1964: Oct. 1964, p. 4).

Imperialism and neo-colonialism are the enemies of the people and, as enemies, they create major tensions in the world. Nkrumah addresses first world tensions: "There are the tensions resulting from the problems left over from the Second World War. Foremost of these is the German issue" (p. 3). Next, "there are the tensions arising out of the striving of the peoples of the developing areas of the world to throw off their burdens of imperialism, colonialism, neo-colonialism and racial discrimination" (p. 4). Third: "There are those divisions resulting from a conflict of ideologies ... . We cannot co-exist with imperialism, we cannot co-exist with colonialism, we cannot co-exist with neo-colonialism. There can never be co-existence between poverty and plenty, between the developing countries and the forces that militate against their progress and development" (p. 4). And, fourth, "there are tensions caused by the possession by the great powers of weapons, the destructive capacity of which there is no parallel in history" (p. 4).

Nkrumah then turns his attention to Africa. Africa is "threatened by two dangerous forces": (1) the desire of foreign powers to penetrate Africa, and establish new forms of colonialism through the vicious system of economic exploitation and economic imperialism, and (2) "the danger of ultra-rightist trends in neo-colonialism, which I would designate as fascist imperialism" (Oct. 1964, p. 4). Nkrumah's use of this term, "fascist imperialism", may have been the first to describe capitalism in its most vulgar form. While today examples abound, the Congo was an example of its existence during the 1960s. The imperialists' operation there was so overtly egregious that Nkrumah used every opportunity to highlight its machinations. This conference was no exception. Nkrumah's message to those 46 countries and 10 observer countries was: "This conference therefore should endorse the demand of the African people: Hands off the Congo, away with the mercenaries" (p. 5). The Congo's problem was an African problem which could only be solved by Africans, united. Also, it was a political problem, first and foremost, that demanded "a political solution", once again a solution that demanded unity.

The second major area of the "Peace and Progress" speech is solutions, for a "country occupied and victimised by a foreign power should have the right to use all means and resources at its disposal to recover its territory and [safeguard] it. This is the basis of the liberation struggle in Africa" (Oct. 7, 1964: p. 6). If a "man-killing" bear is on your back, you will use any means to get the bear off of your back—including the use of violence. So for Nkrumah violence, like non-violence, can be justified as a tactic. Mutual tolerance of others might offer a justifying principle, but not one realistic in a struggle against neo-colonialism. Socialism offers an alternative principle. But unwilling to ruffle the feathers of those neo-colonies not yet committed to socialism, Nkrumah adds, "Ghana accepts socialism as a means of our political and economic development does not and should not place us in opposition to any other country or people". On the contrary, "we who claim to be non-aligned must have the right to choose the political and economic philosophy which we consider most suitable for our rapid development and advancement" (p. 6). As Nkrumah knew, the only economic system that would ensure such rapid development and advancement of all of the people is socialism. A third solution is a declaration of complete disarmament: "Let us declare to the world, here and now, that we demand complete and total disarmament" (p. 7). Fourthly, the United Nations must be reorganized (p. 8). As in the case of Lumumba's Congo, it has been shown to be wanting. The fifth solution is peace in South-East Asia and the Middle East. Finally, "the solidarity achieved by the '77 Group' of developing countries at the Geneva Conference on World Trade and Development" must be consolidated: "Basically, what we want is trade, not aid" (p. 9).

Nkrumah returns to the question of Africa's liberation at the close of this speech:

> The African revolution represents a revolt against the inhuman exploitation and spoliation of Africa and her people by foreign interests. The foundations of the new Africa are based, therefore, on complete emancipation from foreign domination: the political unification of all Africa and a determination to breathe the air of freedom which is theirs to breathe. (p. 10)

Nkrumah's speech, "A New Africa", delivered at the opening of the Summit Conference of the Organization of African Unity in Accra on October 21, 1965—just four months before his overthrow—is illuminating in demonstrating the threat that Nkrumah posed for the neo-colonialists. In Nkrumah's introduction to the speech (*Revolutionary Path*, p. 298), he states:

> As soon as the decision was taken to hold the 1965 OAU Summit Conference in Accra, enemies of the African Revolution set to work to try to prevent the conference taking place in Ghana. Imperialist and neo-colonialist agents did all they could to split the OAU, and whipped up vicious press campaigns. A deputation was sent to visit OAU States in an attempt to persuade them to boycott the conference if it was held in Accra. The excuse was made that Ghana was sheltering political refugees, and was assisting in the subversion of other African States. The governments of Ivory Coast, Upper Volta, Dahomey, Niger (the 'Entente' States), and Togo, used this excuse to declare that they would not attend the conference if it was held in Accra.

Nkrumah continues that "the feverish diplomatic maneuverings before the Accra Summit in 1965, was not between the people of Africa, but between Africa as a whole and imperialism and neocolonialism working through puppet, reactionary regimes representing a small minority of indigenous bourgeois elements" (p. 299). However, these maneuverings were not sufficient to stop this momentous Summit since not only African leaders, but also "representatives of liberation movements throughout Africa met in Accra at the time of the OAU Summit, and discussed common problems", p. 302). Still, the conference was disappointing because "although there were very useful discussions, no unified organization was established to combine strategy and tactics, and to organize the struggle as a whole" (p. 302). It was also a disappointment that the OAU failed "to set up a single African High Command, though a resolution was passed agreeing to the principle of co-ordination in the military field" (p. 302). More and more, the OAU was proving itself to be a bankrupt organization.

In this speech Nkrumah once again shows himself as African spokesman and as a world leader. At the Summit speech were the African presidents and prime ministers, including the recently elected Dawda Jawara, Prime Minister of the Gambia, and, most important for the longevity and the dissemination of Nkrumah's Pan-African ideas, "representatives of our courageous Freedom Fighters in the remaining territories of Africa still under the yoke of colonial rule" as observers (*Revolutionary Path*, p. 298), p. 303).

Nkrumah begins by reminding his audience of those still under colonial rule who are suffering and those heroes who are struggling to free their people in South Africa, Angola, Mozambique, Basutoland [Lesotho], Swaziland, Bechuanaland [Botswana], South West Africa [Namibia] and the so-called Portuguese and Spanish possessions in Africa. He also reminds his audience that their "mounting struggle for freedom and independence is also our struggle" (p. 303). Nkrumah goes on to "salute them" and asks that the audience "allow [him] to assure them in your name, that we stand by them; their struggle is our struggle, and we are determined that they shall soon come to share with us the benefits of freedom and independence, and the responsibilities of managing their own affairs in a united Africa" (p. 303).

Showing himself a world leader, Nkrumah goes on to state that while we address the devastation caused by the imperialist forces operating on our own land, we would be remiss if we did not too criticize these forces "which breed armed conflicts, civil strife and economic impoverishment on other continents" (p. 303). How could Africa be a "thriving continent in the midst of a world convulsed by armed conflicts, tormented by hunger and disease and continually menaced by imperialist intrigue and aggression" (p. 304)? The first such armed conflict that he mentions is the one that was raging in Vietnam; it "presents a grave peril to world peace". So, "we must find a way to end that conflict permanently, if the world is to live in peace" (p. 304). Next, he mentions the conflict between India and Pakistan over Kashmir, a conflict still unresolved today. Third, the arms war commands his attention: "We in Africa … demand the establishment of an Atom Free Zone; we demand the ultimate destruction of nuclear stock-piles wherever they may be and the banning of their manufacture" (p. 304).

On the OAU, Nkrumah states that despite all the resolutions and declarations, "Africa is still an impoverished continent, immobilized by the lack of political cohesion, harassed by imperialism and ransacked by neocolonialism" (p. 304–5). The OAU must devise an "effective political machinery" so that these resolutions and declarations can become "more than words on paper" (p. 304). The Southern Rhodesia problem is a case in point. Great Britain's lack of responsibility in resolving the crisis requires that Africa step forward with the solution. In fact, Nkrumah states that "in the event of the United Kingdom Government failing in its duty, I am sure that the member states of the OAU will take whatever steps are necessary in support of the four million Africans who form the majority in Southern Rhodesia" (p. 305). But how can the OAU step forward without an African High Command in place? Another problem is that of political refugees throughout Africa. This problem cannot be solved as long as Africa is not unified. Nkrumah's words are profound:

> As long as political boundaries persist in Africa, boundaries which we have inherited at independence and were drawn arbitrarily, with no heed to the ethnic, economic, and social realities of Africa, so long shall we be plagued by the political refugee problem. The political refugee problem is a social and political problem, and its only solution lies in an all-African Union Government within which our present boundaries will become links instead of barriers. (p. 306)

Another serious issue involves the disintegrating economies of Africa, for "everywhere in Africa, our economies are crumbling, our treasures are getting empty, we are becoming client [neo-colonial] States, none of us can stand alone" (p. 307). A Union Central Bank is critical.

The only way that Africa will win, he tells his fellow statesmen and fighters of liberation, is if the structure of the OAU is set up and set up immediately. There has to be "now a full-time body or Executive Council of the OAU to act as the Execution arm of the Assembly of the Heads of State and Government" (*RP*, p. 309). Also, there must be an election of "a Union President and a number of Union Vice-Presidents": the "General Secretariat of the OAU shall be the Secretariat of the Executive Council" (p. 309). If we are successful in making the OAU a real functioning body for Africa then "Africa shall be a bright star among the constellation of Nations" (p. 309).

The questions Nkrumah asks of his fellow and potential statesmen are summarized by the following: "Why is it that we are finding it difficult to take this decision in spite of so many resolutions, declarations and attempts?" (p. 308). At one point (p. 307), he answers: "It is courage that we lack, not wealth".

~ ~ ~ ~ ~

6

The *Daily Graphic*

Perhaps one of the best ways of gauging Nkrumah's practice and measuring the influence of his practice is by reviewing the articles which appeared in Ghana's principal newspaper, *The Daily Graphic*. Chronicling a four-month period just prior to his overthrow, November 1965 to February 1966, this review of *The Daily Graphic* provides a useful lens into the danger he represented to the colonialist and neo-colonialist forces in Africa. This short period represents the time during which Nkrumah is most clear on the machinations of capitalism in all of its forms and, therefore, on the necessity for armed struggle as the only means of incising it from the continent. It is the resorting to armed warfare which was most troubling for the enemy, for as the news articles document, Nkrumah was mobilizing African States and people en masse into a people's army. A people's army was the only remaining option, however, as the 1965 Rhodesian conflict illustrates.

Articles referred to in this evaluation may include statements by Nkrumah, a cabinet member, or an educator, but all represent the goals and aspirations of Nkrumah and his party, the Convention People's Party (CPP). These articles reflect Nkrumah's stature as a world statesman, covering such wide-ranging topics as the Rhodesia crisis, socialism, African unity, the OAU, colonialism and neo-colonialism, and world peace.

When British Premier Harold Wilson visited Ghana, the November 1, 1965 issue of *The Daily Graphic*'s front page headline was "UK's move is a betrayal of Africans". The article concerning the United Kingdom states: "Osagyefo the President told British Premier Harold Wilson in Accra yesterday that the proposed appointment of a Royal Commission to inquire into the best means of consulting the Rhodesian people on the proposed constitution was a betrayal of the four million unrepresented Africans in Rhodesia ... . Dr. Nkrumah was speaking to Premier Wilson when he made a brief stop-over at Accra Airport yesterday on his way back home from Salisbury where he and racist Premier Smith agreed on a proposal to set up a Royal Commission to sort out the tangled independence issue".

The problems of Rhodesia (now Zimbabwe) were ones that exemplified the many problems plaguing the whole of Africa, ones that a unified socialist government could solve, in Nkrumah's opinion. In fact, the crisis in Rhodesia afforded Nkrumah the opportunity to act decisively and forthrightly, as he felt he had not done on behalf of the Congo and Lumumba in 1960. Thus, he was determined to act promptly on behalf of a state that was being molded like putty by imperialist forces and shamefully neglected by institutions such as the OAU and the UN. Because this may have been "the straw that broke the camel's back" in regard to compelling the imperialist forces to overthrow Nkrumah, some time should be taken here to offer the background for this Rhodesian crisis.

Nkrumah kept a collection of work on the subject of "Rhodesia" which he intended to develop into a complete history. The collection of letters and papers was published posthumously by Panaf as *Rhodesia File* (1974), with the addition of a 'chronology' (pp. xi-xvi). As briefly laid out in this chronology, the background is as follows. Although in 1965 Rhodesia was still a settler colony, its history is not unlike that of many states in Africa: a history of theft, trickery, violence and domination. In 1888 the land belonged to the Matabele people. Chief Lo Bengula, tricked by the agents of Cecil Rhodes, relinquished all of the mineral rights of his kingdom. In 1889, a royal charter was granted to Rhodes' British South Africa Company, and the first European settlers come into Southern Rhodesia. In 1893 and again in 1895, the Matabele people rebelled, but they were defeated by the armed forces of the British South African Company. By 1904, there were over twelve thousand settlers in Southern Rhodesia. A referendum was held in 1922 for the European settlers, the only people who could vote. Settlers had to decide on whether or not to connect themselves with South Africa or to become self-governing. They voted for the latter. In 1923, there were 34, 000 settlers in Southern Rhodesia. The British Land Apportionment Act in 1930 established European economic control of Southern Rhodesia, granting 52% of fertile land to Europeans and 48% of largely infertile, overcrowded and over-farmed land to more than two million Africans.

With Southern Rhodesia still a British protectorate, the UN General Assembly requested that the UK secure the right to vote for all people of Southern Rhodesia, not just the European settlers. In April 1964, Ian Smith became prime minister of Rhodesia, vowing that there would not be African majority rule in Rhodesia in his lifetime. On October, 27, 1964, British Prime Minister Wilson warned Smith that "serious consequences" would follow any attempt to pass a unilateral declaration of independence (UDI). Wilson further stated that such an act would be regarded as treason. Nevertheless, on November 11, 1965, a UDI was issued by the Smith government. The consequences? Economic sanctions.

Although Nkrumah asked both Great Britain and the UN to "authorize the use of force to end rebellion", not merely economic sanctions, no such military action was taken. This lack of action was just what Nkrumah warned against. Africa, he preached again and again, must create its own African High Command, a military force directed by a centralized government acting on behalf of a united Africa. However, the fact of the non-existence of such a Command did not prevent Nkrumah from devising a military response to the Smith government's military act by creating a people's army. In fact, he saw this creation as a step toward building continental unity. It is another example of Nkrumah's creativity in building Pan-Africanism. Once again, the unwillingness of the African Heads of State to solve Africa's problems forces Nkrumah to begin to erect the structural apparatus that would facilitate continental unity, in this case, a continental, mobile people's army to go anywhere in Africa to fight against colonial and neo-colonial forces.

On Monday, November 8, 1965, on the front page of the *Daily Graphic* in bold print and in all capital letters, the type reads: "Osagyefo the President, Supreme Commander of the Ghana Armed Forces, has reminded officers and men of other ranks of the Ghana Armed Forces that they are citizens of Ghana and of Africa and that the Armed Forces they belong to is a People's Army. 'It is the army of the people and the nation. Your identity therefore with Ghana's revolution and Africa's revolution should remain unquestioned, ' he said". Later, in this speech before the Armed forces, Nkrumah states: "It is through such links between ourselves in Africa that we can forge that enduring sense of brotherhood and solidarity leading to the fulfillment of our cherished ambition, namely, the establishment of a Union Government for Africa".

Kwaw Ampah, Secretary-General of the Ghana Trades Union Congress (TUC), speaks on the relationship between socialism and education in the November 13, 1965 issue of *The Daily Graphic*: "On the mobilisation of the country's human resources, Mr. Ampah said: 'We must develop a socialist consciousness on a mass scale through the effective education of the rank and file of our membership.'"

In this same issue of *The Daily Graphic*, the Rhodesian issue arises again. On the second page, the top headline reads in all caps and bold: "Sékou Touré: We Are at War". In the article, the following statements appear: "President Sékou Touré of Guinea cabled all African Heads of State saying they must consider themselves in a state of war following the illegal declaration of independence by Rhodesia. According to Radio Conakry, the message said the African Heads must consider concrete measures, including 'collective military intervention in Rhodesia'". Touré's action, in fact, shows that he was in synch with Nkrumah on many issues regarding Africa, including the Rhodesian controversy. Together, they would encourage, entreat, pressure other African leaders to join them in their protest. This time, it is Touré who makes the public statement. On the front page of this same issue is the headline: "We Offer Troops": "Ghana has offered to place her troops at the disposal of either the United Nations, the Organisation of African Unity or Britain to restore law and order in Southern Rhodesia". Nkrumah, of course, was always willing to set the example for the rest of Africa—and the world. More, he was readying the continent for unity. Once again he demonstrates that Africa can build unity from the top to the bottom or from the bottom to the top (from its component parts). Africa does not have to wait on African leaders.

Two days later, in the Monday, November 15, 1965 issue of the newspaper, the headlines read, 'Let Africa Send Troops Now': "Four African Heads of State have called on African states to set up a liberation committee for Rhodesia immediately and to send military contingents to the country. The recommendation was in a communiqué issued in Nonakchott, Mauritania, after a private meeting between Presidents Leopold Senghor of Senegal, Modibo Keita of Mali, Sékou Touré of Guinea and Moktar Auld Daddah of Mauritania ... . Ghana and Ethiopia have already offered to place their troops at the disposal of either the OAU or the United Nations to restore law and order in Rhodesia". Nkrumah's example had paid off. On pages 8–9 of the November 16, 1965 *Daily Graphic*, the headline reads, "Our Women Protest ... against Ian Smith". Some of the text of the article reads: "Members of the National Council of Ghana Women yesterday held a big demonstration in Accra against the unilateral declaration of independence in Rhodesia by the racist Ian Smith ... . In a protest note, the executives of the council called on all women of Africa to rally around their leaders in their efforts to crush the illegal and rebellious declaration of independence by the racist minority government of Southern Rhodesia". In addition to building African unity by erecting structures and institutions, unity can be forged by enlisting key sectors of the African population. On this occasion, it is the woman's sector that can band together without the permission of the leaders. This note does not ask the African leadership to allow the women in its various states to rally. The note goes out to "all women of Africa".

The next headline demonstrates that Ghana is prepared to back its theory with practice. The front page story on Thursday, November 18, 1965, No. 4709 is "15, 000 Brigadiers Ready to Fight": "Fifteen thousand members of Ghana's Workers Brigade, including 3,000 women, have volunteered to fight in Southern Rhodesia to help establish majority rule in that African country". By that Saturday, November 20, 1965, No. 4711, the front page article was "Union Government Is the Answer—Kwame": "Osagyefo the President said in Accra yesterday that recent events in Southern Rhodesia had more than ever made it imperative for African states to unite politically. If Africa were so united, the white settler rebels in Southern Rhodesia would not have dared to declare the territory unilaterally independent". Once again, Nkrumah extols the benefits of unity.

No political, continental unity is possible without there first being ideological unity. Thus, on November 25, 1965, the page 11 headline is "Study the Party ideology": "Alhaji M.B. Sulemana, Ashanti Region Party secretary, has called on Party officials in Ashanti to study carefully the Party's socialist ideology based on 'Nkrumaism' and to help educate the masses on the socialist aspirations of the Party". Four days later, No. 4718 *Daily Graphic* reads, "Kwame: Let's Plan on continental basis": "Dr Nkrumah said at the dinner [6th anniversary dinner of the Ghana Academy of Sciences] that the planning for the scientific utilisation of Africa's natural resources on a continental scale would accelerate Africa's development far beyond what any individual African state could ever hope to achieve in isolation".

Nkrumah was not going to relent. In the Tuesday, November 30, 1965, No. 4719 issue of *Daily Graphic*, a bold front page headline reads: "The People answer the Leader's call: Thousands Join Volunteer Force": including a 50-year old man, "large crowds of people thronged various enlistment centres throughout the country yesterday to join the People's Militia being raised by Ghana to help liberate the four million oppressed Africans in Southern Rhodesia". On page six of the same issue appears the following headline: "Big Demand for Books on Socialism": "The annual report of the Ghana Library Board for 1963/64 indicates that there was a sharp increase in the demand for literature on the theory and practice of socialism".

Nkrumah's persistence—and the Ghana people's example—pays off, not only in regard to military action to free Rhodesia, but also in regard to a permanent continental army. On December 4, 1965, No. 4723, front page headlines read: "Selassie opens OAU talks and declares: Let's Unite and Free Rhodesia". Also on this page appears the following headline: "Support Kwame". The first sentence of this article states: "A Kenya Member of Parliament, Mr. J.D. Kali, has called on the Kenya Government to support Osagyefo's constant call for the setting up of an African High Command". But, according to Nkrumah, "practice without theory is blind; theory without practice is empty" (*Consciencism*, p. 78). Africans must know the reason for their actions, and they must act in unison. They cannot do either without study. On December 6, 1965 The *Daily Graphic* reported: "Mr J.A.K. Dougan, senior lecturer at Kwame Nkrumah Ideological Institute, Winneba, has called on teachers to study the party's ideology well so as to be able to impart it to the youth" (p. 10). The next day's headline reads: "Help Achieve Socialism": "Mr. P. K. Kumadey, general secretary of the Industrial, Commercial and Catering Trades Union of the Trades Union Congress (TUC), has called on workers in the country to be dedicated to the tasks ahead and to co-ordinate their efforts towards the achievement of the socialist objectives of the Party" (p.6). In this same issue the headline reads "Close Your Ranks—Fighters Urged": "Representatives of African liberation movements based in Ghana have called on all freedom fighters to close their ranks, and support the freedom struggle in Southern Rhodesia" (p. 10). While some cabinet members and others were aware that "representatives of African liberation movements" were based in Ghana, engaged in Nkrumaist ideological training, now the whole world knew that these young revolutionaries from South Africa, Rhodesia, Angola, the Gambia, and other countries were not only studying in Ghana, but also willing to demonstrate their commitment to Africa by helping to liberate Rhodesia. These representatives issued the preceding statement in Accra and continued by stating:

> It is the historic task of the liberation forces in Africa, Asia, and Latin America as well as progressive forces of the world to mobilise the people towards the total defeat of the war mongering imperialism, that threatens the very existence of mankind. In this big plot, the Verwoerds, Ian Smiths, Salazars, and Francos are but catalysts.

Nkrumah called upon the workers of Africa to do, like the women of Africa, what their leaders refused to do: unite. To celebrate the fourth anniversary of the independence of Tanzania, the Secretary-General of the All-African Trades Union Federation, Mr. J. K. Tettegah, sent a message to the General-Secretary of the National Union of Tanzania Workers. This appears in an article entitled "Our Weapon Is Unity" in the Thursday, December 9, 1965 issue of *Daily Graphic*, p. 3. In the message, Tettegah states that "the unity of workers of Africa is a powerful weapon for opposing the onslaught of both the old and new colonialists" and he "congratulated the national union of Tanzanian Workers for their wonderful contribution in the fight to eliminate all traces of imperialism from the African Labour Movement and to establish a genuinely independent Pan-African Labour Organisation".

Nkrumah must show the African world and the rest of the world that he, and other progressive forces like him, are first capable of acting in unity on behalf of Africa and second determined to achieve Pan-Africanism. To do so, they could not afford to "lose" on the question of Rhodesia. They had to do everything in their power to return Rhodesia to its people. Doing so would encourage others to join in the struggle to achieve Pan-Africanism. On Wednesday, December 15, 1965, No. 4732, the front page bold headlines read: "Rhodesia—Big Protest Against [B.P.], Total". The article begins: "Thousands of people, carrying placards, yesterday held a mammoth demonstration in Accra in protest against British Petroleum and TOTAL, a French oil company, for shipping oil to Ian Smith's white minority regime in Southern Rhodesia in defiance of UN oil embargo on Rhodesia". Other front page articles on Rhodesia appear in the *Daily Graphic*'s next two issues, December 16, 1965 (No. 4733) and December 17, 1965 (No. 4734). In the December 16th paper appears the following statement: "President Sékou Touré of Guinea broke off diplomatic relations in Britain yesterday". In the December 17th issue, it is revealed that Ghana too broke off "diplomatic relations with Britain over the British Government's refusal to quell the Southern Rhodesia rebellion". Also in this issue, Nkrumah "called on all African states to take a definite stand on the Rhodesian crisis … . our policy in Africa has been based on the fundamental necessity to establish an all-African approach to the problems of the African continent. 'This is why I have been advocating the establishment of a Continental Union Government of Africa all these years', he said". This December 17th issue is also important because of another article featuring a speech of Nkrumah on re-groupings: "In the interest of African Unity, there should be no political or economic re-grouping or blocs in Africa in alliance with an ex-colonial power or any foreign power for that matter". Nkrumah continued by suggesting "that the Organisation of African Unity should create and develop essential machinery for African Unity" such as "an African High Command which can defend our continent and ensure the security of the member states". He ends his speech by saying that "the Southern Rhodesian crisis has once again exposed the weakness of the Organisation of African Unity". Nkrumah is fed up with the OAU. It is useless, a paper tiger, in the fight against the colonial and neo-colonial forces in Africa.

On Saturday, December 18, 1965, No. 4735, the front page headline reads: Two more break with U.K". Just as had Ghana and Guinea, the two countries, United Arab Republic and Congo (Brazzaville), break off diplomatic relations over "the Southern Rhodesian issue". On Monday, December 20, 1965, No. 4736, the *Daily Graphic* reports: "Algeria yesterday joined Ghana and seven other countries in severing diplomatic relations with Britain over the explosive Southern Rhodesian issue. The other seven countries are Guinea, Mali, Tanzania, the United Arab Republic, Congo (Brazzaville), Mauritania, and Sudan".

The youth of Africa is the focus of an article in the *Daily Graphic* on Tuesday, December 21, 1965, page 10, No. 4737. Headlined "Help Achieve Union Govt, Youth Told", the article states, "Stressing on the need for the exchange of students between African States, Mr Dei-Anang [Head of the African Affairs Secretariat] said it would ensure brotherly understanding among the youth of Africa by giving them greater responsibility to think in terms of the continent as a whole".

Between November and December 1965, as documented in the *Daily Graphic,* Nkrumah appealed to the three most powerful sectors of the African population: first, African women, then African workers, and finally the African youth. In fact, the youth are the most powerful of all of these sectors, for they serve as the spark which inflames the rest of the population. Women are the most oppressed sector of the African population, and once politically educated and organized they will be determined to throw off their shackles. Workers comprise the essential part of the productive forces in society; they must understand that they are being exploited and that without them the society cannot function. With African youth, women, and workers struggling for the African Revolution, the people of Africa would win, regardless of the sentiments of the African leadership and regardless of the machinations of the capitalist forces. This fact Nkrumah knew; the imperialists were also well aware of this fact since Nkrumah was allowed only two more months in power.

A powerful headline appears in the Friday, December 24, 1965, No. 4740, issue of the *Daily Graphic*: "AATUF Pledges support to Vietnamese". This article documents Nkrumah's willingness to go beyond the borders of Africa. Injustice —in the form of neo- colonialism—everywhere must be thwarted. To do so, workers of the world, in the West as well as in neo-colonies, must rise up. The Secretary General of the All-African Trade Union Federation, J. K. Tettegah, sends a message addressed to "the forces of the National Liberation Front of South Viet Nam on the occasion of the fifth anniversary" in which he states:

> We have consistently stood by the side of the people of South Viet Nam against the forces of U.S. imperialism whose deliberate and wicked acts against the democratic and peace-loving peoples all over the world is causing great uneasiness to world peace.
>
> We renounce all the criminal activities of the U.S. imperialism and call upon workers throughout the world, including those in the U.S., to increase their protest and condemnation of U.S. aggression against the people of South Viet Nam.

The same communiqué also called on the U.S. to withdraw troops and war equipment from the whole of South East Asia to enable peace to be restored.

At the end of 1965, Nkrumah was still entreating African people to unify. And, he was more consistently connecting world justice to African unity. The latter, he believed, would help in the struggle to achieve the former. On Tuesday, December 28, 1965, No. 4741, the headline on the front page is "Africa Must Move in Unity":

> Osagyefo the President declared yesterday that Africa of tomorrow must be a continent effectively united for progress and happiness and completely free from alien domination. He said the continent must also play its full part in establishing a new world order of peace,

harmony and mutual understanding. Without this, Dr. Nkrumah pointed out, all our endeavours for progress in Africa are in danger.

Education in the service of a new African Personality is the focus of the front page article in the December 30, 1965 newspaper. The headline reads "EDUCATION It Must Rescue the People". Dr. N. G. Bakhoom, principal of the University College of Science and Education, Cape Coast, states: "Education in Africa should firstly help rescue the people from the degenerating effect of "colonial mentality" and regenerate in them the African personality … . It is only socialist countries, like Ghana, that could grapple with the situation". What will a socialist Africa mean to African people throughout the world? Instead of acting as a subjugated people, ashamed of their skin color, history, and culture, they will be born again. A socialist Africa will "regenerate in them the African Personality".

As is evidenced by the documented examples appearing in the early December 1965 *Daily Graphic*, the struggle against imperialism, i.e. the Rhodesia struggle, the struggle for the unity of Africa, and the struggle to achieve a socialist economic system, are connected. They are the essential obstacles that must be overcome in the struggle for Pan-Africanism.

On January 3, 1966 the *Daily Graphic* reports on page five a speech made by S. G. Ikoku, senior lecturer at the Kwame Nkrumah Ideological Institute: "African unity is needed for speeding up the liberation struggle in the remaining colonial territories in Africa, including South Africa … . African unity is needed to cover the flanks of the drive to national reconstruction on socialist lines". Nkrumah was convinced that the practical benefits which will accrue from African unity are countless. Already mentioned is the restoration of the African Personality. It will be as if a gigantic weight has been lifted from Africa's, and her people's, shoulders.

"World Freedom Is Our Hope" heads an article on the last page of the January 4, 1966 issue: "Mr. Kwaw Ampah, Secretary-General of the Ghana Trade Union Congress, has said that the success of the world revolutionary movements depended, to a great extent, on the national liberation movements of Africa, Asia and Latin America". On January 12, 1966, a page three headline reads: "Nkrumaism Is to Stay": "'The Nkrumaist' has said that Nkrumaism has provided the formula and basic conditions necessary for the creation of a new Africa—free and united—as a precondition for the rapid development of the entire continent". The page three headline of the January 13, 1966 issue reads: "America Accused": "North Viet Nam has denounced the 'feverish efforts' of the United States to intensify the 'war of extermination' in Viet Nam".

The influence that Nkrumah's Pan-African and socialist policies had on the world is reflected in the January 15, 1966, No. 4757 issue of the *Daily*

Graphic. In one article, entitled 'Ghana Is On the Forefront, ' Premier Lee Kuan Yew of Singapore, on a visit to Ghana, describes "Ghana as a well-known country being in the forefront of the pioneering work in the cause of African freedom. He said all other African countries, whose independence followed Ghana's, take inspiration from and try to follow the pace she had set for African development". On page three of that same issue appears the headline, "Let's Help Free All Peoples": the article reports that "the Tri-Continental Solidarity Conference has called for aid, including arms and munitions for liberation movements fighting to free their peoples from colonial domination". Most interestingly, "the conference also called for a world campaign of economic aid for the National Liberation Front of South Viet Nam and the 'mobilisation' of the people of the United States against the Viet Nam war … . Another resolution supported the Afro-American Civil Rights Movement in America describing it as a "contribution to the general struggle of the peoples against imperialism".

The last page of the *Daily Graphic* for January 22, 1966 is significant in revealing Nkrumah's determination to rid the world of capitalism. In an article entitled "Fight Against Evil Forces", the following statement appears: "The people of Ghana will never rest until they have helped to create conditions in the world which will make the systems of imperialism, colonialism and neo-colonialism impossible". This statement was made by Nkrumah at a state-house dinner held on behalf of Cypress President Archbishop Makarios: "President Nkrumah assured his guest that the people of Ghana were not only against these systems in their own country but in any part of the world where they operate". The front page headline on January 24, 1966, No. 4764, one month before Nkrumah is overthrown, reads: "Osagyefo Appeals to World Powers": "President Nkrumah has called on world powers to invest their enormous capital funds now being wasted on war preparations on projects like the Volta hydro-electric scheme for the benefit of mankind. He said that would in fact eliminate the ever-widening gap between the developed and the developing nations".

On the front page of the February 1, 1966, No. 4771, *Daily Graphic* the headline reads, "HO: Kwame, Come to Hanoi". The article states that "Dr. Nkrumah has accepted an invitation from President Ho Chi Minh of North Viet Nam to visit Hanoi. This will be Ho's second invitation to Osagyefo the President to visit his country". The article continues: "Commenting on the first invitation from President Ho to Dr Nkrumah, the world press hailed it as the brightest hope of bringing a lasting settlement to the Viet Nam war. The London *Times* … recalled Dr. Nkrumah's efforts to bring peace in Viet Nam and said: 'In any event interest in the search for negotiations on Viet Nam appeared to be shifting from London ostensibly to Accra'".

Also in this issue appears the article, "Senegal to Go Socialist": "President Leopold Senghor of Senegal has said that his Government and Party had chosen socialism to bring Senegal to economic and cultural independence" (p. 2). On February 2, 1966, the *Daily Graphic*, p. 7 headline reads: 'Masses Are Final Arbiter': "Let us remember always that in the final analysis, the masses are the final arbiter. They will always choose freedom and justice, as against oppression and corruption. They will always find a way to give expression to their will as against neo-colonialism and against the betrayal of the people by the armed forces". On the front page of the February 15, 1966 issue, the headline reads: "Govt Protests to U.S.": "The Ghana Government has sent a protest to the United States Government against the decision of the US Government to allow the rebel Ian Smith regime to open an information centre in Washington".

Appearing just 4 months before his government was toppled, what do the headlines in *The Daily Graphic* tell us about Nkrumah's commitment to Pan-Africanism and worldwide socialism?

- That a people's army is not only possible to organize, but also that one is already organized.
- That people were encouraged to, and actually did, engage in the study of socialism.
- That heads of state, such as Selassie and Senghor, were advocating African unity.
- That freedom fighters from throughout Africa were living and studying in Ghana.
- That African working class people were encouraged to unite under a "Pan African Labour Organisation".
- That the OAU was, after only two years of existence, a bankrupt organization.
- That youth are the spark of Revolution and, thus, must be organized.
- That Nkrumah (and Ghana) was prepared to have a military force to address the world's problems, not just those of Africa.
- That a new world order of peace, harmony, and mutual respect and understanding must be established.
- That political education is essential for liberation.
- That world leaders, like that of Singapore, recognized the contribution of Nkrumah.
- That the people of Ghana, under Nkrumah's leadership, "will never rest until they have helped to create conditions in the world which will make the systems of imperialism, colonialism and neo-colonialism impossible".
- That Nkrumah had indeed been invited, and had accepted the invitation, to go to Viet Nam to broker a peace agreement between that nation and its enemy, the United States of America.

- That Nkrumah never failed to remind Ghana, Africa and the world that "the masses were the makers of history".

Then, in the Friday, February 25, 1966, No. 4792, issue of the *Daily Graphic*, the front page headline, bold and in all capital letters, reads: "Army Takes Over Government". The article states that "the Ghana Armed Forces in co-operation with the Police, took over the Government of the country yesterday following an early morning coup. A radio announcement said that the coup was led by Col. E. K. Kotoka of the 2nd Infantry Brigade."

7

Conclusion

The question for those struggling today for the African Revolution is "Have the objective and subjective material conditions in the world changed so significantly as to require a change in the focus of the African Revolution?" In other words, are Nkrumah's theory and practice of the African Revolution still viable today? Using the same five indicators that have been used throughout this study—identity, enemy, objective, strategy, and tactics—we can arrive at an answer. The identity question is the same: people of African descent no matter where they were born or happen to live are Africans. The enemy is the same: capitalism in all of its forms. The objective, therefore, must be the same: Pan-Africanism (the liberation and unification of Africa under a socialist economic system). The strategy of organizing to defeat the enemy is still the key. And, finally, the tactic—armed struggle—is clearly necessary to defeat the enemy.

What has changed substantially since Nkrumah's death is the degree of the problem. The suffering of African people is worse today than it was in the 1970s. Capitalism—in all its guises—is more organized, global, vicious and dangerous than ever before. Its counterpart, the socialist world, has shrunk significantly. Unlike in 1966, there is no Soviet Union and socialist hopes for Viet Nam have been dashed in light of its recent efforts to adopt capitalist economic measures. (There is hope, however, in the "winds of change" emanating from Central and South America, even though socialist Cuba's longevity is now being questioned in the wake of Castro's illness.)

Worse, China seems poised to become the new neo-colonialist power in Africa! Too, where the struggle for an African Union remains, it is devoid of any mention of socialism. Also, unlike in Nkrumah's day, there is no thriving Black Power Movement, making demands for justice within capitalist territories. So, not only must today's African Revolutionaries stay the course, but also, they must work more diligently and expeditiously than ever before!

The State of Africa: Worse Today than in Nkrumah's Day

On October 9, 2006, 'Morning Edition' of National Public Radio aired a five-part series entitled "Africa's Lagging Development"[1]. The opening statement was "China, India and parts of Latin America have made progress recently in fighting poverty, disease and illiteracy, but progress in sub-Saharan Africa has been slow and, at times, nonexistent. Over the last two decades, the number of Africans living in extreme poverty has nearly doubled". The examples of this poverty are numerous, including: the lack of access to clean water, the lack of basic health care and primary education; an increase in slums, "growing more than twice as fast as slums anywhere else in the world"; a lack of sufficient food to feed its own people; illnesses/diseases such as HIV/AIDS, and others such as Ebola, Marburg, and "sleeping sickness, river blindness, yellow fever, cholera, bilharzias, tick bite fever, [and] malaria—diseases unheard of in the developed world"[2]; and US and European agricultural subsidies that undercut African farmers.[3] The conclusion drawn is that "the continent risks being left behind even by the rest of the Third World"[4]!

A report by the United Nations Economic Commission for Africa, "*Economic Report on Africa 2005* is just as glum. It is sufficient to highlight ten of the problems identified in the report:

[1] "Empirical evidence suggests that high inequality substantially reduces the rate at which growth is transformed into poverty reduction" [p. 53]

[2] [Although there is evidence of recent strong growth rates of GDP,] "growth has not been accompanied by substantial gains in job creation, which raises serious concerns about the continent's ability to achieve meaningful poverty reduction" [p. 49].

[3] Countries that are still in conflict face even bigger challenges with regard to development, employment creation and poverty reduction. Insecurity in those countries also threatens the economic activity and political stability in neighbouring countries and the region. [p. 56]

[4] "In 2005 … inflation increased in 33 out of 51 countries, including eight of the 13 oil-producing countries: Cameroon, Chad, Côte d'Ivoire, Egypt, Equatorial Guinea, Libya, Nigeria, and Sudan. [p. 43]

[5] Sub-Saharan Africa (SSA) "is the only region in the developing world where the poverty headcount has increased since 1980". In the 2005 *Human Development Report*, 30 of the 32 countries classified in the "low human development" category … are from SSA" [p. 50].

[6] " … many countries are experiencing worsening social conditions" [p. 51].

[7] In addition, "African countries [face] pervasive gender inequality in basic rights, access to productive resources and economic opportunities, and lack of political voice" [p. 53].

[8] "Higher world interest rates will raise the cost of external debt service for African countries, which will dampen growth" [p. 58].

[9] "Agricultural production is expected to be severely affected by climatic shocks, including droughts [especially in Burundi, Rwanda, and Kenya], floods, and desertification in the Sahel". [p. 58]

[10] "Economic growth in many countries will be compromised by the increasing spread of the HIV/AIDS pandemic, which undermines labour supply and labour productivity". [p. 58]

Add to the negative detail of that report a discussion aired on National Public Radio's "Marketplace" on June 13, 2007 addressing the question, "Can a Marshall Plan Work for Africa?". Columbia University's Dean of the Graduate School of Business responded: "Africa is poorer today than twenty years ago". In fact, according to a *New York Times Book Review* article, 'The Least Among Us', seventy per cent of the world's poor live in Africa (Sunday, July 1, 2007).

Conclusion? The suffering of African people is worse today than it was in Nkrumah's day.

What is occasionally implicit but not largely an overt part of the public, in particular the published, discussion about Africa's mal-development and poverty is the role of imperialism. In central Africa alone, over four million people have died in a war over coltan, the heat-resistant mineral used in cell phones, laptops, and other high-tech electronics that are mostly used in the West. (Cabot Inc. of the US is one of the three world purchasers of coltan.) A staggering eighty percent of coltan comes from the Democratic Republic of Congo, a country that has seen so much death and poverty and displacement in the last decade because of its mineral resources. Not the least of the new imperialists exploiting these resources is China (*Nerve*, 2007, p. 45).

China and the Threat of the Re-Colonization of Africa

Walter Rodney, in his classic work, *How Europe Underdeveloped Africa*, makes two important statements. First, that "development and underdevelopment are not only comparative terms, but that they also have a dialectical relationship one to the other: that is to say, the two help produce each other by interaction" (Rodney, p. 75). Second, that at the time of the slave trade "a single African state could not emancipate itself from European control. The small size of African states and the numerous political divisions made it so much easier for Europe to make the decisions as to Africa's role in world population and trade" (Rodney, Chapter 3). In the fifteenth century, during the bustling slave trade period, Africa was dependent on what Europe wanted to buy and sell. Today, still weak, divided and powerless (even more powerless than in Nkrumah's day), Africa is dependent on what stronger, richer nations want to buy and sell.

China's growing interest and involvement in Africa must be seen in this context. China is the third largest investor in Africa. The state-owned Chinese energy company, CNOOC Ltd. has a presence in oil-rich African countries, including Nigeria and the Sudan. According to ISN Security Watch, in its article by Simon Roughneen on May 15, 2006, "China now gets 30 per cent of its oil from Africa, mainly from the Sudan, Angola, and Congo-Brazzaville. [Moreover,] China interests in this sector seem set to grow". Also, according to ISN, "China is helping Ethiopia build the continent's biggest dam; it will launch a communication satellite for Nigeria in 2007; and is introducing a new anti-malaria drug in Uganda. China's state radio station has opened a station in Kenya, delivering 19 hours of broadcasting every day. In 2003, 550 Chinese troops joined a UN peacekeeping operation in Liberia" (*ibid.*).

According to the "Forum on China-Africa Cooperation: Beijing Action Plan (2007–2009) issued on November 16, 2006, after the 3–5 November 2006 Beijing Summit and the Third Ministerial Conference of the Forum on China-Africa Cooperation (FOCAC) held in Beijing, China, heads of state, government and delegation as well as ministers of foreign affairs and ministers in charge of economic cooperation from China and 48 African countries attended the Summit and Conference. According to the action plan, China and Africa "resolved to accomplish" many acts, most very beneficial to China, including the following :

[3.1.2] ... to intensify their exchanges and cooperation in farming, animal husbandry, irrigation, fishery, agricultural machinery, processing of agricultural produce, sanitary and phytosanitary measures, food safety and epidemic control, and actively explore new forms and ways of agricultural cooperation.

[3.2.2] ... to create an enabling environment for investment cooperation and protect the lawful rights and interests of investors from both sides.

[3.3] ... to further open up its market to Africa, increase from 190 to over 440 the number of export items to China eligible for zero-tariff treatment from the least developed countries in Africa having diplomatic relations with China.

[3.4.2] ... to encourage its [China's] financial institutions to set up more branches in Africa.

[3.5.1] ... to keep infrastructure building, particularly transportation, telecommunications, water conservancy and power generation facilities, as a key area of cooperation.

[3.6.1] ... to give encouragement and support to their enterprises in conducting, under the principle of reciprocity, mutual benefit and common development, joint exploration and rational exploitation of energy and other resources through diversified forms of cooperation.

CONCLUSION 159

[3.6.2] ... [to protect] the local environment and promote sustainable social and economic development in the local areas.

[3.7.2] ... to step up scientific and technological cooperation in areas of common interest including agricultural bio-technology, solar energy utilization, geological survey, mining and development of new medicine.

[3.7.4] ... to encourage their aviation and shipping companies to establish more direct air and shipping links between China and Africa.

[4.6] ... to strengthen counter-terrorism cooperation with African countries.

[5.1.2] ... [to] continue to provide development assistance to African countries to the best of its ability and by 2009 double the size of its assistance to African countries in 2006.

[5.4.4] ... to increase the number of Chinese government scholarships to African students from the current 2, 000 per year to 4, 000 per year by 2009.

[5.4.4] ... to establish Confucius Institutes in African countries to meet their needs in the teaching of the Chinese language and encourage the teaching of African languages in relevant Chinese universities and colleges.

[5.5.3] ... to assist African countries in building 30 hospitals and provide RMB300 million of grant for providing anti-malaria drugs to African countries and building 30 demonstration centers for prevention and treatment of malaria in the next three years.

[5.7.2] ... to extend ADS [China's Approved Destination Status] to nine [additional] African countries including Algeria, Cape Verde, Cameroon, Gabon, Rwanda, Mali, Mozambique, Benin and Nigeria, [so that] there are now 26 ADS countries in Africa.

[5.9.3] ... to gradually expand the "Chinese Young Volunteers Serving Africa" program.

Two recent critics of China's presence in Africa are the Council on Foreign Relations (CFR, New York) and National Public Radio (NPR, Washington DC). While the criticism in fact expresses the regret that the US has for not "besting" China in its "trade" with African nations, it is to the point here nevertheless. In its publication on China in January 12, 2006, the CFR states that "by 2045, China is projected to depend on imported oil for 45 percent of its energy needs"[8]. "The country needs to lock in supplies from relatively low-cost African or Middle Eastern sources, experts say. But after the terrorist attacks of September 11, 2001, and the subsequent upheaval throughout the Middle East, China is actively trying to diversify its supply lines away from Middle Eastern crude. Experts say China has adopted an aid-for-oil strategy that has resulted in increasing supplies of oil from African countries" (*ibid.*). According to CFR, there is a link between oil production in Africa and China's arms sales to African countries: "Selling arms to African countries helps China cement relationships with African leaders and helps offset the costs of buying oil from them" (*ibid.*). In some African countries, such as Equatorial Guinea, China has provided "military training and Chinese specialists in heavy military equipment to the leaders of the tiny West African nation" (*ibid.*). On the other hand, CFR admits that "the roads, bridges, and dams built by Chinese firms are low cost, good quality, and completed in a fraction of the time such projects usually take in Africa" (*ibid.*). China has also "undertaken or contributed to construction projects in Ethiopia, Tanzania, Zambia, ... It has cancelled $10 billion in bilateral debt from African countries, sends doctors to treat Africans across the continent, and hosts thousands of African workers and students in Chinese universities and training centers" (*ibid.*).

These contributions, however, must be seen from the perspective of the masses of African people. Do these "benefits" outweigh the exploitive practices of China in Africa? Just as during the first colonial era, it seems as if China is benefiting twofold: exploiting the natural resources of Africa and using Africa as a dumping ground for its low-cost consumer goods. On "Morning Edition" on National Public Radio, November 3, 2006, one segment addressed Chinese goods in Africa: "Cheaper Chinese textiles have muscled in on what used to be a flourishing local industry". Some Africans even complain that the Chinese fabric is of poorer quality than the homemade fabric.

Finally, according to Economy and Monaghan (2006), "Anecdotal evidence also suggests simmering grass roots resentment of the growing Chinese presence" in Africa: "Legal and illegal Chinese immigrants are moving to Africa by the tens and sometimes hundreds of thousands. Chinese laborers are brought in to work in extractive industries, construction and manufacturing projects fueling charges that Chinese investors are taking rather than creating jobs" (*ibid.*). "In Angola, a Chinese $2 billion dollar credit line is contingent on Chinese firms getting 70% of the contracts. In South Africa, where an estimated one hundred to two hundred thousand Chinese dominate the retail and wholesale clothing industry, unions have pressed Pretoria to put quotas on Chinese apparel and textiles imports to protect local industry and jobs" (*ibid.*).

China's presence in Africa is little different from the dialectical relationship that existed between the West and Africa in the fifteenth century. China's presence in a weak and balkanized Africa presents a clear threat of re-colonization. No country, however well-intended, can be in a relationship of power to another country's powerlessness without at some point that relationship metamorphosing into one of dominant and subordinate, superior and inferior, colonizer and colonized. And when the skin color of the dominant power is different from that of those who are dominated then racism is the offspring.

Capitalism today has become global: national borders have disappeared and governments intent on exploitation and capitalist profit-making are endemic around the world. China, though it is still called a socialist country, relates to Africa as any capitalist, neo-colonialist country would and, therefore, must be viewed in the same way.

What is to be done?

There seem two courses that might be followed: that Africa remains on a path of self-destruction, allowing itself to succumb again to the continuing forces of colonialist-style exploitation, domination and ruination; or that the microstates of Africa come together to form a vast continental power that uses its great wealth to promote the health, welfare and development of its people. In keeping with what is in the best interest of African people, and in keeping with the traditional African principles of humanism, collectivism, and egalitarianism, there is only one solution: A Union of Socialist African States. Nkrumah's vision for the African Revolution—his objective of African continental unity and genuine world socialism—must not be altered or forgotten.

"All people of African descent are Africans and belong to the African nation", Nkrumah wrote in 1970 (*Class Struggle in Africa*, p. 87fn). This work has urged that, long after the death of the visionary architect of Pan-Africanism and worldwide socialism, Kwame Nkrumah still offers the only truly viable plan of action for all people of African descent, no matter where they live in the world. To achieve the noble objectives of Pan Africanism, Nkrumah's theory and practice are n eeded now more than ever before.

~ ~ ~ ~ ~

Notes

1 http://www.npr.org/templates/story/story.php?storyId=6213086
2 http://www.npr.org/templates/story/story.php?storyId=6247813
3 http://www.npr.org/templates/story/story.php?storyId=6256274
4 http://www.npr.org/templates/story/story.php?storyId=6213086
5 http://www.uneca.org/eca_resources/publications/books/era2006/index.htm
6 http://www.isn.ethz.ch/news/sw/details_print.cfm?id=15837
7 http://www.fmprc.gov.cn/zflt/eng/zxxx/t280369.htm
8 http://www.nytimes.com/cfr/international/slot2_011806.html. Esther Pan, 'Q and A: China, Africa and Oil'.

1/2   Kwame Nkrumah at the African Freedom Fighters' Conference, June 1962

3   Nkrumah opens the All-African People's Conference in Accra, December 1958

4   Nkrumah speaks at the All-African People's Conference on December 8, 1958

PHOTOGRAPHS 165

5   Nkrumah with Emperor Haile Selassie c. 1960

6   Nkrumah and W.E.B. DuBois c. 1960

7   Nkrumah and Modibo Keita of Mali at the signing of the Ghana-Guinea-Mali pact, April 1961

8   Nkrumah with Gamal Nasser, Sékou Touré and Modibo Keita at the Casablanca Conference, January 1961

9   Nkrumah with Sékou Touré in Conakry, Guinea

10   Nkrumah with Fidel Castro

11   Nkrumah opens the Conference of Pan-African Journalists, November 1963

12   Osagyefo Dr. Kwame Nkrumah

13   Nkrumah with Mohammed Ali (nd)

14   Nkrumah with Chou En-Lai, 1964

15   Nkrumah with Gamal Nasser at the OAU meeting of African Heads of State in Cairo, July 1964

PHOTOGRAPHS 171

16   Nkrumah with Chairman Mao Tse Tung (nd)

17   Nkrumah with Nehru (nd)

18   Kwame Nkrumah Prime Minister of Ghana

19   The casket of Nkrumah at his funeral, May 1972

Bibliography

BOOKS and PAMPHLETS by Kwame Nkrumah

Axioms of Kwame Nkrumah. Panaf Books, 1967.
Class Struggle in Africa. Panaf, 1970.
Consciencism: Philosophy and Ideology for Decolonization. Panaf, 1964.
Dark Days in Ghana (1968) Panaf.
Ghana: Autobiography (1957 Panaf.
Handbook of Revolutionary Warfare: A Guide to the Armed Phase of the African Revolution. Panaf, 1968.
"Message to the Black People of Britain" (reprinted in *The Struggle Continues* (1973) and in *Revolutionary Path* (1973).
Neo-Colonialism: The Last Stage of Imperialism. Panaf, 1965.
Revolutionary Path. Panaf, 1973.
"The Spectre of Black Power" (reprinted in *The Struggle Continues* (1973) and in *Revolutionary Path* (1973).
The Struggle Continues. Panaf, 1968. Collection of Nkrumah pamphlets:
    What I Mean by Positive Action
    The Spectre of Black Power
    The Struggle Continues
    Ghana: The Way Out
    The Big Lie; Two Myths.
Towards Colonial Freedom: Africa in the Struggle Against World Imperialism. Panaf, 1962.

LETTERS

Kwame Nkrumah Letters. June Milne Collection, Box 154. Moorland-Spingarn Research Center. Howard University. Washington, DC.

SPEECHES by Kwame Nkrumah (Ghana National Archives)

March 10, 1959. "Ghana's Struggle to Build a Unified Africa". GNA 13/1/28 (Jan-Dec 1959), Item 6.
March 13, 1959. "On Mr. George Padmore, Adviser on African Affairs to the Prime Minister". GNA 13/1/28, Other Business ii.
August 4, 1959. "The Young Pioneers". GNA 13/1/28, Item viii.
September 22, 1959. "Women Members of Parliament". GNA 13/1/28, Item 2.
December 8, 1959. "The Bureau of African Affairs". GNA 13/1/28, Item 16: Other Business iv.
February 13, 1960. "French Nuclear Tests in the Sahara". GNA 13/1/29 (Jan-Dec 1960).

March 4, 1960. "Earthquake in Morocco". GNA 13/1/29, Item 15: Other Business iv.
April 28, 1960. "Ghana Delegation to Cuba". GNA 13/1/29.
June 3, 1960. "Two Prayers". GNA 13/1/29, Other Business ii.
June 10, 1960. "Ghana-Guinea Union". GNA 13/1/29, Other Business iv.
June 17, 1960. "Financial Provision for Young Pioneers". GNA 13/1/29, Item 2.
June 24, 1960. "Conference for Women of Africa and African Descent". GNA 13/1/29, Item 10: Other Business vii.
July 22, 1960. "Resolutions and Boycott of South Africa". GNA 13/1/29, Item 2: Resolutions of the Second Conference of Independent African States.
July 28, 1960. "Congo Situation". GNA 13/1/29, Item 1: Congo Situation.
August 8, 1960. "Congo Situation, Once Again". GNA 13/1/29, Item 1: Congo Situation.
August 9, 1960. "Assistance to the Congo Republic". GNA 13/1/29, Item 12: Other Business v Assistance to the Congo Republic.
August 19, 1960. "Visit to Vietnam of the Ghana Delegation to the 49th Inter-Parliamentary Conference". GNA 13/1/29, Item 8.
August 26, 1960. "Economic Co-operation with Neighbouring West African Countries". GNA 13/1/29, Item 17: Other Business v.
September 2, 1960. "Legislation Providing for the Ghana Young Pioneers Authority". GNA 13/1/29, Item 3.
November 1, 1960. "Liaison with the Delegation from the U.S.S.R". GNA 13/1/29, Item 37: Other Business ix.
December 30, 1960. "Actions in Regard to French Nuclear Tests in the Sahara". GNA 13/1/29, Item 1.
February 6, 1961. "Government Take Over of Five Gold Mining Companies". GNA 13/1/30, Item 1.
February 13, 1961. "Emergency Meeting Regarding the Murder of Patrice Lumumba". GNA 13/1/30: Murder of Prime Minister Lumumba of the Republic of the Congo.
February 15, 1961. "Visit of President L.I. Brezhnev, President of the U.S.S.R". GNA 13/1/30, Item 10.
February 17, 1961. "Situation in Angola". GNA 13/1/3 0: "Statement on Angola-Portuguese West Africa".
April 18, 1961. "Expulsion of the Union of South Africa from the I.L.O". GNA 13/1/30, Item 2: "International Labour Organisation Conference".
May 30 and 31 1961. "Status of the Union of South Africa". GNA 13/1/30, Item 28: Other Business xi.
June 1, 1961. "Angola and Other Territories in Africa Under Portuguese Domination". GNA 13/1/30, Item 1: "Sanctions Against Portugal".
June 30, 1961. "Radio-Telephone Communication between Ghana-Guinea-Mali". GNA 13/1/30, Item 4: "Radio Telephone Communication between the Capitals of the Union States of Ghana-Guinea-Mali".
February 6, 1962. "Commemorative Stamp in Honour of Lumumba". GNA 13/1/31.
May 5, 1962. "Award of the 1961 Lenin Peace Prize to Osagyefo the President". GNA 13/1/30, Item 3.
May 8, 1962. "Lenin Peace Prize: An Honour to the Whole of Africa". GNA 13/1/31, Item 18: Other Business iv.

June 26, 1962. "Take Over of Gold Mines by the Ghana Government". GNA 13/1/31, Item 12: Other Business v.
June 26, 1962. "The Pattern of Business Organization in Ghana". GNA 13/1/3 1, Item 12: Other Business vii.
July 17, 1962. "Measures Designed to Bring All Classes of People Together". GNA 13/1/3 1, Item 26: Other Business ix.
July 17, 1962. "Progress Report on State Farms". GNA 13/1/3 1, Item 26: Other Business xvi.
July 24, 1962. "Establishing the African Common Market". GNA 13/1/3 1, Item 2: "Ratification of the Treaty Establishing the African Common Market".
October 16, 1962. "Loans Made to Guinea, Mali and the Upper Volta". GNA 13/1/31, Item 17: Other Business.
November 6, 1962. "Conference of Union of African Local Government Councils". GNA 13/1/3 1, Item 3: "Inaugural Conference of Union of African Local Government Councils".
November 20, 1962. "West African Commonwealth Airline". GNA 13/1/3 1, Item 2: "Proposals for a West African Commonwealth Airline".
December 18, 1962. "Management of State Farms". GNA 13/1/3 1, Item 14: Other Business vi.
February 7, 1963. "Construction and Organisation of the Trades Union Congress". GNA 13/1/32, Item 1: "Notes of an Informal Cabinet Meeting Held on Thursday, 7'h Feb, 1963, at Flagstaff House".
March 1, 1963. "State-Owned Enterprises". GNA 13/1/32, Item 3: "Efficiency and Security of State-Owned Enterprises".
June 4, 1963. "African News Agencies". GNA 13/1/32, Item 21: "Conference of Union of African News Agencies in Accra".
June 21, 1963. Speech to Ghana Parliament.
June 25, 1963. Ghana. "Private Members' Motions" section of the Parliamentary Debates.
July 2, 1963. "African Common Market". GNA 13/1/32, Item 17: "African Common Market — Report of Meeting of Experts".
September 3, 1963. "Party Education". GNA 13/1/32, Item 17: Other Business ix.
October 15, 1963. "Economic and Technical Co-operation Between Ghana and the U.S.S.R". GNA 13/1/32, Item 2.
October 15, 1963. Speech to Ghana Parliament.
October 22, 1963. "Ghana-China Economic and Technical Agreement". GNA 13/1/32, Item 14: Other Business iii.
November 19, 1963. "State Enterprises". GNA 13/1/32, Item 16: Other Business v "Participation of Workers in the Management of State Enterprises".
December 12, 1963. "Revision of the Constitution and Referendum". GNA 13/1/32, Item 2.
February 11, 1964. "Organisation of the Young Pioneer Movement". GNA 13/1/30, Item 49: Other Business vii.
February 18, 1964. "Ethiopia-Somalia Border Dispute". GNA 13/1/30, Item 20: Other Business xii.
August 4, 1964. "State Enterprises". GNA 13/1/30, Item 19.
August 11, 1964. "Co-operative Movements in Ghana". GNA 13/1/30, Item 2: "Report of the Cabinet Committee on the Re-organisation of the Co-operative Movements in Ghana".

November 17, 1964. "Organisation of Women's Auxiliary Corps". GNA 13/l/30, Item 3.

December 8, 1964. "Youth Exchange Programme Between the Ghana Young Pioneers and the All-China Youth Federation". GNA 13/l/30, Item 21.

December 15, 1964. "Recommendations Regarding Composition of Boards for State Corporations". GNA 13/l/30, Item 18: Other Business i.

Addresses to Parliament

August 29, 1957. "Ghana's Policy at Home and Abroad". Information Office, Embassy of Ghana, 2139 R Street, N.W., Washington, DC.

December 16, 1959. "Motion to Approve the Government's Foreign Policy". *Parliamentary Debates*. All Parliamentary debates are printed and published by the Government Printing Department, Accra, Ghana and housed in the George Padmore Memorial Library. Accra, Ghana.

June 21, 1963. "Address on the Carter of the OAU". *Parliamentary Debates*. George Padmore Memorial Library. Accra, Ghana.

June 25, 1963. "Private Members' Motions". *Parliamentary Debates*. George Padmore Memorial Library, Accra, Ghana.

October 15, 1963. "Africa Must Unite". *Parliamentary Debates*. George Padmore Memorial Library. Accra, Ghana.

January 12, 1965. "The Role of Armed Forces". *Parliamentary Debates*. George Padmore Memorial Library. Accra, Ghana.

May 25, 1965. "The Necessity for Socialism". *Parliamentary Debates*. George Padmore Memorial Library. Accra, Ghana.

August 24, 1965. "The Struggle for the African Revolution". *Parliamentary Debates. George* Padmore Memorial Library. Accra, Ghana.

September 3, 1965. "International Affairs". *Parliamentary Debates*. George Padmore Memorial Library. Accra, Ghana.

February 1, 1966. "We Are Beset by Forces Created by Neo-Colonialism". *Parliamentary Debates*. George Padmore Memorial Library. Accra, Ghana.

Conference Speeches

April 1958. "Accra Conference of Independent States". *Revolutionary Path*. Panaf, 1973.

December 1958. "All-African People's Conference in Accra". *Revolutionary Path*. Panaf, 1973.

January 1960. "The Second All-African People's Conference". Vincent Thompson, *Africa and Unity*. London: Longman Group Ltd., 1969.

July 1959. "Declaration of Principles of Sanniquellie Conference. *Revolutionary Path*. Panaf, 1973.

July 1960. "Conference of Ghana Women and Women of African Descent". Samuel Obeng. *Selected Speeches of Kwame Nkrumah*. Volume 1. Accra, Ghana: Afram Publications (Ghana) Ltd., 1960.

January 1961. "The Casablanca Conference". *Revolutionary Path*. Panaf, 1973.

May 5 and August 1961. "Cairo Conferences". *Revolutionary Path*. Panaf, 1973.
June 1962. "African Freedom and Unity". Conference of African Freedom Fighters. Supplement with *Ghana Today*, June 20, 1962, pp. 3-8. Published by the Information Section of the Ghana High Commission and printed by Calibri Press Ltd., London.
May 1963. "Unity Now". Founding of the Organisation of African Unity. *Revolutionary Path*. Panaf, 1973.
November 1963. "Opening of the Second Conference of African Journalists". Samuel Obeng. *Selected Speeches of Kwame Nkrumah*. Volume 5. Accra, Ghana: Afram Publications (Ghana) Ltd., 1997.
October 1964. "Peace and Progress". Second Conference of Non-Aligned States. GP/A 1 0044/5, 000/10/64-65, pp. 1–10.
October 1965. "Summit Conference of the Organization of African Unity". *Revolutionary Path*. Panaf, 1973.

Other Sources

Council on Foreign Relations (CFR), January 12, 2006. Esther Pan, 'Q and A: China, Africa and Oil', http://www.nytimes-com/cfrl international/slot2_ Oll806.html
Daily Graphic. The Ghana National Archives. Accra, Ghana. November 1965–February 1966.
Economy, Elizabeth C. and Monaghan, Karen, 'The Perils of Beijing's Africa *Strategy*', *International Herald Tribune* on November 2, 2006. See http://www.cfr.org/publication/11886/perils_of_ beijings_africa _strategy.html
Ghana. Cabinet Minutes. Ghana National Archives. Class Reference AD 13/l/28-13/l/32.
Ghana. Parliamentary Debates. George Padmore Memorial Library. Accra, Ghana. August 29, 1957—February 1, 1966.
"Ghana's Policy at Home and Abroad". Information Office, Embassy of Ghana, 2139 R Street, N.W., Washington, DC, August 29, 1957.
Jangha, Lamin. An interview with author on the Young Pioneers. Milwaukee, Wisconsin (USA). September 28, 1990.
Milne, June. *Sékou Touré*. Panaf, 1978.
Milne, June, ed. *Kwame Nkrumah: The Conakry Years*. London: Panaf, 1990.
Nerve. "Mother Warrior's Voice". Winter 2007. 2711 W. Michigan Street, Milwaukee, WI.
The Nkrumaist. Letter to West Indian Heads of State (7 June, 1962), May–June 1985, Issue No. 4, p. 8.
Rodney, Walter. *How Europe Underdeveloped Africa*. Washington DC, Howard University Press, 1982.
Sherwood, Marika. *Kwame Nkrumah: The Years Abroad 1935-1947*. Legon, Ghana: Freedom Publications, 1996.
Thompson, Vincent B. *Africa and Unity*. London: Longman Group Ltd, 1969, 1971.
United Nations "Overview of the Economic Report on Africa 2006: Recent Economic Trends in Africa and Prospects for 2006". United Nations Economic and Social Council. 3-28 July 2006.
Williams, Eric. *Capitalism and Slavery*. NY: Perigee Books, 1980.

~ ~ ~ ~ ~

Index

A

"A New Africa" Speech (1965)   139–141
Abrahams, Peter   122
Addis Ababa Conference (1963)   101
Africa and Unity   121
Africa and the World   59
African Central Bank   132–133, 141
African Common Market   87, 88, 128
African Consultative Assembly   128
African Currency   132–133
African Diaspora (Diasporan Africans)   25, 53, 57–59, 74
African Economic Development Bank   128
"African Freedom and Unity" Speech (1962)   128–130
African Freedom Fighters   133
African High Command (Joint)   128, 132, 141, 145, 147, 149
African Liberation Front   127
African Monetary Zone   132–133
Africa Must Unite (1963)   1, 11, 15–19, 27
African Non-Violent Revolution   123
African Payments Union   128
African Personality   16, 20–21, 98, 125, 133, 151
African Revolution   1, 3, 6, 7, 11, 27, 29, 31, 32–34, 36–38, 39–42, 44, 46, 48, 51, 54–55, 57–59, 61–62, 66, 68, 72, 74–76, 78–80, 83, 84, 92, 94, 96, 97, 103, 108, 109–110, 121, 123, 126–127, 134–136, 139, 150, 153, 155, 161
African Socialism   21, 37
African Union   154
The African World   62
Afro-Asian Solidarity   54
Agricultural Experimental Stations   91
Aldridge, Dan   68
Alexander, Major General H.T.   85
All-African Committee for Political Coordination (AACPC)   31
All-African Front   57
All-African People's Conference:
   Accra (1958)   87, 123–124
   Cairo (1961)   19
All-African People's Revolutionary Army (AAPRA)   31, 43, 48–49, 56, 70, 74, 76
All-African People's Revolutionary Party (AAPRP)   31, 56, 70, 77
All-African People's Socialist Party (AAPSP)   43
All-African Trade Union Federation   104, 120, 124, 148
All-African Union Government   59, 70, 141
All-China Youth Federation   94
Amoah   53
Ampah, Kwaw   145, 151
Arab State   104
Armah, Kwesi   49
Armed Struggle   2, 6, 11, 39, 47, 59, 65, 143
Arthur, Lt. Samuel   50
Ashanti Goldfields Corporation   89
Atom Free Zone   140
Autobiography of Kwame Nkrumah (1957)   4, 53–54
Axioms of Kwame Nkrumah (1967)   59, 68

B

Bakhoom, N.G.   151
Bandung Conference (1955)   100
Barka, Ben   34
Beijing Action Plan (2007–2009)   157
Belgrade Conference of Non-Aligned Countries (1961)   18
Bengula, Lo   144
Berlin Conference (1884–1885)   36
Black Panther Party (BPP)   51, 60–61, 75

Black Power 3, 32–34, 46, 47, 51–52, 57–59, 61–62, 66, 74, 155
Black Revolution 37, 75
Black Star Line 99, 113
Boggs, Grace 55, 57, 60, 61–62, 68
Boggs, James 55, 57, 61–62, 68
Bolivar, Simon 17
Botsio, Kojo 89
Brezhnev, L.I. 95
British Broadcasting Corporation (BBC) 67
British Land Apportionment Act (1930) 144
British Petroleum (BP) 148–149
British South Africa Company 144
Brown, Ralph [Rap] 58
Bucharest 75, 80
Builder's Brigade 99

C

Cabot Inc. 156
Cabral, Amilcar 39, 49, 50–51, 67–68, 78
The Call at Dawn (The Manifesto of) 49
"A Call to Independence" (1958) 123
Casablanca Conference (1961) 5, 127–128
Casablanca Powers 86, 88
Castro, Fidel 68–69, 70, 154
Central Intelligence Agency (CIA) 26, 45, 51, 55
Charter of African Unity 101–103, 105, 108, 117
Christianborg Castle 50
Civil Rights Movement (U.S.) 152
Class Struggle in Africa (1970) 3, 11, 15, 34, 35–38, 47, 64, 65, 66, 74, 76, 77, 78, 79, 129, 161
Client state(s) 4, 5, 141
CNOOC Ltd 157
The Conakry Letters 39–80
Conference for Women of Africa and African Descent 93
Conference of African Freedom Fighters (1962) 122–123, 128–130
Conference of Heads of State and Government 89

Conference of Independent African States (1958) 33, 101, 123–124
Conference of Union of African Local Government Councils 88
Conference of Ghana Women and Women of African Descent (1960) 109, 126–127
Confucius Institutes 158
Consciencism (1964) 3, 11, 19–25
Continental Union Government of Africa 89, 106, 117–118, 149
Convention People's Party (CPP) 44, 88, 108, 143
Convention People's Party of Ghana Overseas (Moscow) 51
Council on African Affairs 122
Council on Foreign Relations (U.S.) 158–159
Crummell, Alexander 33
Cuffee, Paul 2, 33

D

Daddah, Moktar Auld 146
Daily Times (Nigeria) 77
Dark Days in Ghana (1968) 43, 59, 69
"Declaration for the Colonial Peoples of the World" (1945) 122
Dei-Anang, M.F. 149
Delany, Martin 33
Domestic colonialism 22
Dougan, J.A.K. 147
DuBois, W.E.B. 2, 52

E

Economy, Elizabeth C. 160
Egbuna, Obi 57, 58
Engels, Friedrich 66
En-Lai, Chou 55
Entente States 139
Eshun, Ekow 50

F

Faber, Paul Louis 88
Federation of the West Indies 68
Fifth Pan-African Congress (1945) 121–122
Flagstaff House 50, 95
Fort Knox 131
49th Inter-Parliamentary Conference 94–95

INDEX   181

Forum on China-Africa Cooperation (FOCAC)   158–159
Franco, Francisco   148

G

Garvey, Amy Ashwood   38
Garvey, Amy Jacques   38
Garvey, Marcus   2, 5, 37, 38, 123
Geneva Conference on World Trade and Development   139
Ghana Academy of Sciences   147
Ghana Air Force Training School   109
Ghana Airways   88, 112
Ghana Armed Forces   93, 145, 154
Ghana-Guinea Union (1958)   84
Ghana-Guinea-Mali Union   87, 88
Ghana Library Board   147
Ghana Medical School   119
Ghana Nautical College   113
Ghana School of Journalism on African Affairs   84
Ghana: The Way Out (1968)   59
Ghana's 7-Year Development Plan   112
Ghana's Worker's Brigade   146
Ghanaian Intelligence Service   99
Girls Vocational Training Centres   119
Guevara, Ernesto Che   34

H

Handbook of Revolutionary Warfare (1968)   3, 4, 5, 6, 11, 12, 28–32, 43, 45, 48, 56, 59, 65, 69, 71, 72, 93
Herald Tribune   49
Ho Chi Minh   40, 42, 56, 69, 152
How Europe Underdeveloped Africa   157
Howard University   39
Hunton, Alphaeus, Dr. W.   52

I

Ideological Institute at Winneba   44, 113, 147, 151
Ikoku, S.G.   151
International Labour Organisation (I.L.O.)   86
International Monetary Fund (IMF)   26

Inward Hunger   69
ISN Security Watch   157

J

Jangha, Lamin   77
Jawara, Dawda   140
Johnson, Christine   44, 58, 73–74
June Milne Collection   39–80

K

Kali, J.D.   147
Kalsoum, Senenta   88
Kambona, Oscar   56
Kaunda, Kenneth   52, 67, 72
Keita, Modibo   41, 87, 115, 146
Keita, Seydour   75
Kenyatta, Jomo   43, 54, 122
Kim IL Sung   44
King, Martin L., Jr.   57
Konongo Gold Mines Limited   89
Kotoka, E.K.   154
Kulungugu   63
Kumadey, P.K.   147–148
Kwame Nkrumah: The Conakry Years (1990)   1, 39–80
Kwame Nkrumah University of Science and Technology   112

L

Leballo, Pot lako K.   57
Lenin Peace Prize   95
Lenin, Vladimir I.   1, 55, 66
"Letter to the West Indies"   130
Lewis, Reba   53–54, 60, 62, 63–64, 65, 66–67, 69–70, 71, 72, 80
The London Times   153
Lumumba, Patrice   17, 19, 85, 86, 87, 115, 123, 124, 139, 144

M

Makarios, Archbishop   152
Makonnen, T.R.   122
Malcolm X   24, 34, 37, 57
Malcolm X Liberation University   77–78
Manchester Guardian   122
Mao Tse-Tung   1, 43, 48, 55, 68
Maoism   20
Marshall Plan   156
Marx, Karl   1, 66
Marxist-Leninism   20

Mass Education Women's Groups   119
Mboya, Tom   43
Medlock, Julie   41, 45, 49, 79
"Message to the Black People of Britain" (1968)   3, 32, 34–35, 58
Military Strategy: Soviet Doctrine and Concept   47
Milne, June   39–80
Milne, Peter   73
Mobutu, Joseph Desire (Sese Seko)   52
Mohammed Speaks   58
Monaghan, Karen   159
Morehouse College   78
Moses, Boye   49

N

National Council of Ghana Women   146
National Liberation Council (NLC)   50, 63
National Liberation Front of Algeria (FLN)   127
National Liberation Front of South Viet Nam   151, 153
National Public Radio (NPR)   156–157, 159, 160
National Union of Tanzania Workers   148
Neo-Colonialism: The Last Stage of Imperialism (1965)   4, 11, 25–28, 29, 39, 46, 56
Nerve   157
New York Times Book Review   157
Ngwane [Swaziland] National Liberatory Congress (NNLC)   44, 51
Nkrumah Book Service   68
Nkrumah, Francis Dr.   80
Nkrumaism (Nkrumahism)   11, 20, 22–23, 32, 44, 45, 64, 76, 98, 148, 152
The Nkrumaist   68
Non-alignment   65, 97
North Atlantic Treaty Organization (NATO)   108
Nyamikeh   63
Nyerere, Julius   52, 56–57

O

Organization of African Unity (OAU)   2, 15, 31, 65, 74–75, 101–103, 105, 108, 109, 110, 111, 113, 118, 131, 134, 139–141, 143–144, 146, 147, 149, 153
Osman, Abdullah   89

P

Padmore, George   16, 84, 122
Palais du Peuple   67
Pan African Airways   112–113
Pan-African Congress (1945)   121–122
Pan-African Labour Organisation   148, 153
Pan-African Revolutionary Socialist Party (PRSP)   77
Pan-Africanism   1, 2, 3, 5, 7, 12, 15, 18, 23, 29, 31, 32–34, 39, 43, 44, 83, 84, 88, 89, 95, 96, 100, 104, 109, 111–112, 118, 120, 121–124, 125–127, 129–131, 137, 140, 145, 148, 151, 153, 155, 161
Pan Africanist Congress (PAC)   57
Pan Africanist Youth Movement (PAYM)   44
Pan-American Airways   45
Panaf Books   59, 73, 144
Panchsheel   100
Paper and Pulp Factory (Ghana)   112
Parti Democratique de Guinee (PDG)   35, 79
Party for the Independence of Guinea and the Cape Verde Islands (PAIGC)   50, 67–68
"Peace and Progress" Speech (1964)   137–139
Peace Corps   26
People's Militia   147
People's Republic of Africa   47
Philosophical Consciencism   20–21, 54
Piao, Lin   55
Poku, 2nd Lt. Ebenezer Osei   50
Puppets (of capitalists, colonialists, neo-colonialists)   4, 25, 30, 36, 40, 47, 64, 74

R

Radio Conakry 145
Revolutionary Path (1973) 5, 11, 32–35, 59, 121–123, 125, 127–128, 131–136, 139–141
Rhodes, Cecil 144
Rhodesia File (1974) 144
Rodney, Walter 157
Roughneen, Simon 158

S

Sahara (French Nuclear Tests in) 84, 85
Salazar, Antonio de Oliveira 148
Sanniquellie Conference (1959) 125
Sarraut, Albert 13
Seale, Bobby 75
Second All African People's Conference (1960) 124–125
Second Conference of African Journalists (1963) 30, 134–137
Second Conference of Independent African States 85
Second Conference of Non-Aligned States (1964) 137–139
Seize the Time 75
Selassie, Emperor Haile I 17, 89, 147, 153
Senghor, Leopold 146, 153
77 Group 139
Sisters of the African Liberation Front 127
Sloan, Pat 41, 44–45, 49, 60, 61
Smith, Ian 118, 143–144, 146, 148, 149, 153
Smuts, Jan 12
Socialism 1, 5, 6, 18, 24, 27, 31, 34, 37–38, 42, 43, 46, 60, 69, 70, 83, 90, 92, 94, 95, 99, 104, 107, 110, 111–112, 113, 117, 123, 130, 132, 137–138, 144, 147, 151, 153, 155
Socialist United States of Africa 122
The Spectre of Black Power (1968) 3, 32–34, 52, 58, 127
"Speech at Accra Arena" (1959) 5
Stalin, Joseph 55
The Struggle Continues (1973) 3, 11, 32–35, 52, 59

Sulemana, Alhaji M.B. 147
Swane National Liberatory Congress (NNLC) 51

T

Test Ban Treaty 106
Tettegah, J.K. 148, 150
Thomas, Edgar 78
Thompson, Dudley 44, 65, 68, 71, 80
Thompson, Vincent B. 121–122, 123–124, 134
Tolstoy, Lev 48
TOTAL 148–149
Toure, Ahmed Sekou 40–41, 52, 67, 71, 72, 78, 87, 125, 145–146, 149
Towards Colonial Freedom (1945) 11–15, 88, 122
Trade Union Congress (TUC) 91–92, 145, 147, 151
Tri-Continental Solidarity Conference 152
Tribalism 36
Trotsky, Leon (Lev) 55
Tubman, W.V.S. (Liberia) 125
Ture, Kwame (formerly, Stokely Carmichael) 3, 37, 49, 51, 52, 57–59, 60–61, 67

U

U Thant 52, 69
Unilateral Declaration of Independence (UDI) 144
Union Africaine et Malagache 134
Union Central Bank 141
Union Government of Africa 105, 118, 145, 149
Union of African News Agencies 88
Union of African Socialist Republics 47
Union of African Socialist States 83, 160
Union of African States 124, 133
United Ghana Farmers' Co-operatives Council 93
United Nations (UN) 29, 113–114, 115, 130, 139, 144, 146, 149, 155–156

United Nations Economic
  Commission for Africa   156–157
U.S. Information Agency (USIA)   26
United States of Africa   124
"Unity Now" Speech (1963)   131–134
Universal Negro Improvement
  Association (UNIA)   2, 5, 38
University College of Science [and]
  Education (Cape Coast)   119,
  151
University of Ghana   103
Usoroh, Etop J.   76–77

V

Vanguard party   61
Verwoerd, Hendrik   148
Villa Syli   53, 56, 70
Volta River Project   98–99, 119

W

Washington Post   49
West Africa   62
West African Commonwealth Airline
  88
West and Equatorial African Airline
  112
Williams, Eric   69
Wilson, Harold   143–144
Winters, Mary   79
Women's Auxiliary Corps   93, 109
World Bank   26
Wright, Julia   51–52, 57
Wright, Richard   51

Y

Yankey, Ambrose   52
Yeboah, Lt. Moses   50
Yew, Lee Kuan   152
Young Pioneers   77, 93–94, 105

Z

Zimbabwe News   57
Zonal theory   31
Zwane, S. T.   44, 51

~ ~ ~ ~ ~

About the Author

Doreatha Mbalia is Associate Professor at the University of Wisconsin, Milwaukee. Her research interests are in Pan-Africanism, African women's studies, and comparative African studies, and Africa and the Diaspora. Her published works include: 'Tar Baby: A Reflection of Toni Morrison's Developed Class Consciousness', in Linden Peach (editor) *Toni Morrison*. NY: St. Martin's Press, Inc., 1998; *Heritage: An African-American Reader*. NY: Prentice Hall, 2002; *Toni Morrison's Developing Class Consciousness*. Second Edition. Cranbury, NJ: Susquehanna University Press, 2004.

~ ~ ~ ~ ~

Printed by Libri Plureos GmbH in Hamburg, Germany